The Art of Cinematic Storytelling

The Art of Cinematic Storytelling

A Visual Guide to Planning Shots,
Cuts, and Transitions

Kelly Gordon Brine

OXFORD

UNIVERSITY PRESS

OXFORD
UNIVERSITY PRESS

Oxford University Press is a department of the University of Oxford. It furthers the University's objective of excellence in research, scholarship, and education by publishing worldwide. Oxford is a registered trade mark of Oxford University Press in the UK and certain other countries.

Published in the United States of America by Oxford University Press
198 Madison Avenue, New York, NY 10016, United States of America.

Library of Congress Cataloging-in-Publication Data
Names: Brine, Kelly Gordon, author.
Title: The art of cinematic storytelling: a visual guide to planning shots, cuts and transitions / Kelly Gordon Brine.
Description: New York, NY: Oxford University Press, [2020] | Includes index.
Identifiers: LCCN 2020016476 (print) | LCCN 2020016477 (ebook) |
ISBN 9780190054328 (hardback) | ISBN 9780190054335 (paperback) |
ISBN 9780190054359 (epub) | ISBN 9780190054342 (updf) | ISBN 9780190054366 (online)
Subjects: LCSH: Motion pictures—Production and direction. |
Storyboards. | Framing (Cinematography) | Blocking (Motion pictures) |
Motion pictures—Editing.
Classification: LCC PN1995.9.P7 B648 2020 (print) | LCC PN1995.9.P7(ebook) |
DDC 791.4302/33—dc23
LC record available at https://lccn.loc.gov/2020016476
LC ebook record available at https://lccn.loc.gov/2020016477
ISBN 978–0–19–005432–8

For Malle, James, and Eric.

Contents

Acknowledgments

I wish to thank my wife, Malle, for sharing her expertise and insight, for reading my manuscript, and for providing cheerful support throughout the writing and illustrating of this book. I would like to express my gratitude to my editor at Oxford University Press, Norm Hirschy, for his support throughout the creation of this book.

Much of my film storytelling education has come though the storyboarding I have done for many talented film and television directors over three decades. I would like to thank in particular Steve Surjik and Chris Fisher for all I have learned from them over many years of creative collaboration.

Introduction

Film has the almost magical ability of being able to create the illusion of three-dimensional action on a flat screen. For more than 100 years audiences have been entranced by film's vivid depiction of events both real and imagined. Even though film's storytelling capabilities have long surpassed those of other art forms, advancements continue to be made. Breakthroughs in computer graphics and motion capture continually expand film's storytelling power by augmenting live action and by creating extraordinarily convincing animated worlds.

Films interweave sound and images in elaborate ways. While dialogue, sound effects, and music all contribute immensely, it's the images that are at the heart of film storytelling. The effectiveness of film's visual storytelling powers is based on four elements. The first and most magical of these is the fact that still images that are shown rapidly create the illusion of realistic three-dimensionality and fluid motion, as suggested by the illustration in Figure 0.1.

The second element of film's visual magic relies on the fact that viewers instinctively find connections and meaning in juxtaposed shots. An example illustrates this: imagine a shot of appetizing food that is immediately followed by a boy's close-up as he looks at something just off-screen. Viewers immediately understand the story: the boy is (1) near the food, (2) looking at it, and (3) he finds it just as appealing as we do. These inferences are made even though the food and the boy do not appear together at the same time or in the same shot. A juxtaposition such as this one has the surprising ability to convey story information that is not contained in either of the individual images. It creates a story because viewers' minds draw inferences and project their own thoughts, desires, and emotions into the characters on the screen by connecting the dots from shot to shot.

The third element of film's visual magic is the way in which shot design can create storytelling "spin." This is achieved by the choice of the camera's position, the careful framing of the action, and the artful choreography of the movement of the camera and the actors. The shots that are created can tell different stories and evoke very different emotions in viewers depending on the choices that are made. This gives filmmakers great storytelling power.

The fourth element of film's visual magic is the way in which time and space can be manipulated through shot design and editing. Virtually every film tells its story in a series of scenes that show action occurring at various times in a number of settings. Time can be made to move forward or backward between scenes, and time can be compressed or expanded both within and between scenes. When this is skillfully done, viewers do not find it distracting or artificial. Stories that take place over days or years and in many locations can be condensed into an hour or two and still seem

The Art of Cinematic Storytelling. Kelly Gordon Brine, Oxford University Press (2020). © Oxford University Press.
DOI: 10.1093/oso/9780190054328.001.0001.

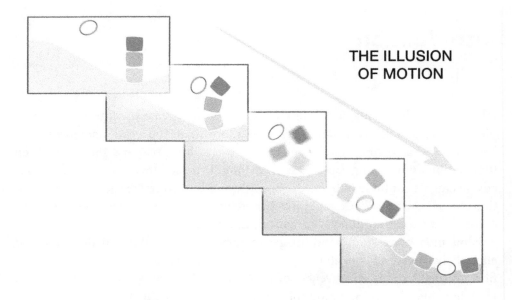

THE ILLUSION
OF MOTION

Figure 0.1 When related images are shown at a rate faster than five frames per second, the human mind perceives motion.

natural. Distance can also be compressed, and characters can be made to travel great distances in a matter of seconds in order to keep the story moving at an exciting pace.

These four elements of film's visual magic provide filmmakers with great storytelling potential. But while film's magic is powerful, if it isn't understood and controlled it can work against good storytelling. This book's aim is to present techniques that will help an aspiring filmmaker control film's visual storytelling power.

The Craft of Visual Storytelling

Every story introduces characters and situations, reveals backstory, creates problems and conflicts for the characters, and then shows how the characters deal with them. Good writing and performances are essential ingredients of a compelling movie, but the story will fall short of its potential if the visual storytelling is not well designed. This is because films are primarily stories told in pictures: even with the sound turned off, a movie's images usually make it fairly clear what's going on.

A large part of a director's job is to use visual storytelling techniques to present story information visually and to manipulate viewers' thoughts and emotions using visual means. Every action shown in a film can convey a range of meanings and elicit a range of emotions depending on how it is shot and edited. For example, a character walking down a street can be shot to seem either safe or threatened simply by changing the camera's angles and motion. Some of these film techniques are obvious, such as the dramatic effect of a close-up, while others are more subtle. Every director must learn the full range of these techniques to master the craft of visual storytelling.

Writing, acting, cinematography, and editing are interdependent. A filmmaker ties these elements together. A director is responsible for the "big picture" view of the storytelling that spans every shot and every scene. Experienced directors have a storytelling plan in mind that is both broad and detailed, and it guides them in the design of virtually every shot and cut.

How the Author Learned about Visual Storytelling

I've learned about film storytelling from over 200 directors through my work as a storyboard artist. Early in my career I was fortunate to work with and learn from Norman Jewison, Haskell Wexler, Michael Moore, Carl Reiner, Jim Sheridan, Peter Pau, and Billie August. The directors I work with are often screenwriters, cinematographers, editors, or actors as well as being directors, and I've learned from their varied approaches to visual storytelling. In this book I've tried to organize, describe and illustrate what I believe are the most important ideas and techniques of visual storytelling in film. Figure 0.2 is a montage of storyboard panels I have drawn for professional directors.

Camera Positions Make a Dramatic Difference

Directors must spend time brainstorming how best to bring scenes to life. What they're doing is imagining how the action should be staged, what the camera angles and shot sizes should be, and how the pieces of several shots will be cut together. A director's early consideration of staging and shooting requirements for the ideal storytelling of a scene can greatly assist the locations manager in finding suitable locations. Once locations have been found a director will spend time imagining where the action will take place and where the camera should be positioned to best tell the story.

To illustrate the importance of camera placement, let's imagine several ways to begin a scene in which a prisoner is alone in a prison cell. We'll look at several ways the camera can be positioned and moved, and consider the storytelling effect of each.

Where do we place the camera? A natural starting point is to use a wide shot. In a prison this probably means placing the camera in the hallway (Figure 0.3). This is an establishing shot, and it introduces the setting of the scene and places the prisoner in context. This shot is very descriptive of the setting but says little about the prisoner. It does not cause viewers to feel much empathy or curiosity about the prisoner. Our wide shot is a little boring because nothing in the shot is moving, and in such cases

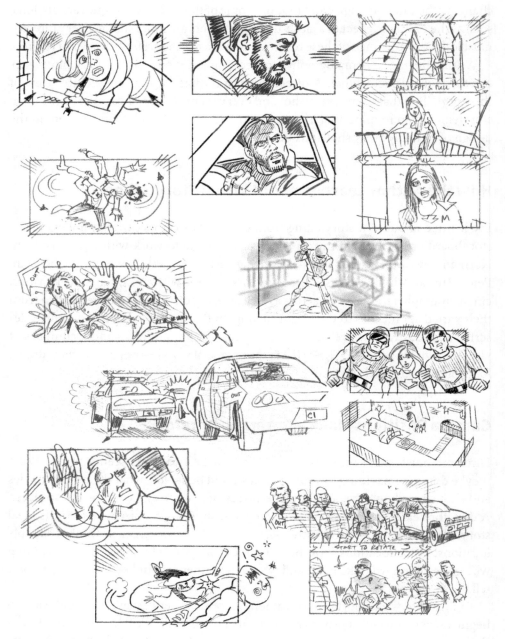

Figure 0.2 These are examples of storyboards drawn by the author for various television productions.

the camera is often moved slowly sideways to create visual interest from the camera's changing perspective. Such camera movement will also create a feeling of suspense.

Suppose our scene starts instead with a close shot of the prisoner as seen from the hallway (Figure 0.4). We see him in more detail and with fewer distractions, and we

Figure 0.3 A wide shot can establish a setting and a mood, and here it puts the prisoner in context. It does not tell us much about the prisoner himself, or create empathy for him.

Figure 0.4 Close shots make viewers think about characters' thoughts and feelings because they dominate the image. Symmetrical shot design can suggest permanence.

start to infer things about his character as we get to know him. But the bars between us emphasize the fact that he's a prisoner: we feel some psychological distance from him because we are outside the cell, while he's inside. If we choose this shot to begin our scene instead of a wide shot, we sacrifice the details of the setting, the spatial depth of the hallway, and the mood of the jail. Note that this shot has a symmetrical composition, which typically suggests permanence, and may be fitting because it suggests that the prisoner will not be free any time soon.

A high-angle shot of the prisoner as he stands behind the bars makes him seem hopeless (Figure 0.5). High-angle shots are often used to make a character seem weak, helpless, confused, or lost. By keeping the camera outside the prisoner's cell for this shot, the director makes viewers feel more detachment than they would if the camera were in the cell with him.

If the prisoner is shown holding the bars in a low-angle shot, we feel that he is defiant. Low-angle shots are often used to make a character seem stronger (Figure 0.6). A low-angle shot such as this starts our scene dramatically. One common reason to begin a scene with a close shot of a character is to create a story link to the character we've cut from. Depending on what took place in the preceding scene, viewers will interpret this visual link as one character thinking about, being oblivious to, or deceiving the other.

Another option is to start our scene with a slow panning shot that scans across some items in the cell that say something about the character (Figure 0.7). Does the cell look lived in, with photos taped to the wall and a collection of books? Are the days recorded as scratches on the wall? By the time the pan finds the prisoner, viewers already know something about his life. Starting a scene in a new setting without a character in the shot, and panning to find the character, is a commonly used transition to a new scene. The choice of placing the camera in the cell with the

Figure 0.5 A high-angle shot can be used to make a character seem weak, trapped, vulnerable, or hopeless. Placing the camera outside the cell makes viewers feel more indifferent than they would if the camera were inside the cell with him.

Figure 0.6 Low-angle shots can be used to make a character seem strong, confident, defiant, or threatening.

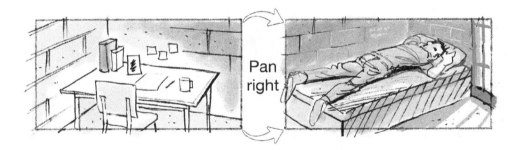

Figure 0.7 Being in the same space as a character makes viewers feel more empathy. Beginning a scene with a pan provides information about the setting and the story before the camera finds the character.

prisoner makes the storytelling more subjective. Viewers empathize with the prisoner because we feel that we are in this cell too.

Our scene could begin close on the prisoner's hands: perhaps he is holding a letter or his dinner tray (Figure 0.8). The shot now tilts up to the prisoner's face. If he's eating, the tilt could follow his spoon upward. Such shots create empathy in viewers because they are close to the character, they emphasize what the character is doing, and they exclude distractions.

Another idea for starting this scene is to begin with a shot that is angled so that the horizon is not level: this is a canted shot. Canted shots make viewers feel uneasy, and this feeling is projected into the character as psychological tension. Here it suggests

Figure 0.8 A tilt up from a character's hands to his face makes viewers think about his activity, thoughts, and feelings, and begin to experience events with him.

that the prisoner's mental state is boredom, anger, or frustration. The effect of the cant can be heightened by combining it with a focus change (Figure 0.9). The shot begins with the bars in focus and the prisoner blurry, and as the prisoner is brought into focus the bars become blurry. We are made to feel that time is moving slowly in this prison cell.

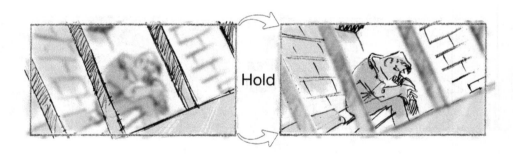

Figure 0.9 A canted shot has a horizon that is not level because the camera is leaning to one side. This creates unease in viewers, and it often suggests a character's negative mental state or foreshadows an unfortunate event.

Another approach to beginning our scene is to use a high-angle shot taken from within the prisoner's cell. This makes him seem caged and his situation seem hopeless (Figure 0.10). Because we are also in the cell we share his despair. A cut to a closer shot at or just below the prisoner's eye level would take us further into his thoughts and feelings.

Our scene could begin with an intense close-up of the prisoner. If we already know he's in prison from an earlier scene, a close-up will make us project our own thoughts and feelings about imprisonment into him, even if his expression is neutral (Figure 0.11). If we don't yet know where he is we may be surprised when the second shot of the scene shows us, or when the camera pulls out to reveal where he is. This may be

Figure 0.10 A high-angle shot taken from within the cell makes us feel we are prisoners too, and thus we feel the prisoner's loss of freedom more intensely.

Figure 0.11 A close-up is the most intense and subjective shot. It makes us share a character's thoughts and feelings. Slowly pushing the camera closer heightens this effect.

done to surprise viewers for either a comedic or dramatic reason. Any close-up can be intensified by slowly pushing the camera closer. This makes viewers feel what a character is experiencing even more deeply.

These examples of various ways to start a prison scene illustrate the storytelling potential that is available simply from choosing where to place the camera. Naturally there are further shot possibilities beyond the ones illustrated. For example, we could tilt down from the ceiling to find the prisoner. Or tilt up from his feet. Or dolly sideways in the hallway close to the bars so they cross the screen until the camera finds the prisoner. The scene could begin with a montage of images such as a dirty dripping tap, the photos on the wall, the barred window, or a fly crawling on a dirty dish. These shots could be followed by a wide shot of the prisoner. The prisoner could step into a shot or roll over in his bed to reveal his face. What's important is to think of a number of possibilities and then choose the ones that seems best for the story, both at each moment and within a sequence of shots.

Reading a scene and visualizing possible ways of shooting it can be both fun and challenging. For each idea that you imagine, you must play the role of your film's first audience. You have to gauge how each proposed sequence of shots affects you, and you can assume that it will have similar effects on viewers. It's important not to be too critical of your ideas at first or you risk discarding something that might be effective with just a little modification. Once you've settled on a plan for the visual storytelling of a scene, it can be saved by using a shot list, by drawing a map, or by creating a simple storyboard. The job of brainstorming and previsualizing shots and sequences is a key part of directing, and it gets easier through practice and by learning more technique.

The Best Direction Is Invisible

This book introduces the craft of visual storytelling in a simple and practical way, without reference to film history. What you learn here has wide application in film, animation, and game design. The techniques described here for designing shots, cuts, and transitions are ones that we have all seen thousands of times in movies and TV shows. A filmmaker who knows these techniques can select the best ones for the drama at every moment. A director's visual style is the result of these many choices.

This book is unusual in that it looks at the meaning and emotional effects of the most common types of shots, cuts, and transitions. It contains practical advice on the basics of shooting common actions and situations in ways that serve various storytelling objectives. This book also shows how to keep time, space, and motion clear. It does not investigate other important artistic and technical areas of filmmaking, including writing, casting, coaching actors, camera technology, lighting, sound, set design, and budgeting, which are all explored in other books. This book focuses on visual storytelling.

Some new directors find it tempting to create "long takes" and other complex and novel shots. I believe that what is most valuable to learn at the beginning are the simple and common types of shots, cuts, and transitions that are the building blocks of the storytelling of most scenes. Some new directors believe it's important to break film "rules" in an effort to show their originality. I believe that a shot or cut that breaks with convention works best when it is done to support a dramatic moment in a story. Breaking rules for no dramatic purpose distracts from the story being told.

A director should never get in the way of the story! It's ironic that the more skillfully a film is directed, the less viewers think about how it was directed. That's the meaning of "The best direction is invisible."

Learning More about Film Storytelling

Unfortunately most jobs in film and television won't help you learn much about directing and editing. The scenes and shots are not created in story order, and therefore an observer has no idea how the shots will be cut together to tell a story. An easy and effective way to study directing, editing, and visual storytelling is by watching scenes from movies with the sound turned off. This allows you to study the shots, cuts, and transitions without being swept up in the story. You'll probably have to watch a scene several times to gain a thorough understanding of it. As you watch, you should ask yourself questions about the design of the shots, cuts, and transitions, the staging of the action, and the camera movement in order to understand how they work together to tell the film's story visually.

Making your own short films is a great way to learn, to be creative, and to put theory into practice. Making your own films will also increase your insight into the techniques of the directors whose films you watch, because you will now have a deeper understanding of the storytelling problems they faced and how they solved them. By absorbing as much as you can from others, and by experimenting and solving the problems you encounter as you make your own films, the more skilled you will become as a film storyteller. Your films will become more polished, more interesting, and more compelling!

1

Seven Film Storytelling Essentials

This chapter introduces seven key concepts of visual storytelling that can give an aspiring filmmaker a quick start. We'll begin with explanations of a few film terms, and other terms will be introduced as needed. The glossary provides a quick reference to all the terms used in this book.

A *scene* consists of a single time and place where one part of a story takes place, such as an office or a park. A *setting* can mean the general time and place of an entire story, but more often it's the specific time and place of one scene.

Locations are places away from the studio that are used as settings for scenes. Locations are typically modified to some degree to suit the needs of a story. Scenes are also often shot in rooms and other environments that are specially built in a studio to save money or because suitable locations don't exist. The term *set* is used to refer to any place at a location or in a studio where a scene is shot. One location may contain several sets, such as the interior and the exterior of a restaurant.

A *shot* is a continuous recording of the story's action taken over several seconds or minutes. Often several *takes* are made of a single shot while attempting to create the best one possible. With guidance from the director, an editor evaluates, selects, trims, and sequences the hundreds of shots that have been created into a single movie. A single shot is often divided into several separate pieces that are then combined with pieces of other shots into one continuous sequence. The total amount of footage that is shot is typically several times what's needed because the bad takes and much of the overlapping footage are discarded.

A video camera may be *static*, which means not moving at all. The camera may be *stationary* but pan or tilt as needed, or it may move dynamically as it *travels* in any direction in space. A type of shot that is used very often is a *point of view* (POV); it's what a character in a scene is looking at as recorded from a camera position close to where that character is. (Sometimes the camera's position is *cheated* to a slightly different angle if this creates a better shot.)

Left and *right* describe the two general directions in which a character may be looking or moving *as seen by the camera*. For editing purposes it's normally only the *general* left or right screen direction of a look or a movement that's important, not the exact angle.

Cuts are the hundreds of times in a film when the currently playing shot is suddenly replaced by a different shot that continues the story (Figure 1.1). Cuts can be quite abrupt, especially when the story continues in a new setting. The techniques of *continuity editing* are used to make cuts less jolting and maintain clarity of time and space. A *transition* is any in-camera or editing-room technique that helps make a change in time or place less abrupt or confusing.

The Art of Cinematic Storytelling. Kelly Gordon Brine, Oxford University Press (2020). © Oxford University Press.
DOI: 10.1093/oso/9780190054328.001.0001.

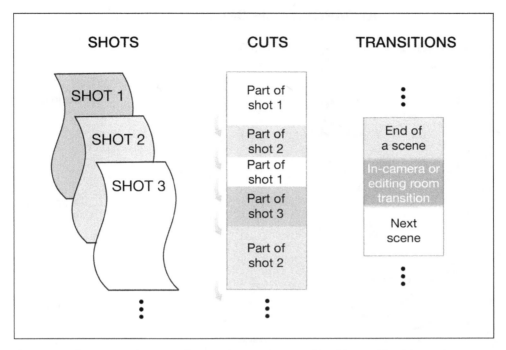

Figure 1.1 Shots cover the action from various angles, usually with considerable overlap. Selected pieces of shots are cut together into storytelling sequences. Transitions include both editing-room effects such as dissolves and in-camera techniques such as tilting down from the sky.

Adding Meaning through Juxtaposition

Juxtaposition is placing two things close together, and in film it describes playing two shots in succession. Juxtaposition often creates new meaning that is not contained in the individual shots, much as words joined in a sentence create meanings that go beyond their individual meanings. When we see a sequence of images, we instinctively create a story in our mind that unites them. As the events of a story unfold we project our thoughts and emotional reactions into the characters we see.

Juxtapositions are very effective at eliciting empathy in viewers. If an image of something meaningful is followed by a close-up of a character, we project our own reaction to the image into the character that we now see, even if that character is expressionless (Figure 1.2). This phenomenon is named the *Kuleshov Effect* after the Russian filmmaker who first demonstrated it on film.

Juxtaposition can add other meanings in addition to empathy. Juxtapositions continue the events of a story and illustrate characters' reactions, but they can also add humor or ironic commentary, or underscore a character's emotional state. A shot of a sad character followed by a shot of the wind blowing fallen leaves or a shot of embers in a fireplace accentuates the character's sadness. Scenes also often begin

JUXTAPOSITIONS CREATE MEANING

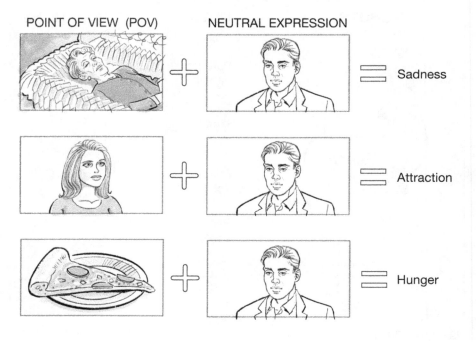

POINT OF VIEW (POV)   NEUTRAL EXPRESSION

Sadness

Attraction

Hunger

Figure 1.2 Viewers react to every image, and they will project their emotional reactions into a character who is seen in a juxtaposed shot, even if that character is expressionless.

with an image of a person, place, or thing that was just referenced directly or indirectly in the previous scene, creating a story link between scenes.

Thinking about possible juxtapositions early in the planning of a film can identify the shots that are needed to create them. A good example of a juxtaposition that connects two scenes is that of a shot of a boy throwing a football that is followed by a shot of the boy as an adult catching a football and running for a touchdown in a professional game. With a single cut viewers can be made to imagine the years of training, practice, and effort that have turned him into a professional! Effective juxtapositions add another dimension of meaning beyond the literal action that they show.

Telling the Story in a Series of Beats

A *dramatic beat* or *story beat* is the smallest division of the story in a film or a play. Anything that viewers hear or see that provides information that moves the story forward is a story beat. Every shot shows one or more beats. Shots are designed to highlight the beats by directing viewers' eyes to what's important to the story at each moment and to show this information with the right emphasis. As a sequence of shots guides viewers' attention, a well-told story unfolds one beat at a time.

It can be helpful to make a list of the beats in a scene on a "beat sheet" prior to visualizing the shots. The script contains most of the story beats, but some aren't mentioned. For instance, the script might not describe a character's "business," such as making coffee during a kitchen scene, and the script may not note the importance of seeing the nonverbal reactions of characters and bystanders. The script also won't describe such details as characters turning their heads, a close-up of raindrops splashing in a puddle, a hand turning a doorknob, or the fact that a scene has to start with a time transition because it's now hours later in the story. Having a list of important beats helps make sure that no essential shots are missed.

Clarity and Composition

Each shot should be designed to illustrate its beat clearly. Being clear doesn't mean revealing who the murderer is in the first scene, or otherwise spoiling the story's mystery and suspense. It means knowing precisely what story beat has to be communicated, and designing the shot to show that beat in the best way possible. Sometimes a shot shows just a single beat, while at other times it might show two or more in succession. A cut is made when there's a better angle to show the next beat.

The images that convey these beats should be well composed and artistically lit, even if the subject matter is a dingy alley or a murder victim. The subject of a shot can be obscured by shadows, fog, or rain, but the shot must still be attractively lit and composed. The shot size that's chosen has to suit the story beat: wider shots emphasize context, while tighter framing isolates the subject, accentuates it, and is more likely to stir viewers' emotions. A useful rule of thumb is that a good composition usually has a pattern that is both simple and strong.

The Order of the Story Beats

The order that story beats are presented to viewers is important to the storytelling. As an example, imagine these three shots: a wide shot of a girl walking in the forest, a shot of a wolf, and a close-up of the girl. If the first shot we see shows the girl walking, we have no reason to worry about her and there is no suspense. If the next two shots are the wolf and the girl's close-up, we experience the girl's encounter with the wolf along with her, and we share her surprise and fear.

The beats could be reordered to present the shot of the wolf *before* the wide shot of the girl walking. This immediately creates suspense because we know that the wolf is a threat to anyone who is nearby. When we first see the girl walking, we feel suspense because we know the wolf is nearby. When we see the girl's close-up we understand immediately that she sees the wolf. In this simple example we can see that the order of the story beats can be critical to the storytelling.

Whose Scene Is It?

Usually one character is the focus of a scene: this character is sometimes described as "driving the scene" dramatically. A scene is often said to "belong to" a specific character. This character is not necessarily the most active or the one with the most lines, but may instead be mainly observing events and reacting to events. The character whose scene it is may be the parent or the child, the boss or the employee, the assailant or the victim, the pursuer or the pursued, the good guy or the bad guy. Each scene should be presented from the point of view of the character whose scene it is, and fortunately the script usually makes this clear. The reason it's important to identify the character that a scene belongs to is because this character must be favored by the camera.

Two Versions of the Same Simple Scene

Here's a simple scene: an assassin arrives at an office, shoots a businessman, and leaves. This description of the scene does not say whether viewers should experience these events from the assassin's POV or his victim's, but this is a crucial question. Normally it is clear from the context of the larger story in the full script which POV is the best choice. Although the action described is simple, there are still several beats to this scene. This action could be shown in a single wide shot or a panning shot that swings left and right as needed, but the result would not be dramatic. It would not allow us to live these events through one character, which is more interesting and more exciting than action that is seen by a witness at some distance. It's essential to good storytelling to design shots that tell the story in a way that makes a scene belong dramatically to the character who is most important in that scene.

Suppose it seems best that this scene belong dramatically to the assassin. We might begin the story with a shot of elevator doors opening to reveal the assassin. He steps out, and we follow him down the hall to an office door. We're accompanying the assassin and this feels exciting. Perhaps we see the assassin ready his gun before entering. We now either enter the office with him, or we cut inside to see the door open and reveal him. Next we cut to the killer's POV of the shocked businessman at his desk. The assassin fires and the businessman is hit. We follow the killer out the door, or we are already in the hall and we lead him for a moment and then let him exit close to the camera. This scene is the assassin's because the camera is with him

IT'S THE ASSASSIN'S SCENE

Elevator doors reveal assassin

Pan with

Follow assassin along hallway

Follow

He opens office door and enters

Door opens revealing assassin

Push in as victim reacts

Assassin fires

BLAM BLAM

Victim is hit

OUT

Assassin comes into hallway and exits

Figure 1.3 In this storyboard a short assassination scene is visualized as being from the point of view of the assassin.

as he arrives, it shows him in tighter shots, it shows his POV, and it leaves with him. This plan is storyboarded in Figure 1.3.

What if this is the businessman's scene, as shown in Figure 1.4? We could start with a shot of the unsuspecting businessman as he finishes a phone call, sits down, and resumes his work. Now we hear the door open, and as the businessman looks up we cut to his POV of the door opening and the assassin coming in and firing at him. We see the businessman as he's hit and as he slumps in his chair.

If we had wanted suspense instead of surprise, we could have cut briefly to the hallway earlier to show the elevator doors opening and the assassin stepping out. Then we could have returned to the businessman, and we would feel suspense as we await the assassin's arrival. Of course for this to work, we would have to know that the man in the elevator is an assassin. Note that the action is essentially the same in both of these versions, yet the storytelling is quite different.

IT'S THE VICTIM'S SCENE

Door opens revealing intruder

Hold

Intruder steps in and draws gun

Office worker reacts

Intruder draws gun and fires

Office worker is hit

Intruder leaves

Scene ends on victim

Figure 1.4 In this storyboard the same scene presented in Figure 1.3 is now visualized and storyboarded from the point of view of the victim.

Putting the Audience Where the Story Is

When theatergoers watch a play from their chosen seats, their angle on the action never changes. Film is very different because viewers can be positioned anywhere for each shot. Filmmakers take advantage of this by being selective about the angle from which viewers see the action in every shot. A key part of a director's job is to choose camera positions that will make viewers experience thoughts and feelings that will advance the story.

Emphasis and Visual Interest

A scene typically builds to a climax. In general the best way to support the drama graphically is to start with wide shots and gradually introduce tighter shots as the drama progresses. This introduces the setting and the characters early, and as events build to the climax of a scene, the important characters appear in tighter shots. Closer shots make viewers identify more with the experience of a character while excluding distractions in the surroundings. Of course not every scene has to start wide and end in close-ups, but having this template in mind is a good starting point. You can make exceptions when you feel it helps the storytelling.

How screen images affect our thoughts and emotions parallels our reactions to what happens around us in life. These general observations are helpful rules of thumb when deciding where to put the camera:

- What's close to us seems important.
- Close shots emphasize a character's action and psychology, while wide shots emphasize the setting (Figure 1.5).
- What we look up at seems important and powerful.
- What we look down on seems less important and weaker.

Objectivity and Subjectivity

Objective shots are ones that portray events in a detached way. They show us the action from the point of view of an observer who is not participating in the scene's action. Wide shots, shots in which the camera is stationary, and shots that are not at the eye level of the characters are generally more objective shots. *Subjective* shots make us experience events with a character, and share the character's thoughts and emotions (Figure 1.6). A close-up isolates a character from the setting and from other characters and is the most subjective type of shot. To create subjective shots of a moving character, the camera must travel with the character.

The degree of subjectivity of a shot reflects how we experience what we see in life. When we watch someone at a distance we tend to feel detached, but when we

Wide shots are about the setting   Close shots are about the character

Figure 1.5 Wide shots emphasize the setting, while close shots emphasize a character's actions and psychology.

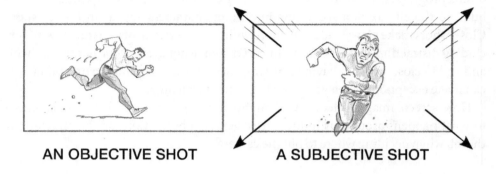

Figure 1.6 Objective shots are wide, do not move with the character, and do not show the character's point of view. Subjective shots are close, move with the character, and show the world through the character's eyes.

accompany someone who is going somewhere, we feel connected to that person. We often share the person's thoughts and feelings during the trip. In a film a character's action can always be shot objectively or subjectively. The most subjective coverage in a scene is generally given to the character who drives the scene dramatically.

Tie-Up Shots

A tie-up shot helps us understand and be immersed in the space that two characters (or a character and an object) are in. This makes events seem more real and dramatic. For instance, if a shot of a man is followed by a shot of a bear in what appears to be the same setting, we assume they are near each other. But our reaction to the action is not as strong if we don't see them together in the same shot. A shot over the shoulder of the man to the bear ties them together convincingly and makes the bear seem more threatening (Figure 1.7).

Making Shots Exciting and Immersive through Movement

Action and visual changes are exciting, and scenes without them can be boring. These are ways that movement is used to make shots more exciting and immersive, and they are illustrated in Figure 1.8:

- A moving character (including one who is entering or exiting a shot) is more interesting than a stationary one.
- Movement toward the camera is the most exciting direction.

**TIE-UP SHOTS
UNIFY SPACE**

Figure 1.7 A tie-up shot unites two characters or objects in the same physical space. This makes a scene seem more real and dramatic than would be possible by using only juxtaposed shots that show things separately.

- Extras or vehicles crossing the foreground and background make a shot seem more real and exciting.
- The camera can push closer to a character for dramatic emphasis.
- A character or vehicle's action seems more exciting when the camera moves with it because we feel that we are on the trip too.
- Wide shots can be made more interesting, suspenseful, and immersive by moving the camera slowly sideways.

Making Cuts Smoother

A cut is an instantaneous change from one image to another. The cut can be unexpected and abrupt. Fortunately, cuts can be made less noticeable. Perhaps the best cutting points occur when someone or something exits the frame, a door closes, someone looks off-screen, or when something big happens such as a splash, an explosion, or something hits the ground. Motivated cuts, cutting on action, and using

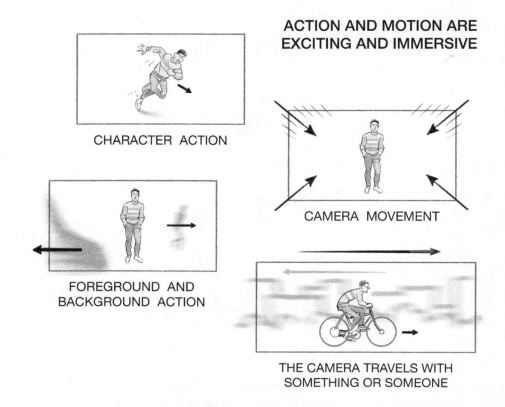

ACTION AND MOTION ARE EXCITING AND IMMERSIVE

CHARACTER ACTION

FOREGROUND AND BACKGROUND ACTION

CAMERA MOVEMENT

THE CAMERA TRAVELS WITH SOMETHING OR SOMEONE

Figure 1.8 A shot can be made more cinematic, immersive and exciting by having the characters move, having the camera move, or having both move.

compositional instability as a distraction are three common ways to make cuts seem smoother and more natural.

Motivated Cuts

Cuts are less noticeable when the story makes viewers want to see something that can't be seen in the current shot. Cuts made to satisfy the audience's curiosity are called *motivated cuts*. The motivation can be created in several ways. A character looking off-screen motivates a cut to find out what the person is looking at. An off-screen noise, such as a voice or the sound of a door opening, makes viewers curious, and a cut can satisfy their curiosity. When a character exits, we often want to see a new shot that shows where the character is going. Any direct or indirect verbal or visual reference to a person or a place can motivate a cut to what was referenced.

Prelapped music, sound effects, or dialogue that comes in advance of the arrival of the next scene makes viewers interested in seeing the new setting. A dramatic motivation occurs when something very significant occurs and viewers want to see its consequences, including how the characters in the scene are reacting. The dramatic event could be anything from an explosion to someone's startling confession.

Cutting on Action That Can Bridge Two Shots

An action that spans two shots makes a cut less noticeable. We might see someone approach a door, open it, and start to step through; the following shot shows the character coming through the doorway on the other side. Action can bridge a cut from a wide to a closer shot at a new angle. Cutting on action can be done when a character sits down, stands up, raises a glass, lights a cigarette, or turns to look in a new direction. About one-third of the action occurs in the first shot, and the second shot shows the remaining two-thirds. Actors usually repeat the entire action for each shot, because this *overlapping action* is more likely to cut smoothly. Cutting on action is often used for punches: the cut to a new angle accentuates the violence while masking the fact that no contact was made (Figure 1.9).

A weaker but still effective way to use action to help hide a cut is to cut at the moment a character performs a small action. Some examples of small actions are slight movements of a character's eyes, head, or hands, or an object being picked up or put down. In this case the action is completed in the first shot, and the shot that follows is of a different subject in the same scene or a new scene.

CUTTING ON ACTION

Figure 1.9 Cutting on action makes a cut less noticeable. The action links the two shots and distracts attention from the abruptness of the cut.

Using Stable and Unstable Compositions

A shot can be compositionally stable or unstable. In a stable composition the subject of the shot maintains its size and position within the frame. Viewers prefer pleasing compositions over unattractive ones, and they also prefer stable compositions over unstable ones.

The subject of any shot is normally stable in its position in the composition at some point during the shot, while other objects in the shot may appear to move within the frame. The subject of a shot naturally appears stable when the subject and the camera are not moving, but it will also appear stable if both the subject and the camera are synchronized in their movement (Figure 1.10).

An unstable composition is one that is changing rapidly, usually because of motion. An object may be moving into, out of, or across the frame, and this compositional instability is what makes entrances and exits such good cutting points

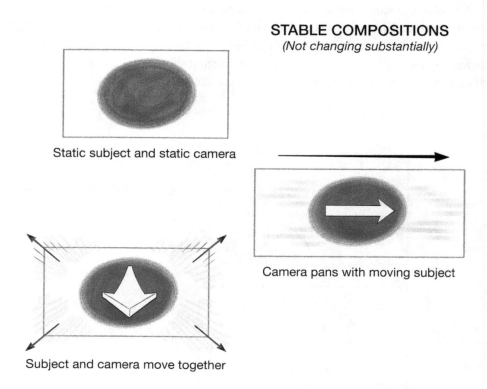

STABLE COMPOSITIONS
(Not changing substantially)

Static subject and static camera

Camera pans with moving subject

Subject and camera move together

Figure 1.10 A composition is stable when the subject maintains its size and position and the composition is largely unchanging. The subject and the camera may both be stationary, or the subject and the camera may be synchronized.

(Figure 1.11). Other examples of sudden radical changes that make a composition unstable are splashes, explosions, the image going out of focus, and the lights being switched off.

Note that what appears to be moving within the frame of an unstable composition may or may not be an object that is actually in motion. Movement by the camera can make a still object appear to move. For example, a shot taken through the window of a moving train that looks down at a wheat field racing past is an unstable composition. A hand holding a gun could reach into this shot and give the shot stability, or the camera could pan a little to find the face of a character.

Viewers' preference for visual stability can be exploited to help hide cuts in two basic ways. The first method is to use motion to make a shot's composition become unstable and then cut to a stable shot. Viewers are happy that stability has been restored. This distraction has tricked them into not thinking about the cut. Examples of ways to create compositional instability at the end of a shot are the exit

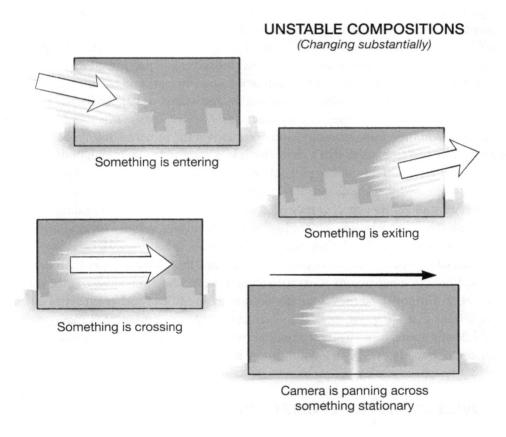

UNSTABLE COMPOSITIONS
(Changing substantially)

Something is entering

Something is exiting

Something is crossing

Camera is panning across
something stationary

Figure 1.11 A composition is unstable when it is changing quickly and substantially. This is usually the result of something entering, exiting, or crossing the frame, but also happens when the camera pans over stationary objects.

of a character or the sudden wipe of the image as a person, vehicle, or other object crosses the screen close to the camera.

The second method of hiding a cut is to cut from a stable shot to a new one that is unstable but quickly stabilizes. The motion and instability at the beginning of the second shot distract viewers' attention from the cut that was just made. The new shot quickly stabilizes, leaving viewers satisfied. Some examples are starting a shot with a character's entrance or with a bus wiping across the frame to reveal someone by the side of the road. Chapters 6 and 7 explore the design of smooth cuts in more detail.

Using Motivated and Unmotivated Camera Movement

The camera has complete freedom of movement. It can rotate on an axis to tilt or pan, or the entire camera can travel in any direction. Camera movement can be considered *motivated* or *unmotivated*. When an object within the frame starts to leave the shot, the camera can pan or move so that the object remains visible. This type of camera movement is motivated by the action of the object. Camera movement can also be motivated by a character's look in the direction of something that's off screen: the camera pans to find what the character is looking at. This type of motivated pan can also start on what is being looked at and pan to find the observer. In this case viewers understand the motivation once the pan lands on the character.

Camera movement can also be motivated by the drama, as happens when a character reacts to events and the camera pushes closer to visually intensify the character's reaction. Another dramatic motivation occurs when the camera slowly pulls back to a wider shot to emphasize that a character is in a specific environment, perhaps as a movie's final shot. If this type of pull out occurs midway through a story, it has the effect of emphasizing that a character is lost, or trapped physically or psychologically or by circumstances. We expect to return later to see how the character is dealing with it.

Unmotivated camera movement begins for no obvious reason. An unmotivated camera move is very effective when used to begin a scene because it signals to viewers that the story is continuing in a different location and that time has passed. An unmotivated camera move usually starts with something hidden from view, and the move reveals it. Unmotivated moves are not used in the middle of scenes except as quick transitions that compress time. If the camera makes an unmotivated move in the middle of a scene, it can distract attention from the story, as it usually seems like an unseen character's POV. Camera movement is discussed in more detail in Chapter 5.

Staying on One Side of the Action

Good storytelling requires several camera angles on the action of most scenes. Several shots are taken that record the same action from various camera positions. The actors repeat the action as accurately as possible so that the only difference in the shots is the camera's vantage point. But even if the actors do a perfect job of recreating a scene's action for every shot, if the camera positions are not well chosen the shots won't cut together smoothly. Poorly chosen camera positions create shots that do not fit together well because they make characters and objects seem to jump or turn at the cuts. The most important rule for creating shots that will cut without introducing such unintended movement is to position the camera on only one side of a scene's action.

What is shown on the left and right of the screen is very important in filmmaking. Every shot has a left side and a right side, which is the view of both the camera and the audience. A shot with two characters will usually have one character positioned on the left side of frame and the other on the right. A line can be imagined running between the two characters on the set. If all shots are taken from just one side of this line, then the left-right orientation of the two characters will be the same in all the shots. This means that all of the shots will have the same *screen geography*. This is very helpful for keeping viewers spatially oriented.

In Figure 1.12 the action is between two characters who are interacting physically or verbally. An *action line* can be imagined to run between the two characters.

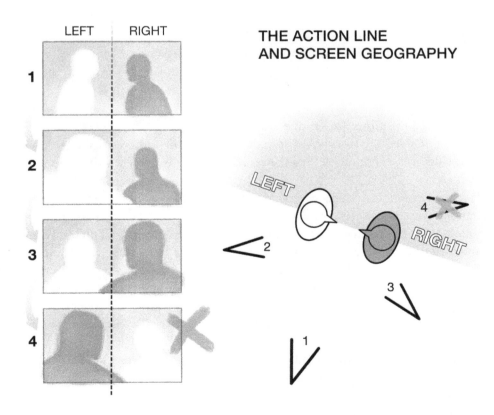

Figure 1.12 These storyboard frames show how moving the camera across the action line flips the left-right orientation of the two characters on the screen. Consistent screen geography helps keep spatial relationships clear.

A THREE-WALLED SET

Figure 1.13 Staying on one side of the action is like shooting in a three-walled set. By avoiding shooting toward the fourth wall, camera angles and lighting are simplified, and cuts will not upset the established screen geography.

Three camera positions are on one side of this line, and one camera position is on the other side. The storyboard frames show that the lone camera position on the far side of the action line flips the screen geography, which is disorienting to viewers.

When all the shots in a sequence share the same screen geography, the cuts work better because space as it appears on the screen remains familiar to viewers. Staying on one side of the action keeps characters' positions, their looks and their direction of movement consistent from shot to shot. It simplifies shooting, saves time, and makes it much more likely that the shots will cut together well. Most directors and editors try to avoid flipping screen geography. Those directors who do flip screen geography usually try to make the flip less jarring by designing the composition of the second shot to look quite different. Screen geography is discussed in more detail in Chapters 6 and 7.

Another way of thinking about camera placement and screen geography is to think of a scene as being shot against a three-walled set. The camera can't be allowed to look in the direction of the nonexistent fourth wall, and this restricts the camera angles to those that see just three walls (Figure 1.13). Viewers are generally unaware that they never see the fourth wall. Thinking of a set as having three walls is a good way to simplify the shooting and create shots that will cut better. It also simplifies the lighting. Complicated scenes may have action that takes place along several lines that run in several directions, and shots in the direction of the fourth wall may become necessary. Yet even when this happens, a scene may still be able to be thought of as consisting of several smaller parts, each of which can be shot as though staged against a three-walled set.

Starting a New Scene

A new scene begins with a shot in a new setting. It sometimes seems confusing or abrupt if a scene starts with a simple *hard cut* to a shot in the new scene's setting. *Transitions* are used either to introduce new scenes more gently and gracefully, or to distract or intrigue viewers so that they are not concerned with jumps in time and space. Some transition techniques suggest longer time intervals between two scenes, even though the scenes play continuously on the screen. These are called *time transitions*.

Helping Viewers Understand and Become Immersed in the New Setting

A wide establishing shot can introduce a new setting, but it can be jarring if a new scene starts suddenly with a hard cut to a shot in which action is already underway. A shot that begins by framing a part of the set that serves to establish the mood of the new setting without yet introducing the action of the scene can be a gentler way to start. Such a shot can immediately pan or tilt across elements of the setting until it finds a character who begins the scene. Imagine a pan across a beach or a market, or a tilt down from treetops or skyscrapers. In each case the camera stops when the character is framed and the action of the scene begins. This type of introduction of a scene gracefully establishes a new and interesting environment, and puts a time interval between the two scenes. Several such time transitions are illustrated in Figure 1.14. They are explored in detail in Chapter 9.

Starting on Something Nondescript

A shot can start on an unimportant person, vehicle, or object that quickly moves out of the way to reveal the characters as a new scene begins. Alternatively, the camera can pan off or move off something in the foreground to find the characters who start the scene. The foreground object could be a wall, fence, or bushes, for example. Starting in this way puts the previous scene out of viewers' minds, gives them the feeling of anticipation that is felt whenever curtains open in a theater, and suggests that some time has passed since the previous scene ended.

IN-CAMERA TRANSITIONS

Wipe in

Tilt down

Tilt up

Rack focus

Reveal

Wipe out

Move off to reveal

Figure 1.14 A transition can be created while shooting to make jumps in time and space between scenes less noticeable. Many in-camera transitions begin a shot with a character not yet visible, and then reveal the character.

A Distraction Can Begin a New Scene

A scene can begin on a peripheral character such as a pedestrian, a waiter, or a girl on a bicycle. The camera pans with that character until it lands on the characters who are in the scene. A scene can begin with a character's entrance or a dramatic event, such as a dish smashing against a door. A scene can start with a dramatic close-up of a person or thing. Sometimes the camera starts close on something and pulls out to reveal the context. These are a few examples of shots that are captivating and serve to distract viewers from the jump in time and space that happens at the beginning of every new scene.

Linking Two Scenes with Meaning

The first image of a new scene can be the person, place, or thing referenced at the very end of the previous scene. A new scene can begin with an image that abstractly emphasizes the emotional state of the character last seen. Examples are rain, machinery operating, or something smashing. The first image of a new scene can be something that contrasts with the image last seen, or which seems ironic, comical, or frightening in relation to it.

2

Using Storyboards

Many directors find it useful to develop storyboards to help work out a film's visual storytelling and to present their ideas and plans to others to facilitate discussion and collaboration. When an animated film is being planned, storyboards are always developed, but for live action they are used mainly to plan visual effects, stunts, and special effects. Some directors go beyond this and storyboard most scenes, occasionally even drawing their own sketches. The quality of the drawings is not important: they only have to be good enough to help with planning the visual storytelling. This chapter takes a closer look at storyboards because they are used throughout this book.

Shooting on Paper

Storyboard panels show an approximation of what the camera will frame for every story beat, they indicate the action and the dialogue of the characters, and they show camera movement. All of this is presented in story order just like the script (and unlike the shooting schedule, which is designed for maximum efficiency).

Storyboards are designed with continuity editing in mind, so the juxtapositions of images are just as important as the images themselves. A superficial look at a well-designed storyboard will miss the continuity editing plan that is built into it. Careful study of a storyboard can reveal storytelling and continuity problems. Storyboards are very different from *shot lists*, which are simply written lists of the shots that are needed for a scene in whatever order they occur to the director to write them down in.

When a film is edited, pieces of various shots are *intercut* with pieces of other shots for storytelling purposes, so it is common for several pieces from a single shot to be used at different points with pieces of other shots in between. Storyboards intercut shots in a similar way. Intercutting is possible because several different shots are used to cover the same action. These shots may be taken at the same time using two or three cameras, or a single camera may be repositioned and the action is repeated. Because there is so much overlapping coverage of the same action, usually only small pieces of any shot become part of the edited film, and most footage is discarded. Large amounts of overlapping coverage give the director and the editor many choices when editing the film (Figure 2.1).

The Art of Cinematic Storytelling. Kelly Gordon Brine, Oxford University Press (2020). © Oxford University Press.
DOI: 10.1093/oso/9780190054328.001.0001.

THE SHOTS FOR ONE SCENE

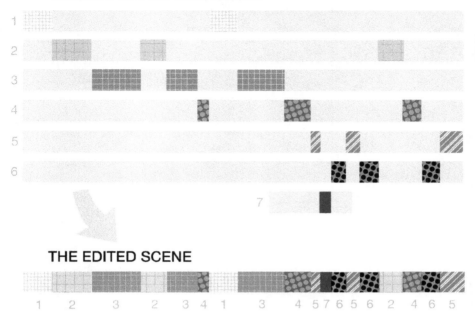

THE EDITED SCENE

Figure 2.1 Usually several shots cover the same action. An edited scene uses only small pieces of each shot, as is shown here schematically. A storyboard is intended to be a preview of the edited film.

Because a storyboard represents the plan for the essential visual storytelling of a film, it is sometimes said that it is a version of the film that is "shot on paper." By using storyboards, directors can develop sequences visually at low expense before anything is shot. During preproduction storyboards help in planning, communicating, and budgeting. During production storyboards are a roadmap and a communication tool. They also help the director stay focused on the storytelling while dealing with the demands and stresses of shooting. The final use of the storyboards is to guide the editors as they assemble a rough cut to show to the director. Figure 2.2 shows a template of storyboard frames, which is the starting point for any hand-drawn or digital storyboard. Figures 2.3 and 2.4 show sample hand-drawn storyboard pages that are parts of several longer sequences. The originals were drawn using a template like the one shown.

Storyboards are simple sketches and not finished illustrations intended for publication. They have to be drawn fast to meet tight preproduction deadlines, and capturing likenesses and details is not important. Storyboards can be very simple

Figure 2.2 A storyboard template may be photocopied for pencil drawing, or it may be in digital form for drawing on a tablet. This template uses the HDTV aspect ratio of 16:9.

and cartoon-like, yet still record and communicate what's essential. What they have to show is the framing, the action including entrances and exits camera movement, and the cuts. Storyboards are sometimes updated to reflect changes to the script, changes to the sets, and changes to the storytelling.

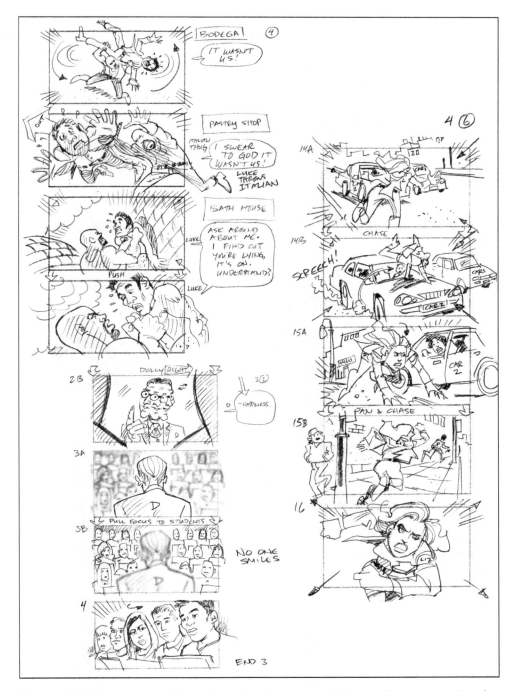

Figure 2.3 This is a montage of several storyboard sequences that were drawn on preprinted paper templates by the author.

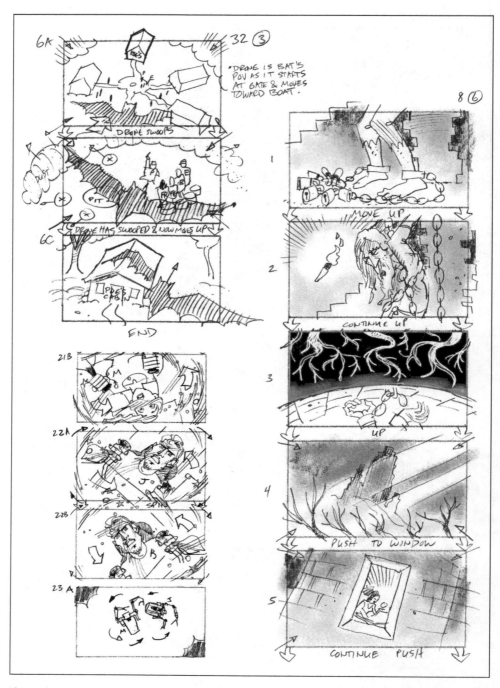

Figure 2.4 Through the use of storyboards, visual storytelling options can be explored and sequences planned before shooting begins.

Sometimes a storyboard is taken a step further to provide a more vivid previsualization of a sequence in the form of an *animatic*. Originally an animatic was a videoed storyboard. A rough soundtrack was added that included dialogue and sound effects. Nowadays computer animation is commonly used because it makes the process easier, faster, more detailed, and more easily modified. Animatics are used in the planning of high-budget movies with complex sequences involving stunts, special effects or visual effects. They are also used to test commercials and to develop video games.

Aspect Ratios

The *aspect ratio* of a rectangular image is the proportion of its width to its height. In the earliest decades of motion pictures, movies were shot on film to have a 4:3 aspect ratio. In the 1950s televisions were introduced that adopted the same standard, but as they became widespread, movie-theater ticket sales declined. The movie industry responded by creating *widescreen* movies to attract audiences by offering them a more immersive experience than televisions could provide.

The movie industry settled on aspect ratios of 1.85:1 for widescreen movies and 2.39:1 for very wide *anamorphic* widescreen movies. In 1996 the *HDTV* aspect ratio of 1.78:1 was adopted for high-definition television. This shape was designed to be midway between television's 4:3 aspect ratio and 1:85:1 aspect ratio that was the most common for movies. The goal of this new screen shape was to minimize the *letterboxing* black bands on the top and bottom or sides that mask the unused portions of the screen when movies or older television shows are displayed. Today's television shows are often shot using the HDTV standard, and thus no black bands are needed.

The newer 2:1 *Univisium* format was designed as a size that could be used in theaters, on televisions, and on smartphones with minimal letterboxing and no cropping. Univisium's aspect ratio is approximately midway between those of the HDTV and anamorphic formats. Most video cameras can record in a variety of aspect ratios.

Storyboards are sketched on paper or on a tablet within the boundaries of rectangles that have the same aspect ratio as the video format that is going to be used for the film that is being planned. A master page can be created with four or five rectangles having the required aspect ratio, and then these can be photocopied or replicated on a tablet as needed. Figure 2.5 shows the most common aspect ratios.

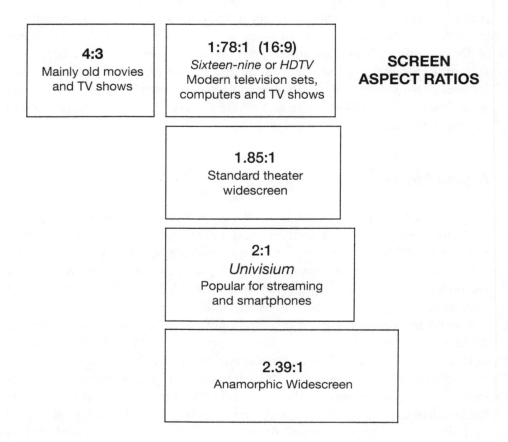

Figure 2.5 Storyboard frames should reflect the aspect ratio chosen for a film because shots are composed differently depending on the width of the camera image.

Indicating Action Using Arrows

Arrows can be used to show the movement of a character, a vehicle, an animal, or an object that is moving. They can indicate walking, running, driving, sitting down, lifting, and so on, as well as entering and exiting the frame. An arrow drawn in perspective can show action away from or toward the camera. If an arrow breaks the frame, it indicates an entrance or an exit. Figure 2.6 illustrates the uses of arrows in storyboards.

Illustrating One Shot in Two Panels

Storyboard panels are always read down the page from top to bottom. When two panels are not directly connected by arrows, this indicates a cut to a different shot

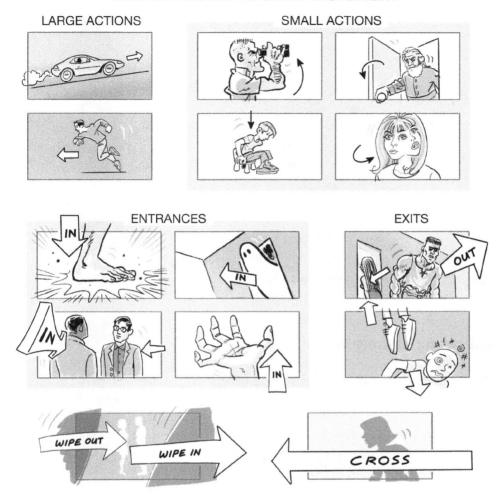

Figure 2.6 Storyboards are easier to understand if large and small actions are clarified using arrows. If the arrow breaks the frame it indicates that there is an entrance or an exit.

from a new camera position. Throughout this book I've added gray arrows to the left side of the storyboard panels wherever there is a cut to help suggest the flow of the shots and the story.

Sometimes the action in a shot is better described by using two panels: one panel might show a character starting to fall and the second might show the character hitting the ground. In these cases two panels illustrate a single shot. Two panels that illustrate a single shot are connected by a pair of arrows that touch and join the corners of the two panels together on the left and right sides. Figure 2.7 shows three stationary shots that are illustrated in two connected panels to clarify the action. This makes it clear what the shot looks like at its beginning and its end.

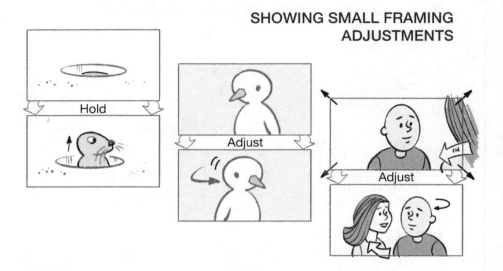

Figure 2.7 A single stationary shot is drawn using two connected panels when it helps make the action, the framing, and the cuts more clear.

Indicating Camera Movement

The shots that most often need several panels to illustrate are those involving camera movement. Camera rotation records pans and tilts, and a traveling camera records dolly, tracking, crane, handheld, and drone shots. These are all drawn using connected panels and a few printed words. When it seems more descriptive, a pan may be drawn in a single wide panel. These camera moves are all easy to understand, with the exception of "tilt up," which may look odd but is drawn in this order to be consistent with the top-to-bottom order in which storyboards are read. Figure 2.8 shows several storyboard panels of pans and tilts.

If the camera itself travels up, down, left, or right through space, it is also shown using two or more panels that are connected by arrows. To keep the storyboard drawings from becoming cluttered, arrows that indicate camera movement are shown only in the four corners or outside the panels (Figure 2.9).

Adding Labels, Dialogue, and Notes

Storyboards are easier to follow if dialogue is written in and if the characters are labeled with an initial for easy identification. This is much easier than trying to sketch a likeness. If there is an notable characteristic such as a beard or a hat, this can also be used to identify a character visually. Another option is to use tones or patterns to identify characters by making their clothing appear different from other characters'.

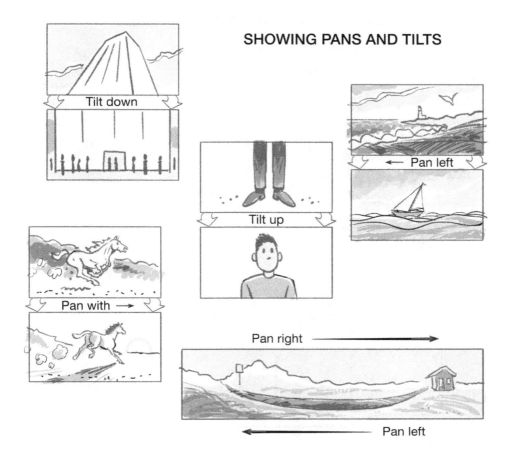

Figure 2.8 Pans and tilts are usually shown using two storyboard frames connected by arrows. These illustrate the framing of the beginning and the end of the shot. A pan can also be shown in one wide panel.

Enclosing dialogue in bubbles is not always done on storyboards, but it makes it obvious which text is dialogue. Using characters' initials to label the bubbles makes it clear who is speaking. Unlike comics, it's best to keep the bubbles out of the panels so that they do not affect the composition of the shots. Notes in the margins can show special information, such as "stunt double," "slow motion," "handheld camera," or "VFX." Figure 2.10 illustrates the use of dialogue bubbles.

Numbering Scenes, Shots, Panels, and Pages

Each new scene starts at the top of a new storyboard page. The setting of the scene is written in the upper right-hand corner, for example: "Ext. Park—Night."

SHOWING THAT THE CAMERA TRAVELS

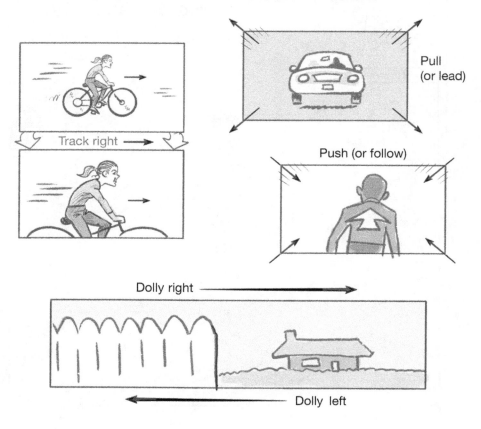

Figure 2.9 Camera movement up, down, left, or right is illustrated using multiple panels or an elongated panel, arrows in the four corners or outside the panels, and descriptive text.

Figure 2.10 Dialogue bubbles are an effective way of highlighting dialogue on storyboards and separating it from other text.

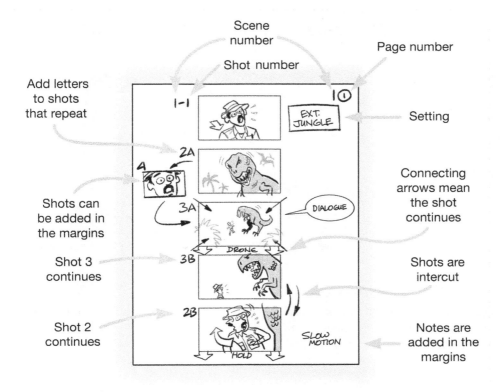

Figure 2.11 In addition to the drawings, a storyboard page includes the scene, shot, and page number, as well as text including the setting, camera movements, dialogue, and other notes.

Every storyboard page is numbered in the upper right-hand corner. The first number is the scene, and it's followed by a circled number indicating the storyboard page number, for example, ①, ②, ③ etc. Every storyboard panel is labeled with its shot number. If more than one panel is used for one shot, then each one is given a letter of the alphabet appended to the shot number, such as *3A, 3B, 3C,* etc. Figure 2.11 shows how scenes, shots, panels, and pages are numbered.

Drawing Maps

Hand-drawn maps of the action of actors and of the camera positions are a helpful addition to any storyboard. They depict the important elements of the geography of a setting, show how the action is staged, and mark the camera positions. Complicated action can be drawn as a series of maps.

Each actor or extra is indicated by an oval icon that represents a top view of the person's position. A circle within an oval is sometimes added to suggest an actor's

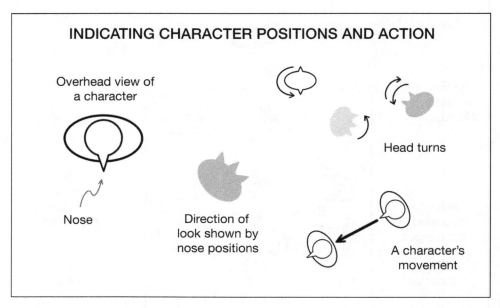

Figure 2.12 On maps the positions and movements of actors are shown by using ovals with a circle for the head and a pointed nose that indicates the direction of the actor's look. Solid arrows are used to indicate movement.

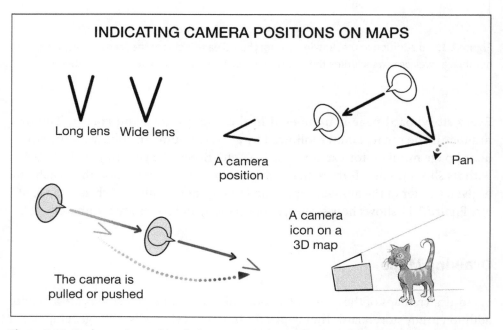

Figure 2.13 Each camera position is drawn as a V whose opening is broad to indicate a wide lens or narrow to indicate a long lens. Dotted arrows indicate camera movement. A few 3D maps in this book used simple 3D camera icons.

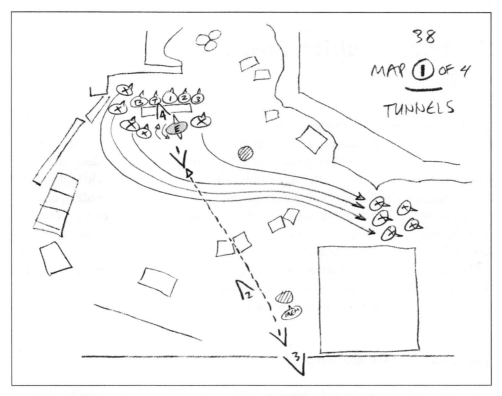

Figure 2.14 This is an example of a typical hand-drawn map. It was used to supplement a storyboard for a television production.

head, and a small "V" suggests the position and direction of an actor's nose, which serves to indicate the direction in which the person is looking, which can be an important element of the design of a shot (Figure 2.12). Ovals are usually labeled with the initial of the character, and extras are labeled "X." Solid lines with arrows are used to indicate the paths actors follow when they move.

On maps every camera position is shown very simply as a numbered "V" in which the letter "V" opens up toward the action in the direction in which the camera points (Figure 2.13). If a shot involves camera movement, a dashed line with an arrow is used to indicate camera movement along that line. Figure 2.14 is an example of a map drawn to supplement a storyboard that was created for a scene in a television show.

3

Shot Composition Basics

One way to keep viewers interested in a story is to present shots that are visually appealing. To achieve this, even shots of unattractive subject matter, such as a dumpster in a dingy alley, should be artistically lit and composed. When designing shots it helps to think of them as both images of the three-dimensional world and abstract two-dimensional patterns of colored shapes and lines. The abstract pattern of a shot should be attractive and at the same time support the mood of the story beat that the shot illustrates. This chapter offers some guidelines on making shots work abstractly so that they support the action and the drama.

To create a good composition the action, camera movement, framing, focus, and lighting have to be carefully designed to work together to achieve a pleasing composition throughout a shot from start to finish.

Composition Guidelines

A strong composition usually has a simple abstract pattern that can be seen by squinting at it. Squinting eliminates the details and reveals the essential elements, and this is a useful way to evaluate a composition's strengths and weaknesses. Often a shot can be improved by making adjustments to what's in view, whether by moving the camera, changing the lens, repositioning the actors, adding foreground, or altering the lighting. Some experimentation is usually required to find the right composition for the storytelling.

The Subject and the Center of Interest

Most compositions have a center of interest that viewers' eyes are drawn to. The person or thing that is the subject of the storytelling is in this spot. For example, a woman may be the subject of a portrait, and the center of interest is her face. In film a shot's center of interest usually changes when the subject moves or exits, something enters the shot, or the camera moves. The subject may or may not be the largest visual element in a shot. Two areas of interest in one shot may compete for viewers' attention. Viewers may glance back and forth between two characters, or between a character's hands and eyes. But most of the time one center of interest is dominant in a composition, and while viewers will study various parts of the image, their eyes will return to the center of interest. Most often this is the face of a character, and within any face the eyes are normally what is looked at most.

The Art of Cinematic Storytelling. Kelly Gordon Brine, Oxford University Press (2020). © Oxford University Press.
DOI: 10.1093/oso/9780190054328.001.0001.

The Rule of Thirds

When we look at something our tendency is to look directly at it by keeping it in the center of our vision. This is our most comfortable and natural viewing angle, and in the center of our vision we see the most detail. This instinctive way of looking at the world carries over into how we compose photographs: we want to position the subject of a photo in the middle of the frame. Unfortunately, having the center of interest in the middle can make the resulting photograph seem too symmetrical and too repetitive. A centered subject can also weaken a composition by seeming to divide it in half horizontally or vertically. It's a fact that an off-center composition often seems more unified and visually interesting. This is no doubt why traditionally the professional approach to composition in painting and photography is to avoid centering the subject, although paintings of religious figures are sometimes centered for emphasis and to imply permanence.

The *rule of thirds* is a method that is used to help overcome our natural tendency to center a composition's subject by encouraging us to move it away from the center. This rule is most useful for wide shots and establishing shots, and is less applicable to close-ups and POV shots, which in film are often more effective if they *are* more centered.

To use the rule of thirds, start by imagining the frame being divided into thirds horizontally and vertically. These horizontal and vertical lines have four points of intersection. By slightly repositioning the camera, we can move the subject of the shot from the center to a point closer to one of these four intersection points. The subject does not have to be placed precisely on a point of intersection: it just has to be moved to a visually pleasing position a little away from the center and toward one of these points to remove the subject from the crosshairs of the composition. Off-center framing of the subject encourages viewers' eyes to explore the composition. This makes a shot more interesting and the viewing experience more immersive. Experimentation can help you determine which of the four intersection points to use to create the most attractive composition for a particular shot. Figure 3.1 shows several subjects in centered compositions and in compositions based on thirds.

When to Center the Subject

The rule of thirds is helpful when composing wide shots, which tend to emphasize an environment and a mood. For a closer shot that emphasizes a person or an object, the shot should usually be more centered, although not necessarily perfectly geometrically centered. Good visual centering often means that the subject is near the middle of the frame horizontally but a little above the middle vertically. For instance, the eyes are usually the center of interest in a close shot of a person, and in a close shot they should be positioned higher than the middle of the frame.

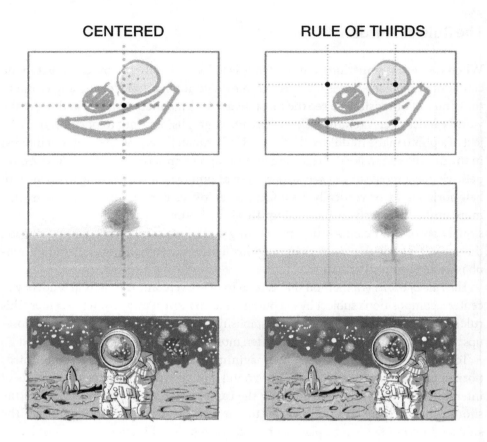

Figure 3.1 The rule of thirds suggests placing the subject of a shot near one of the four intersection points of lines that divide a composition into vertical and horizontal thirds.

Two common examples of shots that should be framed with the center of interest close to the middle of the frame are a character's close-up as the person looks off screen, and the POV of that character (Figure 3.2). This simulates how people look at things: what is of most interest is kept in the center of one's vision. Exactly how centered should an observer's POV be? If the observer is seen in a close-up that is followed by that person's POV, then both subjects should be slightly off center, one to the left and one to the right. The subjects' positions within the frame should mirror each other. An observer who is looking just to the side of the camera lens should be almost centered, as should that person's POV. But if an observer is looking farther from the camera, then both shots should have their subjects framed farther from the center. Viewer's eyes travel a short distance left or right when a cut is made between these shots, and this helps create the illusion of three-dimensional space between the observer and what's in their POV.

There are other uses of centered shots. A frontal close-up of a character thinking or reacting should have them positioned close to the center of the frame. A shot that

CLOSE-UP   POV

Figure 3.2 Close-ups and POVs are often framed so that the subject is near the center of the composition.

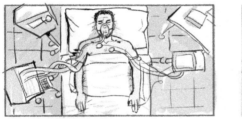   

Great importance; life or death   Permanence, power and authority

Figure 3.3 A centered and symmetrical composition can suggest seriousness, peacefulness, permanence, power, or authority.

leads or follows a walking or running character or a moving vehicle must be centered in order not to seem unbalanced. A cutaway to an important object such as a phone, a clock, a bomb or a weapon is generally centered. The condition of a person lying unconscious in a hospital bed can be made to seem more serious and important by using a symmetrical centered shot taken from directly overhead.

Wide shots are not usually centered, but a centered and symmetrical establishing shot of a building can be used to convey a feeling of power, permanence, or authority, and is therefore often used for courthouses, legislatures and houses of worship. Centered compositions seem formal and can suggest peacefulness or an order to things. Subsequent events may confirm or upset this order. Finally, sometimes an establishing shot is symmetrical simply because it's the most attractive shot available in a particular setting, or contrasts nicely with some of the other shots in a scene. Figure 3.3 illustrates two applications of symmetrical framing.

The Rule of Odds

For small groups of objects, odd-numbered sets are more visually attractive than even-numbered ones (Figure 3.4). The *rule of odds* serves to remind us to avoid composing shots that contain a group of two or four if a group of three or five is an option. Odd numbers make a composition seem more dynamic because the objects cannot be evenly divided or paired. With sets of eight or more viewers don't readily see whether the count is odd or even, so the rule of odds is not important for larger sets.

Grouping Things Together

When the elements in a composition are grouped the composition is usually stronger than when they are scattered. This is because grouping simplifies and unifies a composition (Figure 3.5). Anything can be grouped to improve a composition, whether people, objects or a combination of both.

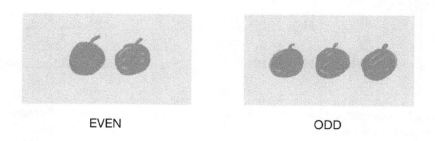

EVEN   ODD

Figure 3.4 The rule of odds states that odd numbers of objects in a composition are more interesting than even numbers.

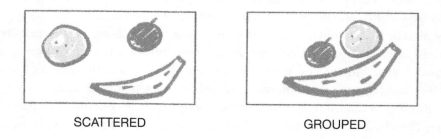

SCATTERED   GROUPED

Figure 3.5 When scattered elements in a shot are grouped the composition is strengthened by becoming unified and simplified.

Overlapping People and Objects

Overlapping elements in a composition can make it more interesting and three-dimensional. It also adds interesting intersections and shapes to the two-dimensional pattern of the composition. At times overlapping adds mystery because certain things are partially hidden (Figure 3.6).

Visual Balance

When a composition has something large on one side but nothing significant on the other, it can look unbalanced and create an uneasy feeling. What is needed is something on the other side to balance the composition. An object of a similar size will balance the composition, but it may now look symmetrical, stationary and uninteresting (Figure 3.7). (Note that for composition *size* means the *apparent* size of an

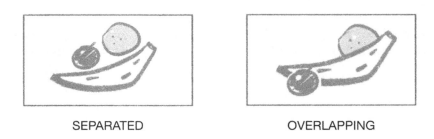

SEPARATED   OVERLAPPING

Figure 3.6 Overlapped elements can make a composition more interesting and three-dimensional. When something is not entirely seen, it sometimes adds mystery.

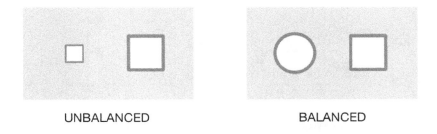

UNBALANCED   BALANCED

Figure 3.7 A composition can look unbalanced if the visual weights of the objects on each side are not equal. Making the two objects equal in size will create balance, but the composition may become so symmetrical that it seems uninteresting.

object, not its *actual* size. How big it looks in the picture is all that matters, and this depends on how close it is to the camera.)

To make a composition balanced and interesting both sides need something with the same visual weight but not the same apparent size. Visual weight is the perceived weight of a visual element, meaning how important it seems visually. A small and a large object can be balanced visually in several ways. One approach is to move the large object a little closer to the center and move the small object a little farther from the center (Figure 3.8). Another approach is to make the smaller object stand out because it has either an interesting shape, greater contrast or more color. One further technique is to make lines in the composition run to the small object to draw attention to it. All of these methods achieve the same goal of balancing the composition while keeping it varied and interesting.

Unity and Variety

A good composition has both unity and variety in its design. Unity makes an image striking and memorable when first seen. This is often achieved through grouping elements in the composition and creating a simple pattern. A certain amount of variety within the unity of a composition helps hold a viewer's interest as their eyes scan over it. The variety can result from differences in position, shape, size, height, tone, color, and texture (Figure 3.9). A rule that serves as a useful reminder to look

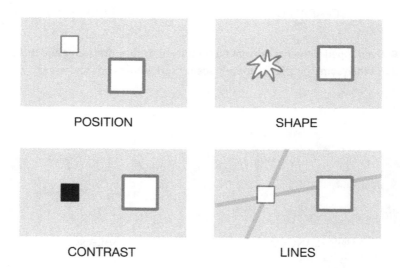

POSITION   SHAPE

CONTRAST   LINES

Figure 3.8 A small object on one side of the image can be made to balance visually with a larger one opposite through careful positioning or by making the smaller object stand out visually.

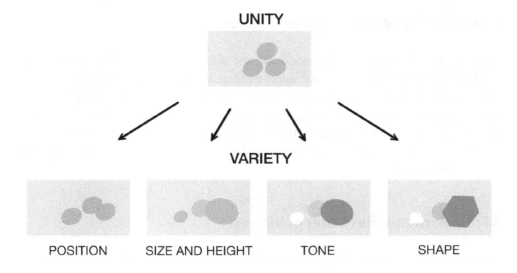

Figure 3.9 A strong composition is simple and unified. Variety can add visual interest when unity seems too monotonous.

for variety when arranging objects, positioning actors, and framing shots is "never half or the same".

An easy way to create variety in the heights and sizes of people and objects is to have them positioned at different distances from the camera. Differences in height can also be created or exaggerated by lowering or raising the camera. Finding the right composition may involve experimenting with different angles, repositioning the actors or rearranging objects in the shot. If there are distracting elements they can often be removed or hidden behind objects that are added in the foreground.

Contrast and Color to Highlight the Center of Interest

Often the center of interest can be made to stand out by using contrast. There are three ways of creating contrast. *Tonal contrast* is greatest when adjacent parts of the image are very different on the gray scale. Lighting can increase this contrast. A silhouetted figure standing at the end of a dark alley can be made to stand out vividly using tonal contrast. An example of the use of *color contrast* is to make one person in a crowd stand out because their jacket is a different color from all the others. *Textural contrast* makes something stand out because its pattern is distinctive. These types of contrast can also work against a good composition if they do not occur at the center of interest.

Lines Leading to the Center of Interest

Lines such as the edges of walls, windows and sidewalks in the background can be used to lead viewers' eyes to the subject of a composition (Figure 3.10). These *leading lines* may be horizontal, vertical or diagonal. Sometimes two intersecting lines can be positioned to meet behind the subject, and this intersection reinforces the effect of leading lines. To use this technique either the camera's position must be adjusted or the actor must be repositioned. There are often but not always lines available that can be used as leading lines.

A Frame around the Center of Interest

People tend to look at what is contained within any frame, just as the concentric rings of a dartboard make people look toward its center. The compositional technique that takes advantage of this tendency is called creating a *frame within a frame*. Doorways, window frames, pillars, arches and branches can be used to partially surround the subject of a shot. Apart from this making a shot more interesting and attractive, characters and events that are framed seem more important (Figure 3.11).

LEADING LINES

Figure 3.10 Lines in the background can be used to lead viewers' eyes to the center of interest.

Figure 3.11 A frame within a frame makes a shot more interesting and attractive, as well as increasing the importance of what's framed.

A frame within a frame can even be created by adding something to the shot, such as a cut branch held near the camera that dangles into the shot.

Avoiding Unwanted Focal Points

Any area of a composition that is made to stand out visually draws the attention of viewers' eyes. The area may stand out due to movement, converging or intersecting lines, high contrast, or bright colors. Such a focal point is a distracting hot spot that draws attention away from the subject of a shot. This distracts viewers from the storytelling of the shot.

One example of a distracting and unwanted focal point is any diagonal line that intersects the corner of the frame. A minor adjustment to the framing of a shot can move a diagonal line away from a corner (Figure 3.12). Unwanted focal points can be dealt with by moving or angling the camera, rearranging the objects in view, adjusting the lighting, decreasing background action, or using foreground objects to hide busy or distracting areas.

Making Screen Space Seem Wider with Curves and Crosses

The screen is limited in size, but there are sometimes ways of making it seem wider. One way is to find shots where a curve or a zigzag can be used instead of something that is straight. This can be applied to roads and pathways (Figure 3.13). Unfortunately there are many occasions where something straight has to be used because there are no alternatives. Another way to make the screen seem wider is

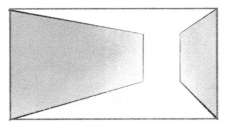
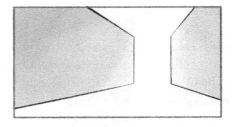

Lines that lead to corners
are distracting

Unobtrusive lines lead to edges

Figure 3.12 Diagonal lines that run to the corners create unwanted focal points that draw attention away from the center of interest. A minor adjustment to the framing will move a diagonal line away from a corner.

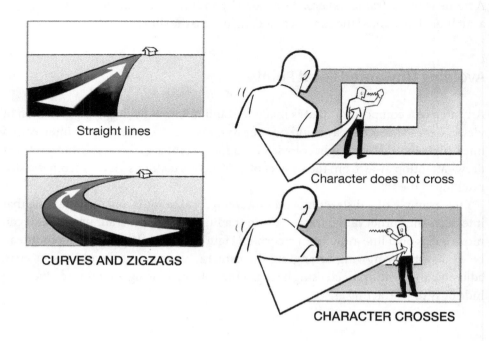

Straight lines

CURVES AND ZIGZAGS

Character does not cross

CHARACTER CROSSES

Figure 3.13 One way of making the screen seem wider and less constrained is to use curved and zigzag paths that redirect viewers' eyes to the center of the composition. Another technique is to have an entering character cross to the opposite of the an turn.

to have a character who enters a shot cross the middle of the screen to the opposite side before coming to a stop. For example, if a character enters a shot to walk up to a blackboard, the character can cross the middle of the screen and stop at the black-board on the opposite side of the frame and turn to face the opposite direction.

Distracting Backgrounds

A background can steal focus from the subject of a shot by calling attention to itself. This can happen in various ways. One is if there is persistent background move-ment, such as a fluttering flag. Accidental and distracting alignments of objects in the foreground and background can also easily occur. Sometimes a window frame, door frame, tree, or pole seems to grow from a person's head or otherwise line up with a figure in a misleading way (Figure 3.14). The camera, the subject, or both can be moved to eliminate such distractions.

Sometimes the subject of a shot doesn't stand out because its colors, tones, or patterns are visually similar to the background, or the background is too busy (Figure 3.15). One solution is to move the camera, the subject, or both so that there is a different background behind the subject. Lowering the camera and recomposing

MISLEADING ALIGNMENTS

Figure 3.14 Care should be taken to avoid inadvertently making objects in the background line up with a foreground figure in misleading ways.

The subject is hidden by a busy background and low contrast

Figure 3.15 A busy background or a lack of contrast can hide the subject. Some options are repositioning the subject or the camera, using a low angle, or moving the camera farther back and using a longer lens to throw the background out of focus.

the shot as a low angle can be a quick way of eliminating distractions that are seen at eye level. Another solution is to move the camera farther back and use a longer lens that will throw the background out of focus.

Three-Dimensional Angles

All objects have the three physical dimensions of height, width, and depth. A shot that shows only one side of an object seems flat, while a view of two or three sides makes it seem three-dimensional (Figure 3.16). For variety and for dramatic effect flat shots are sometimes good, but more three-dimensional shots are more cinematic. When designing a shot there are usually many choices of angles that create images with varying degrees of three-dimensionality.

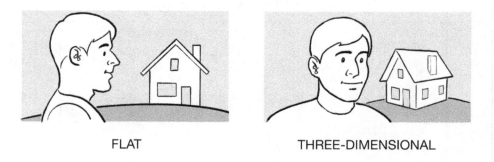

FLAT   THREE-DIMENSIONAL

Figure 3.16 The illusion of three dimensions is always greater when two or three sides of an object can be seen, although flat compositions are sometimes effective for storytelling.

The three-dimensionality of a shot can change throughout its length. For example, the camera may shoot a character who at first is walking more or less toward the camera, but who then stops beside it. At first the camera will record a wider and more three-dimensional shot of the character's approach, but at the end of the 90-degree pan the character will be framed in a flat profile shot. This adds visual variety to the shot.

Planes of Depth

What the camera sees is often divided into the *foreground, middle ground,* and *background.* Shots that are composed to show more than one of these planes of depth seem more three-dimensional and immersive. Often a shot can be improved by adding some foreground or by changing the camera angle so that there is more depth in the background behind the actors. When the camera moves, these planes move at varying speeds within the frame, which adds to the illusion of three-dimensionality and motion (Figure 3.17).

Framing and Reframing

What the camera sees is seldom motionless. As the action takes place the camera operator typically has to make continuous small adjustments to the framing of each shot to maintain a pleasing composition. Reframing is also needed when there is a major change to the composition, such as a when a character enters or exits a shot.

FOREGROUND, MIDDLE GROUND, AND BACKGROUND

Figure 3.17 Foreground, middle ground, and background can be used to make a shot more three-dimensional and immersive. The effect is greatest when the camera is moving and when some planes are out of focus.

Cheating to Improve the Composition

When a second shot is set up to cover the same action, sometimes actors and objects such as pieces of furniture or bottles on a table are slightly repositioned to improve the composition. Because the second shot is from a different angle, the perspective change from the camera's new vantage point hides these small differences between the two shots. Changes that are made to improve the compositions and the cuts are known as *cheating*. This word is often used in the phrases "cheating something into" or "out of" a shot. Another kind of cheat occurs when an actor is slightly repositioned for his or her closeup in order to improve the background of a shot.

POV's can be cheated by moving the camera slightly to create a more pleasing or more descriptive shot than one recorded from the actor's actual position. Cheating is also done to make room for the camera: one example is moving an actor out from a wall so that the camera has room to shoot over the actor's shoulder.

Framing People

Most shots have people in them, so it is important to know how to position actors to create attractive storytelling shots. Important areas of concern are how to frame and crop characters, how to visually balance their looks and movement, and what the storytelling effects are of both their placement within the frame and their on-screen direction of movement.

Left and Right Placement

Where the subject of a shot is placed often makes a difference to the storytelling. Most viewers have a subconscious preference for the right-hand side of the frame, and placement of a composition's subject in the upper right quadrant seems to be the most natural and restful placement. Viewers' eyes are drawn to this quadrant. Why this is so is uncertain, but even if it is only a habit reinforced by culture, a knowledge of this fact can help when composing shots. An consequence of this phenomenon is that a character who is seen standing on the left side of the frame seems more likely to be starting a trip, while one seen standing on the right side seems to have arrived at the destination (Figure 3.18).

What's on the right of the frame is more likely to be considered the subject of a shot. In Figure 3.19 are pairs of mirrored images. In each set of two, what's on the right side seems more important and seems to be what the shot's story is about. Of course it would be monotonous if the center of interest were always on the right in every shot, but knowing that the right side has a small advantage can influence shot design when it will make an important difference to the storytelling. Sometimes it's worthwhile to change the blocking so that the subject can be on the right at an important dramatic moment.

Look-Space

A character can seem cramped if there is not enough space between his or her eyes and the frame. A shot can be reframed to achieve visual balance by moving the

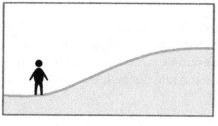
Just about to climb

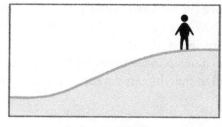
Arrived at the top

Figure 3.18 Our subconscious tendency to favor the right side of the frame makes us believe that a stationary character on the left is about to start to travel, while a stationary character on the right seems to have reached the destination.

About the door   About the man

About the trail   About the man

Figure 3.19 Viewers subconsciously favor what's on the right side of the screen. The character or object on the right side often seems to be what a shot's story is about.

LOOKSPACE (LEADING LOOKS)

Figure 3.20 Look-space gives a composition more balance by positioning the figure farther away from the edge of the frame that is in the direction of the character's look.

character slightly back from the edge they are looking toward. Adding such *look-space* is also called giving a *leading look* to a character (Figure 3.20).

As shown in Figure 3.21, the closer a character's look comes toward the camera lens, the less look-space is needed. Intentionally framing a character without look-space is called *short-siding*. This can sometimes help the composition, such as when

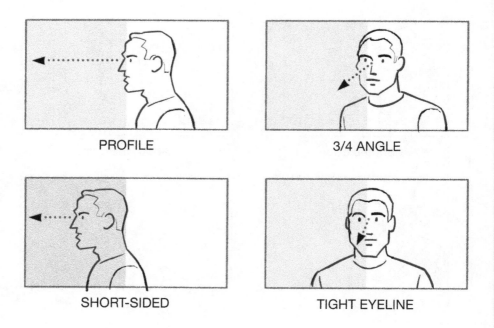

PROFILE   3/4 ANGLE

SHORT-SIDED   TIGHT EYELINE

Figure 3.21 The amount of look-space to give characters depends on the angle of their look relative to the camera. Short-siding intentionally crams the character on one side, usually to create a feeling of conflict.

a character is listening at a door. Short-siding can also work well when used at the beginning of a shot in which a character soon turns away from the closest edge of the frame to face the opposite direction. Storytelling uses of short-siding are to emphasize that a character is confused, upset, or disoriented. Some directors short-side characters during confrontational conversations.

Walk-Space

A person who is walking or running is given a little extra space to move into in order to help balance the composition. This is *walk-space*, and it serves the same compositional purpose as look-space. The more that a character's path is angled toward the camera, the less walk-space is needed (Figure 3.22). Walk-space is applied to all types of motion of a person, an animal, or a vehicle (Figure 3.23).

The Frame, Headroom, and Cropping

Close shots of people must be framed attractively. The tops and sides of heads should not seem to rest against or only just touch the frame, as this is distracting

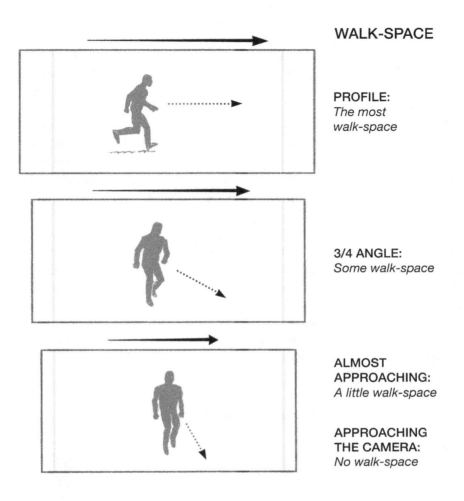

WALK-SPACE

PROFILE:
The most walk-space

3/4 ANGLE:
Some walk-space

ALMOST APPROACHING:
A little walk-space

APPROACHING THE CAMERA:
No walk-space

Figure 3.22 Anything that is in motion toward the left or the right needs walk-space for a balanced composition. The more the movement is angled toward or away from the camera, the less walk-space is needed.

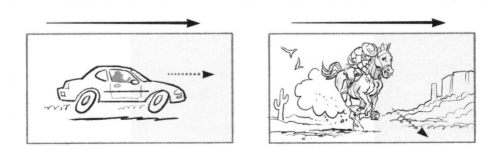

Figure 3.23 Walk-space should be given to anything that's moving left, right, up, or down. More than half of what's moving will appear on the side of the frame opposite the side towards which the object is headed.

and emphasizes the limitations of the screen. To prevent this, a small gap can be used to separate the outline of the head from the frame: this is called *headroom* (Figure 3.24). The idea of headroom can be generalized into the compositional guideline that nothing in a shot should seem to rest against any edge of the frame.

In tight shots the frame can crop the head, and the amount of cropping should be chosen to be substantial and not just a sliver. An important rule of good cropping is not to let the frame cut the figure precisely at a joint, but to show a small piece of the figure beyond the joint. This rule can be applied to cropping at the neck, the elbows, the wrists, the knees, and the ankles. Showing a piece of the figure past a joint implies that the world of the film extends beyond the window of the frame.

A figure should not seem to be standing on the lower edge of the frame. A small gap can be introduced for separation. When the legs of a standing or moving figure must be cropped it looks best when this is done mid-thigh instead of below the knees, although this looks fine if the character is seated. In group shots it can be difficult to frame everyone perfectly, and some compromises may be necessary. Luckily the busyness of a group shot will make minor framing problems less noticeable. Even so, the group as a whole must either be attractively cropped or be given some space to separate it from the frame's edges.

HEADROOM AND CROPPING

CONTOURS TOUCH EDGES   USING CROPPING AND HEADSPACE

Figure 3.24 The contours of figures and objects should not seem to touch or rest against the frame. They must either be cropped noticeably or be given some space to separate their contours from the frame.

Shot Sizes

There are several standard ways that characters are framed (Figure 3.25). The various sizes have different uses that are explored in Chapter 5.

- *Very extreme close-up*: This is a very close shot that consists mainly of the eyes.
- *Extreme close-up*: The shot consists of the center of the face from the forehead to below the lips.
- *Close-up:* This usually crops the top of the head and includes the neck and some of the shoulders. It's sometimes called a "collar-tips" shot and will include the knot of a tie.
- *Medium close-up*: This shot includes both the head and chest, although the top of the head may be cropped.
- *Medium shot:* This shot crops the figure just below the belt.

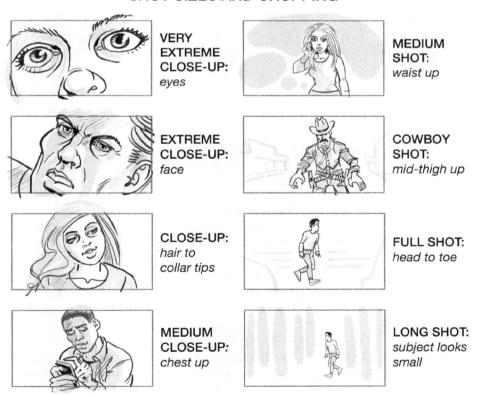

SHOT SIZES AND CROPPING

VERY EXTREME CLOSE-UP: *eyes*

EXTREME CLOSE-UP: *face*

CLOSE-UP: *hair to collar tips*

MEDIUM CLOSE-UP: *chest up*

MEDIUM SHOT: *waist up*

COWBOY SHOT: *mid-thigh up*

FULL SHOT: *head to toe*

LONG SHOT: *subject looks small*

Figure 3.25 These sketches are examples of the standard shot sizes. There is always some latitude to exactly how the figure is framed and cropped.

- *Cowboy shot*: The figure is cropped in the middle of the thigh. The name reflects the fact that holsters would be visible.
- *Full shot*: A head-to-toe shot shows the figure at roughly 90 percent of the height of the frame.
- *Long shot*: The figure is two-thirds of the height of the frame or less.

Some Classic Composition Techniques

Some types of composition are used often because they are so effective. The following list describes some classic types of composition that are widely used, and several of them are illustrated in Figure 3.26.

- Symmetrical framing can suggest authority, power, permanence, or peacefulness.
- Soft focus behind the subject draws attention to it.

SOME CLASSIC COMPOSITIONAL TECHNIQUES

SYMMETRICAL
Authority, permanence

SOFT FOCUS BACKGROUND
Beauty, emphasis

FOREGROUND
Beauty, tranquility, context

PERSPECTIVE
Excitement, depth, distance

OVERLAPPING
Beauty, immersiveness

SILHOUETTED
Mystery, fear

FRAME WITHIN A FRAME
Power, emphasis,
timelessness

THROUGH A WINDOW
Context, isolation,
vulnerability

BACKLIGHTING
Beauty, separation
from background

Figure 3.26 Certain types of composition are frequently employed to create beauty and emphasize the drama. Some of the most popular methods are illustrated.

- Foreground in a composition is attractive and makes a shot more immersive.
- Converging perspective lines draw viewers in and emphasize depth and distance.
- Overlapping shapes create visual interest and emphasize three-dimensionality.
- High-contrast or silhouetted figures and action are more vivid and mysterious.
- A frame within a frame gives added emphasis to the subject.
- Action seen through a window can be attractive and suspenseful.
- Backlit shots are eye-catching and make the subject stand out from the background.
- Haze is used to create beauty and a mood of mystery by partially obscuring the background. It makes beams of light visible.
- Cast shadows and shafts of light can be thrown onto walls, floors, furniture, and people.
- Wet surfaces reflect light better and can make an otherwise uninteresting surface such as a street more attractive.

Unconventional Framing

Some directors and cinematographers use unconventional framing to create unusual compositions. Unconventional framing can be used with the aim of supporting the story by creating a feeling of danger, fear, urgency, or loneliness, or it can be used to help create a distinctive visual style that may or may not help the story.

Probably the most useful and common type of unconventional framing is canting a shot, which means angling the camera so that the horizon is not level. This turns vertical and horizontal lines into diagonals. Canting is useful in two ways. It can increase suspense or make viewers feel psychological unease when a normal uncanted shot would look ordinary, and it can also be used to create a more interesting composition when mundane subject matter looks boring when shot normally. For example, a plain residential street or parking lot that is shot with a canted camera creates a sense of foreboding when an uncanted shot might seem dull.

Most professional directors use unconventional framing sparingly. Some of the ways that a shot can be composed unconventionally are illustrated in Figure 3.27, and these and several others are listed below:

- Intentionally making the image unstable ("shaky cam") and incompletely framing the action to simulate the nervous, dynamic, and urgent feeling of unrehearsed and authentic news-gathering footage. Many viewers find this distracting when used excessively
- Unusual camera angles such as straight-down shots
- Shooting entire scenes as wide shots
- Short-siding characters by not giving them look-space
- Placing characters or the center of interest very close to the edge of the frame
- Positioning characters only in the lower half of the frame and showing more ceiling or sky

UNCONVENTIONAL FRAMING

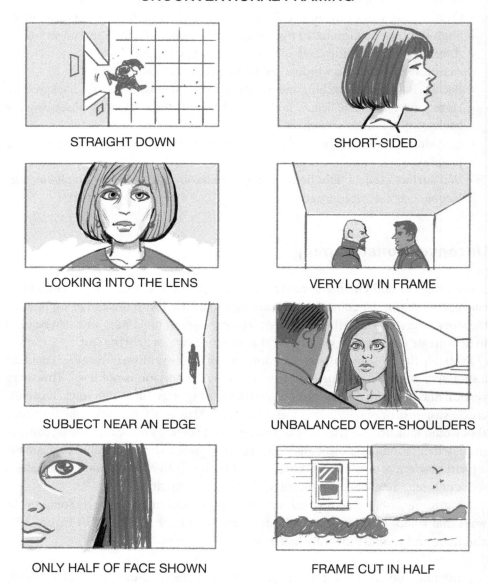

Figure 3.27 Several common types of unconventional framing are shown. These techniques can be visually interesting and sometimes they support the storytelling, but they can also be distracting.

- Centering shots, for instance by not using look-space with close-ups
- Cutting close-ups in half down the center of the face at the edge of frame
- Having characters look directly into the lens at the audience
- Cutting the frame in half, whether horizontally or vertically

4

Camera Angles, Lenses, and Storytelling

In the previous chapter we looked at the composition of shots generally, but did not explore the effects of lenses, focus, and perspective. This chapter looks at how these affect composition and how they can be used for film storytelling.

Camera Height and Perspective

Most shots are recorded with the camera at or just below the level of an important character's face, but high- and low-angle shots are also used. Low-angle shots are dramatic because they make nearby characters and tall objects tower over the camera. When characters and objects are further from the camera, a low angle will make them appear lower in the frame. Low-angle shots make vertical lines converge toward the top of the composition (Figure 4.1). When seen in a low-angle shot, characters and buildings seem stronger and more impressive, and sometimes they seem threatening. A lower angle can also be used to eliminate something from the background of a shot that is visually distracting, not appropriate for the shot, or outside the film production's control, such as signage or traffic.

High-angle shots tend to reduce the drama, presenting a scene more like pieces on a chessboard. Vertical lines converge toward the bottom of the composition. In general high-angle shots feel more detached and present a more objective view of both the arrangement of people and objects and the activity that is underway, although they can be frightening if the view shows that a character is in danger of falling. A high-angle view can make a character seem weaker and more vulnerable.

A high angle can sometimes create a novel composition that provides interest in an environment that is otherwise plain and uninteresting. Examples are overhead shots of people exiting through doors, riding in elevators, or hiding in washroom stalls. Low-angle and high-angle shots in stairwells are often the most visually interesting environments available in buildings. Sometimes a static dialogue scene planned for an office can be relocated to a staircase, where it provides much more potential for interesting coverage. Crane and drone shots can provide interesting high-angle views and perspective changes for establishing shots as well as to show the movement of a vehicle.

The Art of Cinematic Storytelling. Kelly Gordon Brine, Oxford University Press (2020). © Oxford University Press.
DOI: 10.1093/oso/9780190054328.001.0001.

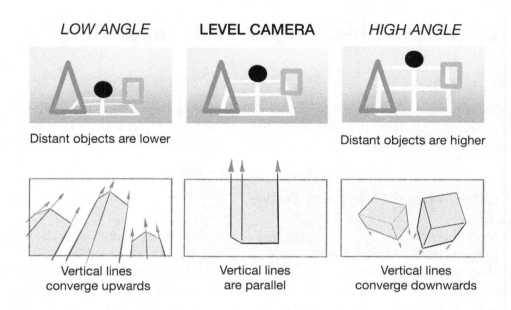

Figure 4.1 Camera height has a significant effect on the composition of a shot, and this affects the storytelling.

Depth of Field

A lens can be made to focus on an object at any distance from the camera. The point along the camera's line of sight where the focus is sharpest is called the *focal point*. The plane that extends outward from this point at a right angle to the line of sight is called the *focal plane*. Objects that are somewhat closer or somewhat farther away from that object will also be in focus, while objects that fall outside this range will be out of focus and appear fuzzy and soft. The zone in which objects are in focus is called the *depth of field*. An object that lies in the focal plane is not in the middle of the depth of field: one-third of the depth of field lies on the camera side of the object, while two-thirds of it lies behind the object. For example, if the camera is focused on someone standing 10 feet in front of the lens, then everything between about eight feet and 14 feet from the camera will be in focus.

A large depth of field is one in which objects are still in focus at greater distances from the focal plane. This is called deep focus. A shallow depth of field is one in which objects quickly appear soft unless they are located quite close to the focal plane. By making the depth of field more limited, the object that the camera is focused on can be isolated from what's in the foreground and background. This draws more attention to the subject of a shot, which makes an image more attractive and

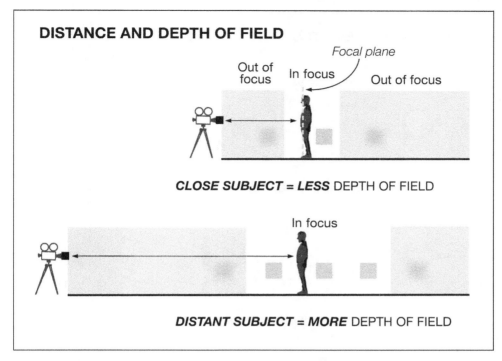

Figure 4.2 A subject that is near the camera will be within a smaller depth of field, while a subject that is more distant will be within a greater depth of field.

helps highlight what's important for the storytelling. The depth of field can be made deep or shallow in several ways:

- The farther the subject that is in focus is positioned from the camera, the greater the depth of field (Figure 4.2).
- Depth of field increases as the aperture size is made smaller (Figure 4.3).
- Depth of field decreases as the focal length of the lens increases (Figure 4.4).
- A smaller or less expensive camera will have a larger depth of field because of the ways in which a smaller sensor affects the optics of the conversion of light to a digital image.

Constant Object Size

The lens length and the distance of a camera from its subject can be chosen together in various combinations that all show the subject with a *constant object size*. For example, a wide lens on a camera that is close to its subject can make the subject appear to be the same size as it appears when seen through a long lens on a camera that's farther away. Note that while the subject can be made to remain the same size, wide lenses push the background farther away, while long lenses draw it closer (Figure 4.5).

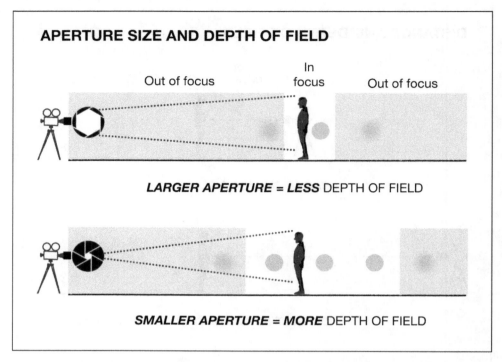

APERTURE SIZE AND DEPTH OF FIELD

Out of focus   In focus   Out of focus

LARGER APERTURE = LESS DEPTH OF FIELD

SMALLER APERTURE = MORE DEPTH OF FIELD

Figure 4.3 A larger aperture size reduces the depth of field, while a smaller aperture size increases it.

Normal Lens (50mm) and Storytelling

A 50mm lens is called normal because it has a viewing angle similar to that of the human eye. When we look through a 50mm lens the image looks undistorted and natural. The further that the length of a lens is from 50mm, the more the image looks distorted and unnatural. These distortions can be used creatively to help with a film's storytelling, but too much distortion draws attention to itself and distracts from the story.

Wide Lenses (under 50mm) and Storytelling

Wide lenses increase the field of view by pulling more in at the top, bottom, and sides than would be seen with a normal lens. The wider a lens is the more it exaggerates perspective by making more distant objects appear smaller. This can be useful for such things as making a room seem larger, a hallway seem longer, an elevator shaft seem deeper, or a potential fall from a height seem more dangerous. Wide lenses are not flattering when used for close-ups because they distort the appearance of the head, most noticeably by making noses appear larger (Figure 4.6).

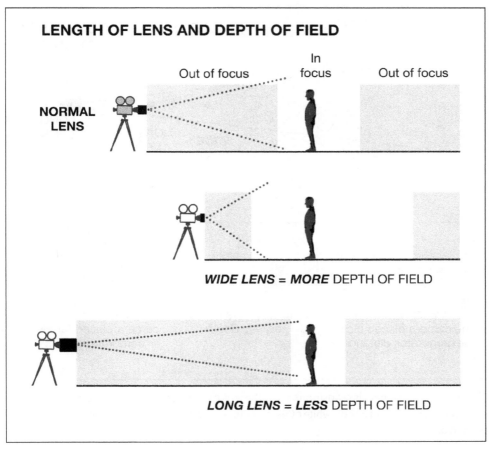

LENGTH OF LENS AND DEPTH OF FIELD

In
focus
Out of focus   Out of focus

**NORMAL
LENS**

WIDE LENS = MORE DEPTH OF FIELD

LONG LENS = LESS DEPTH OF FIELD

Figure 4.4 A wider lens increases the depth of field, while a longer lens decreases it.

Wide-lens shots seem more three-dimensional and intense than longer lens shots. They exaggerate depth and distances (Figure 4.7). A wide-lens shot of a person reaching toward the camera will make the hand look quite large compared to the head. Wide lenses exaggerate the speed of movement toward and away from the camera by making moving objects appear to grow or shrink faster, and therefore entrances and exits are quicker and more dramatic. For handheld shots, a wide lens is usually used because wide-lens shots look less shaky. Wide lenses provide greater depth of field.

Long Lenses (over 50mm) and Storytelling

The magnified view of long-lens shots does not seem as three-dimensional or immediate as wide-lens shots. They narrow the field of view by cropping the image at the top, bottom, and sides. Long lenses flatten perspective by bringing more distant objects

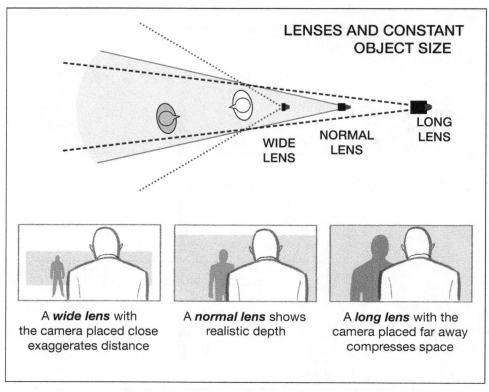

Figure 4.5 If the camera is repositioned and the lens changed, the subject can be made to remain the same size in a shot, while other objects at different distances are brought forward or pushed back.

closer and making spaces seem smaller. This has the effect of stacking people and objects at various depths so that they seem closer to each other than they actually are. Movement toward and away from the camera seems slower because moving objects do not change apparent size quickly. This can make action seem less intense (Figure 4.8). Long-lens shots can look shakier and are therefore avoided for handheld shots.

Long lenses flatten facial features and are therefore more flattering for close-ups. They reduce how much of the setting is visible, which can have the effect of separating characters from their environment and making conversation seem more private. A long-lens shot can give the feeling of the subject being under surveillance. A long lens's limited depth of field throws the foreground and background more out of focus, which can make a shot more beautiful and allows more opportunities to change the focus from one subject to another at a different depth during a shot.

Pans, Tilts, and Lenses

The choice of lens makes a big difference to a pan. When a normal lens is used to pan a character who is walking across the camera's line of sight, the character's

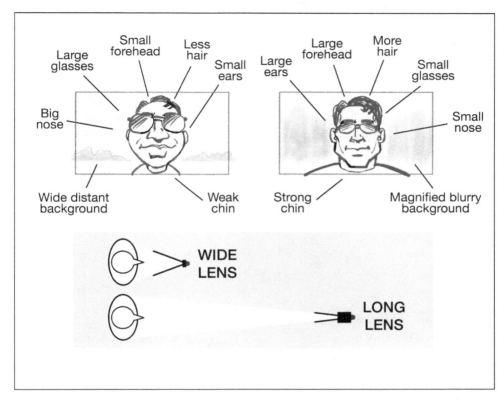

Figure 4.6 Wide lenses enlarge what is closest to the camera, and this exaggerates facial features in close shots. Longer lenses are more flattering.

size does not change significantly if the pan is short. A longer pan with a character who is covering more ground will show the character change more in apparent size, and more of the background will be seen because the camera rotates more. The camera can be set farther back and a longer lens can be used to reduce the apparent size change of the character and to limit the amount of the background that's seen.

A wide lens positioned close to a moving actor has to rotate quite far to keep the actor within the frame during a pan. This will record a substantial size change in the character as well as a significant change in the background during the pan. This contrasts with the much more limited changes to the background and character size when action is shot through a long lens (Figure 4.9).

When shooting in a room, a nearby wall may prevent the camera from being positioned far enough away from a character to use a longer lens, so a wider lens must be used. To avoid the effect just described, the actor is directed to walk in a slight arc so as not to come too close to the camera in the middle of the walk. This is sometimes called a "banana." It prevents the very noticeable distortion of the character growing unnaturally large and then becoming small again as the actor travels past the camera.

A *wide lens* exaggerates distance

A *long lens* reduces distance,
flattens space and stacks objects

HOW LENSES CHANGE DEPTH

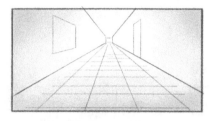

A *wide lens* makes a
hallway seem longer

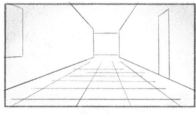

A *long lens* makes a
hallway seem shorter

Figure 4.7 Wide lenses exaggerate depth, making distances seem greater.

The length of the lens makes a big difference when creating a tilted shot. Imagine a tilt up from a person's shoes to a close-up. If we use a wide lens on a camera that is close to the character, the shoes and floor will be seen in a down shot, and at the end of the tilt up the person's face will be seen in an up shot against the ceiling. But if a longer lens is used and the camera is positioned across the room, the tilt will involve much less rotation. This means that the angle will change less from the beginning to the end of the shot, and consequently much less of the floor and ceiling will be seen.

Focus and Storytelling

Viewers' eyes are drawn to the part of a shot that is in focus. Most of what is closer to and farther from the camera is blurry because it is out of focus. This is often called *soft focus*. In general the subject of a shot is what's in focus, and the lens is adjusted to maintain focus when a character moves or the camera moves.

A shot can begin with a character in soft focus, and the character can then be brought into focus in three ways. The first technique is to adjust the lens to bring the character into focus, perhaps suggesting that the character is regaining consciousness. (An alternative storytelling approach is to begin instead on the character's

LENSES CAN CHANGE APPARENT DEPTH AND SPEED

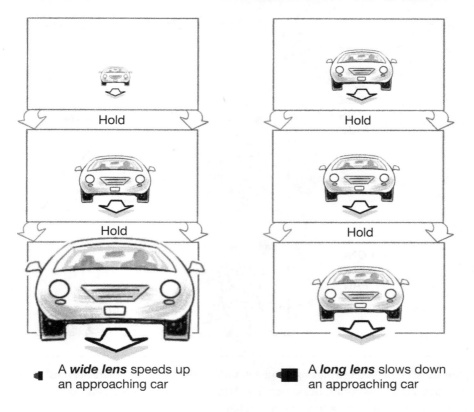

Figure 4.8 Lenses can exaggerate perspective and speed up or slow down apparent speed toward and away from the camera.

POV and bring this into focus.) The second technique is to begin the shot with the character out of focus, but as the character moves closer to the camera, the actor enters the focal plane and becomes sharp. This technique creates a mood of mystery. In the third technique the shot begins with a foreground or background character (or object) in focus, and then the focus is shifted to a second character (or object) at a different distance from the camera. This is called a *rack focus* (Figure 4.10), and it allows a single shot to first highlight one subject and then another for storytelling purposes.

Zooming and Storytelling

A *zoom* is most often used to go quickly from a wide shot to a close-up for emphasis instead of using a match cut or a punch in. Some directors also use short, fast zooms

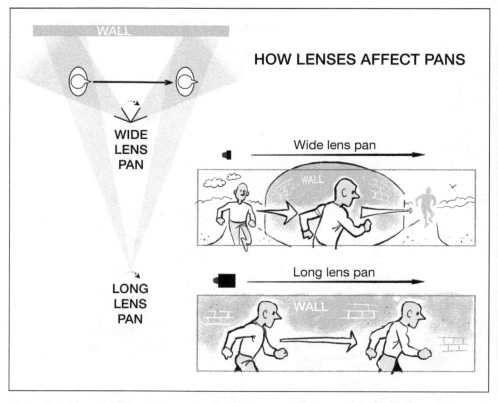

Figure 4.9 When shooting a moving character, a wide lens close to the character must rotate much farther than a more distant long lens needs to. The wide lens produces greater changes to the character's size and to the background, and the distortion is noticeable.

in action sequences and to highlight characters' reactions. Such zooms are one element of the cinéma-vérité style, which favors handheld shots, casual framing, and sudden zooms and pans. The goal of cinéma-vérité is an appearance of spontaneity and authenticity. This is achieved by appropriating the impromptu style of the camerawork of documentaries, which out of necessity is sloppier, since documentary filmmakers typically record unfolding events without having much control over them. Here are some additional uses of zooms:

- A small zoom in is often hidden in a panning shot to improve the composition at the end of the pan.
- A zoom can zero in on one window of a building that is being surveilled to clearly identify it.
- A snap zoom is a quick zoom that is used to tighten a close-up in order to motivate a flashback, or to draw the audience's attention to something.

Figure 4.10 A shift in focus can be used to direct viewers' attention between objects at different distances from the camera. A rack focus can be done between characters or between a characters and an object.

- If a frightened character turns back suddenly to look near the camera, a zoom out can reveal that no one is there.
- A zoom out can be used to highlight that a character is trapped in a particular situation or environment.

5

Designing Shots for Storytelling

The simplest approach to shooting the action of an entire scene would be to use a single stationary wide shot, a single medium shot that pans left and right as needed, or a handheld camera that follows the characters around. Unfortunately these approaches are usually not ideal for visually heightening the drama of a scene. To effectively dramatize most scenes, the camera has to record several shots that are designed to emphasize specific dramatic beats, and these shots will all have different characteristics. During editing the shots are cut together in a way to make the story-telling as effective as possible.

During any shot, the camera may move or be stationary, pan or tilt, and be positioned at any height and distance. It may be positioned to show a moving character traveling in any direction. The characters may be framed in many ways. As this chapter will show, all of these choices have a great influence on the storytelling. For a story to have impact, the shots must be carefully designed to support the drama.

Types of Camera Movement

A camera has great freedom of movement. The phrase "six degrees of freedom" is sometimes used to precisely describe freedom of movement in three-dimensional space. The six degrees of freedom comprise three types of *rotation* and three types of *translation*, which is typically referred to as the camera *traveling*. Rotations involve movement around a fixed axis that runs through an object, while translations involve an object traveling to a new position at a different point in space.

Rotating the Camera While Recording

A camera can be rotated on three axes. Rotation on the camera's vertical axis is a *pan*, which gives a range of views to the left and right. Rotation of the camera on its horizontal axis *tilts* it up and down and gives it a range of views from a high angle through eye level to a low angle (Figure 5.1). Pans and tilts are often used to keep a moving character or vehicle visible in the frame for longer as it travels past. Pans and tilts are also often used to give a wider view of something large. For example a pan across a landscape is a common type of establishing shot that starts a scene by introducing the setting.

The third way that the camera can be rotated is along its line of sight, which is the axis that runs through the center of its lens. This creates a *canted* (or *Dutched*) view,

The Art of Cinematic Storytelling. Kelly Gordon Brine, Oxford University Press (2020). © Oxford University Press.
DOI: 10.1093/oso/9780190054328.001.0001.

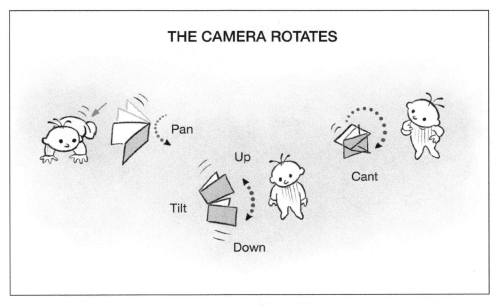

Figure 5.1 A camera can rotate on three axes. This can be done while the camera is stationary or traveling. Rotation on the vertical axis is a pan, and rotation on the horizontal axis is a tilt. Canting the camera is tipping it sideways by rotating it using its line of sight as the axis.

which is like the off-balance view you have when you tip your head toward your shoulder. The horizon is no longer horizontal. Although stationary shots taken at a canted angle are fairly common, shots taken during a canted rotation are not Such shots could be characters' POV's as they peek around corners, as they fall to the side, or as they sit up from lying on their side.

The Camera Travels While Recording

The camera is often made to travel through space while it's recording. The three axes of movement for travel through space are forward and backward, left and right, and up and down (Figure 5.2). This movement can be created either by carrying the camera or by using equipment such as dollies, jibs, booms, cranes, and drones. The continuous change of perspective of a shot recorded from a moving camera can make it more interesting, exciting, and immersive. Moving shots are often used to stay with a moving character and to show the moving character's POV. Sometimes shots are taken in which the camera moves even though it is not traveling with someone. This is most often done to highlight a character's reaction or to introduce a new scene.

A camera move is often combined with a camera rotation such as a pan. One example is when the camera dollies to the right while the lens rotates to left. This is called a *counter*. A counter is useful because it keeps a stationary subject framed throughout a sideways camera move.

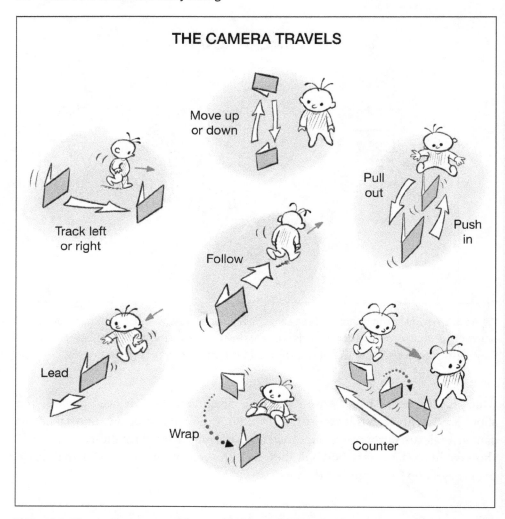

Figure 5.2 The camera can travel forward, backward, left, right, up, or down. Camera movements can be combined with rotations, such as panning while traveling, or dollying left while panning right to create a countering movement.

Camera movement is smooth when a camera is mounted on a crane or dolly. A handheld camera creates shaky shots because it's impossible for an operator to carry a normal camera and keep it steady while walking. A certain amount of optical and digital smoothing is provided by some video cameras, but for smooth handheld shots a camera stabilizer must be used. A *Steadicam* makes use of counterweights to record very smooth shots while the camera is being carried by an operator. It is ideal for shooting on steps or rough terrain, during complex moves, and where dolly tracks cannot be used because they would be visible in the shot. A Steadicam can even be used to record low-angle shots from a height that is barely above the floor.

Motivated and Unmotivated Camera Movement

When considering whether the camera should move, the question of its *motivation* must be addressed. The motivation is the reason for the camera's movement, and it may be in response to either the action or the drama. An example of action motivating the camera occurs when a character starts to walk: the camera must pan or dolly if the character is to be kept in the shot. A character who is shown receiving bad news provides a dramatic motivation for camera movement: the camera pushes closer to increase viewers' empathy for the character.

What if the camera starts to move but there is no motivation provided by either the action or the drama? This is called an *unmotivated* camera move. An example is the camera panning off the characters it has in view to scan the room and find another character. Unmotivated moves can be confusing for viewers, as it may seem like the camera is a character who is looking around. This can make a scene seem less real.

Unmotivated camera moves are normally used only to begin scenes, and for this purpose they are very effective. An unmotivated move that finds the subject of the shot is usually understood by viewers as a signal that a new scene is beginning. When this technique is used it makes the cut from scene to scene visually smoother, while also suggesting a distance from the previous scene in time and space. An unmotivated move that begins a new scene is a transition technique that is created in the camera and not in the editing room.

Examples of Motivated Camera Moves

Motivated camera moves are a response to the action or the drama.

- Action across the screen motivates camera movement that will keep the person or thing framed in the shot or at a constant distance from the camera.
- A character's head turn or look motivates a pan or tilt to see the character's POV (Figure 5.3).
- A close shot that starts on the action of a character's hands can tilt up to the character's face. The shot's beginning serves as the character's POV of the character's own hands, and when the tilt lands on the face, this link is understood to have been the motivation.
- The camera can push in as a character reacts to events.
- A short pan between two side-by-side characters who are looking in the same direction is motivated by an understanding of the context. They might be visiting a patient in a hospital, or be seated side by side at a dinner table or in a car. The advantages of a pan in these situations are avoiding a cut, linking the characters psychologically, and adding movement to an otherwise static scene.

MOTIVATING A CUT WITH A LOOK OR A HEAD TURN

Figure 5.3 A pan can be motivated by a character's look or head turn.

- To create a wrap the camera must circle or partially circle a character in one direction while it pans the opposite way to keep the character framed. The motivation for this move is a dramatic one: the character is reacting to events. Sometimes a wrap is intensified by having the character rotate slowly in the opposite direction.
- A wide master shot can slowly creep sideways or closer to the subject to add visual variety to an otherwise static scene, as well as to create suspense. This move is motivated by the drama.
- Pulling the camera away from a character at the end of a scene leaves that character at the mercy of the environment. This tells viewers that the character faces challenges, and can underscore that the character is overworked, lost, alone, trapped, or hopeless. The effect is heightened by moving the camera upward as well as backward.

Using Unmotivated Camera Moves to Introduce Scenes

Introducing new scenes is almost the only use of unmotivated camera moves. Viewers understand an unmotivated move as a signal that a new scene is beginning. Although there are other ways to open a scene, unmotivated camera moves do "open the curtains" very effectively. The camera may pan, dolly, or tilt until what starts the new scene comes into view. The camera often starts on something nondescript in the foreground, such as a wall, and the camera's movement off it reveals the subject of the shot, and the action of the scene begins if it is not already underway. When an unmotivated pan is used to begin a scene, it may optionally be given a slight nudge from background movement such as birds in flight or pedestrians. In these cases the camera movement is not entirely unmotivated.

Unmotivated moves in the middle of a scene are usually avoided because they make the camera have a personality, but sometimes an exception is made. The camera can pan to something very unusual that the audience must see, such as an unexpected witness to the events of a scene, a clue that has been overlooked, or an angle where something magical starts to happen. The camera may also pan away in modesty when a scene is about to become intimate, or if a character's grief or other emotion is too intense, and the pan ends the scene.

Deciding Whose Scene It Is

In almost every scene there is one character who drives the story. Viewers should experience the drama of a scene from the perspective of the character whose scene it is, as this affects how they feel about it. The fact that the events of a scene should be shown mainly from this character's perspective affects the way the action is staged and where the camera is positioned. It also affects the cuts and the transitions into and out of the scene.

A Story Told from Three Perspectives

Suppose there is a scene in which one man assaults another at night on a quiet street. This story could be told in four ways: through the eyes of the attacker, through the eyes of the victim, through the eyes of a witness, or objectively.

To tell the story objectively requires wide, stationary camera angles that are not from the perspective of any of the characters and are not synchronized with a character's movement. A surveillance camera is an example of objective coverage. Covering a scene objectively feels cold and detached. The shots record the action of the scene, but little about the emotions and psychology of the characters. Because we are not experiencing the events with and through a character, we feel no passion.

If our story is told through the eyes of a witness, the assault must be shot from the witness's vantage point. The witness might be looking through a window or from behind an obstruction such as a wall or a vehicle. We see the witness's reaction in close-up, and we feel the witness's emotions. Although the assault might be covered in two sizes from the witness's angle, neither is close enough to elicit great sympathy from viewers for the victim.

If our story is told from the attacker's point of view, we move with this character as he approaches his victim, recording shots as the camera travels with him, both leading and following. We also shoot the attacker's moving POV to intercut it with the other two moving shots. Several close, slightly low-angle shots could dramatically record the assault. In this version of the attack the emphasis is more on the attacker than the victim, and the attacker should be the character who is seen in tighter shots. We escape with the attacker by once again using moving cameras. The attacker could exit close to the camera as it records a moving shot that is leading him. In this version the story is told subjectively from the attacker's viewpoint.

If this is the victim's scene, we should be with the victim before, during, and after the attack. We should get to know the victim before the assault. The camera should travel with the victim. The attack itself emphasizes the victim more than the killer. A menacing shot of the attacker is seen from the victim's angle, and there could be a low-angle shot from the victim's POV lying on the pavement. When the attacker leaves, the camera stays with the victim. The story in this case is told subjectively from the victim's POV, and we feel sympathy for the victim.

Occasionally the character whose scene it is changes as a scene progresses. For example, the scene just described could be told from the attacker's POV until the attack is over. But then as the scene seems to be ending in a wide shot that shows the attacker leaving, the camera moves backward slightly to surprise us by revealing the shoulder of someone we did not realize was watching. It is now this witness's scene, and the final shot is the witness's close-up reaction.

Highlighting the Character Whose Scene It Is

As seen in the previous examples, specific techniques can be used to throw the spotlight on the character whose scene it is. Here is a summary of the main ones:

- The character whose scene it is will often be present throughout the scene.
- The important action of the scene is shown largely from the main character's POV.
- We see the main character's reactions in close-up.
- The main character has tight eyelines to the camera.
- The camera height is close to the main character's eye level.
- When the main character moves, the camera often moves too.
- There may be a push in as the main character reacts, usually at the scene's end.
- The scene often ends on the reaction or exit of the character whose scene it is.

Creating Objective and Subjective Shots

To experience events with characters and share their thoughts and feelings, we have to be close to them, travel with them, and see what they see. In general the character whose scene it is is the one who will be given the most subjective shots. These subjective shots parallel how we feel in life: we often feel more emotionally connected to people we are near. Objective shots are from a greater distance and do not move with the character. They give us more of a feeling of detachment.

Often a scene starts objectively and gradually becomes more subjective. This is mainly achieved by gradually positioning the camera closer and by starting to move the camera in a way that's synchronized with the movements of the scene's main character. The characteristics of objective and subjective shots are illustrated in Figure 5.4.

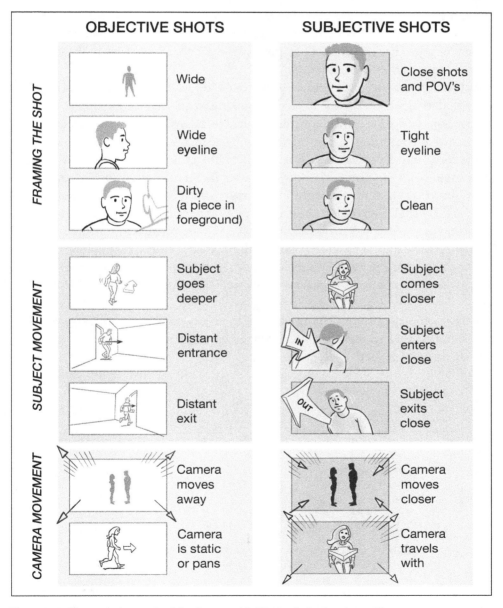

Figure 5.4 Shots can be made objective or subjective to help the storytelling.

Shot Size and Storytelling

The shot size of a character is the key indicator of how important a character is at a particular point in a story. When characters are large on the screen, we feel that we are close to them. Most of the background is excluded, and this helps us concentrate on the character without being distracted by thoughts about the character's surroundings.

A close-up makes us feel a strong relationship with a character. The shot size and how it affects viewers can vary during a shot if the actor approaches the camera or if the camera approaches the actor, but if the camera moves in sync with a character, the shot size and the feeling it causes do not change. When the apparent size of a character does change, the shot's emphasis swings either more toward the character or more toward the environment.

When designing a close-up there is often a choice whether foreground is included or excluded in a shot. If one character is talking to another, or looking at a nearby object, a part of the second character or the object may appear in the foreground of the first character's shot. If it's a person, the piece that is shown could be a shoulder. If the foreground element is a computer monitor or other equipment, one corner of it could be in the frame. Keeping a piece of foreground in a close-up makes it a *dirty shot*. If there is no element in the foreground it is called a *clean shot* (Figure 5.5). A dirty shot is a type of tie-up shot. It unites two characters or a character and an object in space, and it maintains a spatial and story relationship between the two elements of the shot. A clean shot isolates the character and is more subjective.

For convenience, the various shot sizes have been given names. They are listed here, along with descriptions of their effects on storytelling. Examples are shown in Figure 5.6.

- *Very extreme close-up:* This is a shot of the eyes only. It's an intensely subjective shot that is often used to show a strong negative reaction such as shock, terror, disorientation, or disbelief.

DIRTY SHOT   CLEAN SHOT

Figure 5.5 A clean shot does not contain a foreground piece of another character or an object, and this isolation emphasizes thoughts and feelings. A dirty shot contains foreground and ties things together spatially and dramatically.

SHOT SIZE AND STORYTELLING

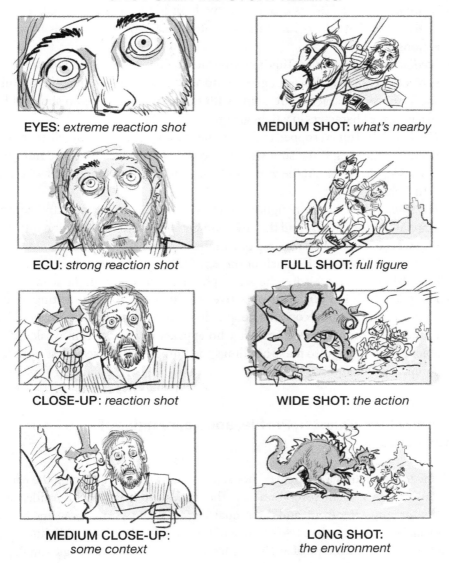

EYES: *extreme reaction shot*

MEDIUM SHOT: *what's nearby*

ECU: *strong reaction shot*

FULL SHOT: *full figure*

CLOSE-UP: *reaction shot*

WIDE SHOT: *the action*

MEDIUM CLOSE-UP:
some context

LONG SHOT:
the environment

Figure 5.6 Shot size is the single most important design element of a shot. The tightest shots are the most psychological, while the widest shots emphasize the environment and the context. Intermediate-sized shots emphasize the action.

- *Extreme close-up:* This is cropped somewhere on both the forehead and the chin. An ECU is a very subjective shot of a character who is observing or reacting. Viewers feel that they share the character's thoughts and feelings.
- *Close-up:* This is cropped at the collar-tips. A CU is a subjective shot that is a detailed view of the character's face. We are with the character in thought

and feeling. Movement must be limited so that the character does not leave the frame.

- *Medium close-up:* This is cropped at the base of the chest. An MCU is a subjective shot that allows more movement and can show the hands for certain actions.
- *Medium shot or half shot:* This is cropped just below the belt. This is a moderately subjective shot that allows for greater movement, such as walking. It is useful for showing what characters are doing with their hands. A medium shot can hold two or three characters in a tight group.
- *Cowboy shot:* This is cropped in the middle of the thigh, just below where holsters would be hanging if the shot were of a cowboy. It is as tight as the framing of a moving character can be while still showing leg movement, so it is a useful action shot.
- *Full shot:* This is the entire figure from head to toe. This is an objective shot that emphasizes the context and the environment. It is useful for showing full-figure physical action, such as dancing or running.
- *Wide shot:* This takes in much of the set, and may include many characters. It establishes or re-establishes the geography and atmosphere of the scene.
- *Long shot:* This is a very wide objective shot. It emphasizes the setting over the characters. If the shot contains people they will appear small and insignificant in their environment. A character who appears in it may seem weak, vulnerable, or lost. It may also make buildings and human activity seem less significant compared to nature.

Frontal, Three-Quarter, Profile, and Rear Angles of One Character

A character framed in a particular shot size does not have to be facing the camera, but can be shown from several angles. The angles are front, back, profile, three-quarter, three-quarter front, and three-quarter rear. In any particular scene it would be unusual to use more than two or three of these angles. This list highlights some of the advantages of each type of angle (Figure 5.7). The choice of an angle can depend on what is seen in the background. For these shots the camera may be placed one side or the other of the figure due to a physical restriction, such as which way a door swings open.

- *Front:* This is the most subjective angle on a character.
- *Three-quarter angle*: This is a subjective and three-dimensional angle that may improve the background. A three-quarter angle is a good starting point for a shot of a character who turns and walks away.
- *Profile*: This angle may improve the background. It can suggest graphically that the character is nervous or faces a challenge.

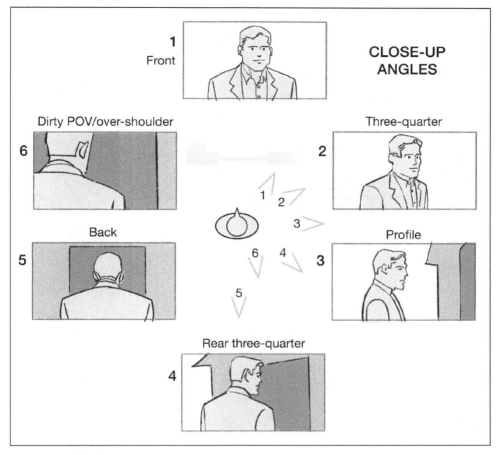

Figure 5.7 Which angle is best for a close-up depends on the action, on what the background looks like, and on the storytelling effect of each angle.

- *Rear three-quarter angle:* This angle ties together the character's POV and face. It can be used for a shot in which a second character opens a door. It can also set up a character's turn toward the camera.
- *Back:* This symmetrical shot can emphasize the importance or uncertainty of what a character is about to face or find. The camera also often follows the character from this angle to allow viewers to experience the character's journey.
- *Dirty POV:* This combines a character's POV with a piece of the character and is the basis of over-shoulder shots.

Shots of Two and Three People

Shots of two and three characters are often needed. Figure 5.8 shows several shot types and their uses.

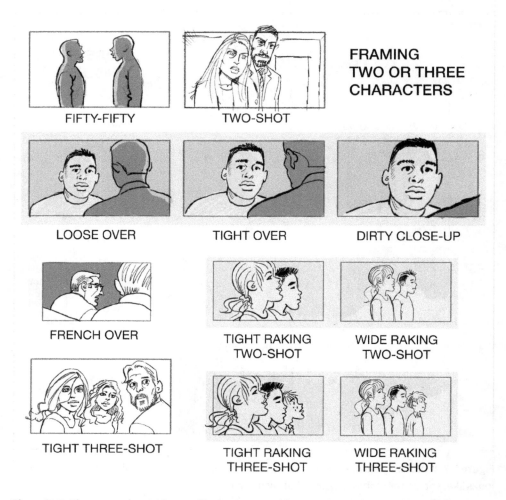

Figure 5.8 These storyboard frames illustrate several frequently used ways of framing two or three characters.

- *Fifty-fifty shot*: A balanced and graphically strong shot of two characters facing each other. The characters may be positioned in front of an attractive or striking background. It may also be shot against a background that reinforces the story beat literally or symbolically, such as a new factory or crashing waves.
- *Two-shot* or *three-shot*: Two or three characters are framed tightly and attractively. It unites the characters in space and in the story.
- *Raking shot*: This frames the characters nearly in profile. It can suggest that the characters are acting as a team. It allows a tighter shot of two or more characters by overlapping and stacking them. It makes a more interesting composition than a frontal two-shot.
- *Over-shoulder shot*: A close shot of a character that holds a piece of the person the character is talking to in the foreground. It can be framed looser to emphasize their relationship or tighter to emphasize a reaction.

- *French over* (or *negative over*): This is an over-shoulder shot of two characters who are standing or seated side by side, with the camera behind their backs.

Camera Height and Storytelling

Camera height has a significant influence on the story that a shot tells. Most of the time the camera is set close to the level of the characters' eyes. This is more or less the height of an adult observer in the room, as well as being suitable when the coverage must be subjective. In practice the camera is often set slightly lower than the characters' eyes because this creates a more flattering angle, it makes the characters seem more important, and it improves the composition.

A *high angle* looks down on a character or a scene, and it tends to make the character depicted seem immersed in the environment. A character may seem smaller, weaker, less in control, a fish out of water, threatened by something, or at the mercy of others or of the environment (Figure 5.9). A high angle is also often a good descriptive angle. It can be used as an establishing shot or as a wide shot when an elevated view makes the geography and the situation clearer. A high-angle shot could show a crowded street or military officers studying a map spread out on a table. A high angle is sometimes used for interesting and stylish shots of

Figure 5.9 A high angle can make a character seem small, weak, vulnerable, lost, confused, isolated, or immersed in the environment. Low angles make a character seem tall, powerful, confident, or threatening. Both can make heights seem more dangerous.

someone lying in bed, swimming, and many other things. A high angle is usually an objective angle.

A *low angle* makes a character seem taller, stronger, more important, more determined, more authoritative, or more threatening. A low angle can also show something important, attractive, or frightening. Low angles often introduce dramatic diagonal perspective lines into a composition.

How the Direction of Movement Affects Storytelling

The direction of the movement of characters, vehicles, and other things relative to the camera affects the storytelling.

Movement toward the Left or Right Side of the Screen

On-screen movement can be in any direction, but the most important aspect of screen movement is whether it's toward the left or the right or neither. If movement is directly into or out of the screen it is said to be headed in a *neutral* direction. Movement in a neutral direction occurs when a character or vehicle travels along the camera's line of sight (Figure 5.10).

Whether movement is toward the left or the right side of the screen influences the mood of a shot and thus affects the storytelling. Movement toward the left side usually seems a little more uncertain to viewers, and may even seem frightening.

MOVEMENT IN A NEUTRAL DIRECTION

The camera's line of sight

Figure 5.10 A neutral angle of movement occurs when something moves directly toward or away from the camera along the camera's line of sight. The on-screen movement is directly toward or away from the audience with no left or right component.

Movement toward the right seems more positive, and a character headed in that direction seems more likely to succeed (Figure 5.11). Because of this effect, directors often choose to have the good guys moving to the right, and the bad guys moving to the left. On the other hand, the good guys should move left if they are headed toward trouble. The direction of their movement can suggest that the characters are in peril even if the they are not yet aware of any danger.

The storytelling effects of the direction of screen movement apply to anything that's moving, including people, animals, vehicles, and cyborgs. This includes the on-screen movement of stationary people or objects that is created by camera movement, such as when people, trees, shelving units, or planks in a fence travel across the screen in one direction because the camera is panning or dollying in the other. In general a camera that dollies sideways across soldiers standing at attention seems to work better when the camera moves to the left, which makes the stationary soldiers move across the screen toward the right.

The physical layout of a location and the need for continuity between shots and scenes may limit directional choices, but where there is an option it's worth considering what feeling the movement gives in each direction and determining which suits the drama best. Although this is not generally the main consideration when designing a shot, the effect of direction can be important. One example is choosing which direction a character should head who is entering a dark and foreboding cave. Ideally that direction should be to the left on the screen.

There is also a geographical meaning to the direction of screen movement. This is based on the way maps are oriented: a character headed west moves to the left, while a character headed east moves to the right. This convention is used mainly for longer trips involving familiar geography, such as the westward journeys of American pioneers and flights from the Americas to Europe.

LEFT AND RIGHT MOVEMENT

A journey toward
the left seems riskier

A journey toward
the right seems more certain

Figure 5.11 Movement toward the left can suggest that things will not go well for a character, while movement toward the right suggests a better outcome.

Movement toward the Camera

Movement toward the camera is more interesting and more intense than movement across the screen. As the subject of a shot grows in size it becomes more important to the story and to viewers, whether it's a person, a train, or a boulder rolling down a hill. This is the same reaction that we feel in everyday life when something or someone approaches us.

When evil characters approach the camera, they grow more threatening, but when sympathetic characters approach, the effect is to make us identify more with their experience and their situation, as well as with their thoughts and emotions. As the subject approaches us and grows bigger in the frame, more of the background is blocked from view, which increases our focus on what is approaching. A similar effect can be achieved with stationary characters by slowly moving the camera toward them.

Movement Away from the Camera

A character's movement away from the camera reduces dramatic intensity. If the camera is not following the character then the environment grows in importance, which may underscore that the character is exploring or confronting what lies ahead, that a journey is starting, or that a scene is ending.

Movement up or down in the Frame

In general movement upward seems more positive than movement downward, whether on screen or in life. Movement to the right and upward can be combined, and this combined movement from the lower left of the screen toward the upper right is the most positive direction of travel. This parallels the direction people like to see a graph of the stock market heading. On-screen movement down in the frame and especially toward the lower left is more suspenseful than movement in other directions.

The camera position determines the on-screen direction of movement of whatever is being recorded. A high-angle shot of people walking along a sidewalk will show them moving down on the screen if they are getting closer to the camera, but will show them moving up on the screen if they are moving away from the camera. There is often a choice to be made whether a moving character will appear to travel upward or downward in the frame.

It may seem strange, but there are choices even for the screen direction of an ascent or a descent. A high angle can be found that makes a character climbing up a ladder or a mountain trail appear on screen to be moving downward in the frame and on the screen. A high angle can also be found to make a character climbing down a ladder or a hiking down a mountain trail appear to be moving up in the frame. This paradox goes unnoticed by viewers and is not important; what's important is that the angles be dramatic and attractive and support the story. Figure 5.12 summarizes the storytelling effects of the direction of movement on the screen.

Increasing the Illusion of Depth

Part of people's enjoyment of cinema is the experience of entering a different three-dimensional world. Emphasizing this illusion makes a film more realistic, immersive, and engaging. Figure 5.13 illustrates some techniques for increasing cinematic depth, and some of these are described in what follows.

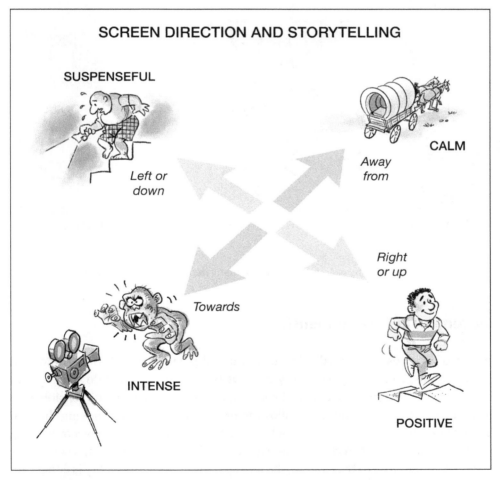

Figure 5.12 The direction of on-screen movement often influences how viewers feel about a story.

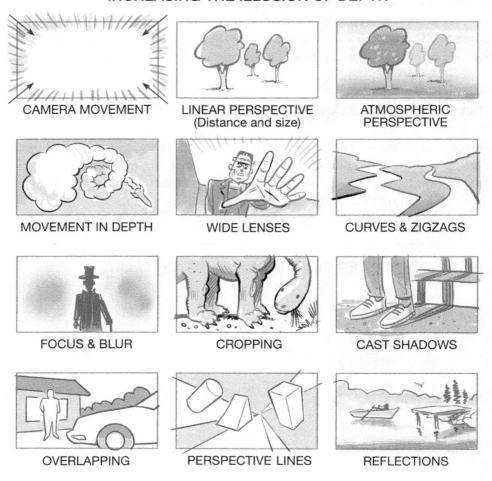

Figure 5.13 There are many ways to increase cinematic depth through shot design.

Movement in Three Dimensions

Action of all kinds enhances the illusion of three-dimensionality. Action toward and away from the camera is particularly effective because objects that do so change in apparent size. Camera movement through space has a very three-dimensional effect. Some extreme examples are following or leading a character moving through a crowd or within a narrow space such as a submarine. People and objects crossing the frame add to the three-dimensional effect. When people and objects enter or leave the frame close to the camera, the feeling of three-dimensionality is enhanced. Entrances and exits from the top of the frame are particularly dramatic. Examples are a spaceship or a car entering or exiting over the camera.

Perspective Depth Cues

Perspective creates the illusion of the convergence of the lines found in streets, sidewalks, and architecture, and this accentuates the illusion of depth on the screen. These lines are most striking in low- and high-angle shots because the vertical lines that normally appear parallel now converge dramatically. Another spatial depth cue is the overlapping of people and objects and of the foreground, middle ground, and background of an image. When a raking angle is used, perspective creates apparent size differences in people and objects that are in fact of similar size.

Lighting Depth Cues

Several lighting techniques can increase the illusion of depth. Backlighting puts an edge of light on objects, separating them from their background. A fog machine can create haze that creates atmospheric perspective in which more distant objects lack color, contrast, and detail. Reflections on wet surfaces and in water add to the illusion of depth. When characters step into and out of pools or shafts of light the space they are in seems more real. Strong shadows cast by blinds, poles, or figures can be compositionally striking while enhancing the three-dimensionality of an image.

Lens Choices and Cinematic Depth

A lens that is wider than a normal lens forces the perspective of a shot by exaggerating the size differences of people and objects at various distances from the camera. This increases the apparent speed of movement toward and away from the camera, and one common use is to make the arrival and departure of cars more dramatic.

Shots That Capture Attention

Viewers like shots with action. This is not possible for every shot, but many shots can be enhanced, and it's worth taking the time to consider whether action can be added.

Adding Entrances, Reveals, and Wipes

Entrances, reveals, and wipes are all ways of bringing characters into scenes. They add action, excitement, and sometimes a small amount of mystery to what might otherwise be stationary shots and static scenes. When used to begin the first shot of a new scene, they create the feeling of time having passed since the events of the previous scene.

Entrances are dramatic. Live theater makes frequent use of entrances from the wings as well as from around corners and through doors on the set. In film similar techniques are used, including walking into a shot from off-camera, entering from behind a wall or other obstruction, coming through a door, turning on a light, or walking to a point where a character is in focus.

The term *reveal* describes anything that brings a hidden or unrecognizable character into view without the character actually making an entrance. The theatrical equivalents are a rising curtain, a spotlight coming on, an object being lowered, or a character turning to face the audience. In film a reveal can be created by using either action or camera movement. A reveal through action can be created by such things as a refrigerator door opening (with the camera inside), the removal of a mask, the lowering of a newspaper, or a character stepping into the light. Camera movement can create reveals in several ways, including moving sideways to be able to see beyond a corner or moving backward to create a wider view that pulls a character into the frame. An advantage of reveals is that characters are given something similar to an entrance, yet they do not have to be actually arriving, but may be discovered already in the middle of an activity. Reveals are often used to begin scenes.

A *wipe* occurs when a foreground object, vehicle, or person crosses in front of the camera, momentarily blocking the camera's view. A *wipe in* occurs at the beginning of a shot. Something moves out of the way to reveal the scene. A *wipe out* ends a scene as something moves in front of the frame to block the camera's view. Wipes increase the feeling of a busy environment, depth, and sometimes urgency. Ending a shot with a wipe makes the cut that follows immediately seem more natural. Wipes have a function that is similar to the opening and closing of theater curtains.

Action

Shots with action are more interesting than shots without. Action is most exciting when it is seen from a low angle, when it's close to the camera, and when it's directed toward the camera. Action can be added to a shot in various ways, such as by giving characters business or having them walk while they talk to each other.

Other Movement within a Shot

The movement of extras and traffic across the frame in the foreground or background is exciting and adds to the verisimilitude of a scene. Other options for motion include using a wind to blow foliage, fallen leaves, or laundry on a line, as well as well as rain and machinery that is operating. These can make a setting more immersive and help create a mood. When no movement is available in a setting, the camera can create motion artificially by creeping slowly sideways in a wide shot of the scene.

Shots That Create Mystery

When viewers are unable to identify someone, when they see only part of something, and when they hear something off-screen, their curiosity is piqued. They pay more attention because there is a mystery. Here are a few examples of mysterious shots that intrigue viewers:

- A shot begins on a character's back and we must wait a moment before he turns to reveal who he is.
- The camera starts on a leg sticking out from under the sheets and slowly dollies to find the sleeping figure's face.
- We see hands or feet first, and then tilt up to find the character's face.
- A character cannot be identified immediately due to being obscured by objects, lighting, or fog, or due to the camera angle.
- A shadow enters a shot on the floor or a wall.
- We hear an off-camera voice or a sound such as a shower running. The camera slowly pans or travels to find the source.
- The camera follows a trail of blood, clothing, or other items.
- A pan or dolly lands unexpectedly on a character's close-up.
- We see the lower part of a door (or car door) swing open and feet step into view.
- A fender and tire suddenly enter the frame and stop in a close shot.

Designing Shots That Create Moods

The actions and dialogue of characters are the essence of a film, but the drama can fall flat if the shots don't suit the story. Shown in what follows are some types of shots and techniques that are commonly used in several kinds of scenes.

Building Suspense

Suspense generally comes when viewers know something important and perhaps threatening before a character does. These techniques help increase a story's suspense visually:

- Viewers see something threatening, such an evil person's presence, before a character does.
- A character is seen partly obscured through foreground such as a fence, a window, foliage, or blinds, or seen through a window.
- A wide shot of the scene slowly moves sideways, passing foreground such as diners, laboratory equipment, sculptures, columns, trees, or fencing.
- Shots may suggest they are someone's POV because they include a piece of foreground and are slightly unsteady. This is sometimes done even when there is no one watching.
- A long lens that holds two people in conversation while cars or people cross the foreground is unsettling and suggests that the characters are not entirely in control of events.
- High and low angles can generate strong diagonal lines in a composition. These create an uneasy feeling compared to peaceful horizontal and vertical lines.
- Shadows in a composition can create a threatening feeling.
- A quick falloff of light to a dark background can create a sinister or foreboding feeling. (Sunlight has no measurable falloff, but light from vastly weaker artificial sources quickly loses its intensity with distance.)
- A shot can re-establish how isolated a character is, such as a cutaway outside that re-establishes a lonely farmhouse at night.

Increasing the Feeling of Mystery and Foreboding

Mystery is when something is not explained or understood. In a film we may not know who characters are or what their intentions are, or who is responsible for something that has happened. The feeling of mystery can be enhanced visually.

- The wind blows leaves, flags, an empty swing, a wind chime, or laundry on a clothesline.
- A normally happy place such as a playground or home is closed and empty.
- Scenes take place in the fall, at night, or during a storm.

Intensifying a Character's Action or Psychology

These are examples of visual possibilities to intensify a character's action or psychology:

- Subjective shots are more psychologically intense than objective ones.
- A shot starts on the hands of a character, and tilts up to the face.

- Cutting from a character's close-up to an abstract shot can imply something about the character's psychology. Cuts can be made between a preoccupied driver and shots of rain hitting the windshield while the wipers sweep across, or shiny wet pavement racing past, or the movement of out-of-focus taillights as seen through a long lens.
- Events in nature can mirror events in the plot, such as rain, wind, and nightfall, and shots of nature can reflect a character's mood.
- The camera circles a character. The character may rotate slowly in the opposite direction.
- The camera follows an in-focus character, but what's ahead is out of focus.
- A character's POV goes out of focus and this ends the scene.

Emphasizing Urgent and Important Action

These are examples of visual possibilities to emphasize action:

- Jump cuts within scenes and to new scenes
- Low-angle shots
- Subjective shots that lead and follow a character
- Shots with a moving POV that a character steps into and the shot continues
- Scenes that open with a close shot of feet on the move and tilting up
- Handheld shots that make characters and events seem more agitated
- Swish pans from one character to another in a related scene
- Exaggeration of action and movement, including arrivals and departures, through the use of a wide lens
- Wipes and crosses by people and vehicles to make an environment seem busier

6

Continuity Editing Basics

Trimming and sequencing shots with the goal of telling a story that seems to flow continuously, clearly, and logically in time and space is called *continuity editing*. Continuity editing respects viewers' natural assumption that time and space are contiguous from shot to shot, and it achieves this by using techniques that minimize discontinuities. Continuity editing helps filmmakers satisfy their viewers' expectation that people and objects should not seem to jump instantaneously and unrealistically within a setting or to a new place and time. Even directors who have a style in which they frequently use jump cuts and "cross the axis" nevertheless employ continuity editing much of the time.

Continuity editing can make a story's unavoidable changes of time and place seem smooth and natural, but this is only possible if the director has created shots with continuity in mind. The small set of continuity rules that guide directors, cinematographers, and editors is called film grammar. This chapter introduces continuity editing and film grammar, and these ideas are explored further in the next two chapters, as well as being interwoven with the storytelling theme throughout this book.

The Importance of Left and Right to Editing

Screen motion can be in six directions: left or right, up or down, and into or out of the screen. For continuity editing the left and the right of the screen are most important because they are the foundation of viewers' understanding of a film's space. An example illustrates this fact. In a film a mountain climber ascending a peak may sometimes be seen in a high-angle shot that is framed such that the climber appears to move downward on the screen, but viewers are not confused as long as the climber continues to move consistently in just one direction across the screen. If on the other hand, the climber is seen moving to the right in one shot and to the left in the next, it may seem like the climber has turned around.

Questions of left and right are concerned with characters' positions on the two-dimensional screen, where they are looking, and the direction of their movement. Whether screen movement is angled toward or away from the camera, or upward or downward, is far less important than the consideration of whether motion is toward the left or right side of the flat movie or television screen. In other words the exact degree of a character's look or movement relative to the camera's line of sight is of much less importance than the fact that it is to the left or the right. Movement that appears to be *directly* into or out of the screen is movement in a *neutral* direction (Figure 6.1).

The Art of Cinematic Storytelling. Kelly Gordon Brine, Oxford University Press (2020). © Oxford University Press. DOI: 10.1093/oso/9780190054328.001.0001.

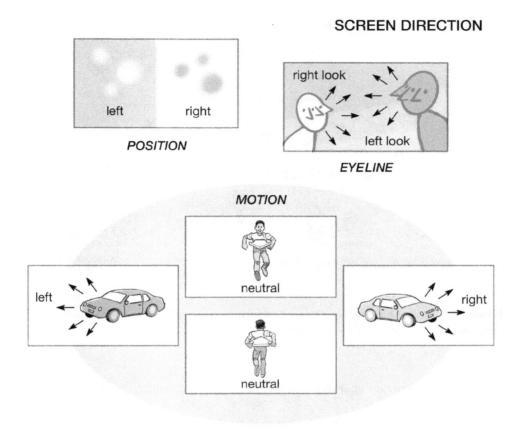

Figure 6.1 Viewers' understanding of a film's spatial relationships is based on the left and right of the flat screen. This applies to characters' positions, where they're looking, and the direction they are moving in. This is important for continuity editing.

Characters, Settings, and Cuts

Almost every shot has a subject (usually a character) and a setting, such as a room. Every few seconds a cut occurs as the current shot is replaced by a different shot. The new shot may change the subject, the setting, or both. The four types of changes that are possible when cutting are illustrated in Figure 6.2. This example uses two characters, a rabbit and a fox, and two settings, a field and a forest. The conclusions about time that viewers would instinctively make when shown this example can be generalized to all combinations of subjects and settings. Here are the four types of cuts that can be made:

1. The cut is to a new camera angle on the same rabbit in the same field. We infer that time is continuous.

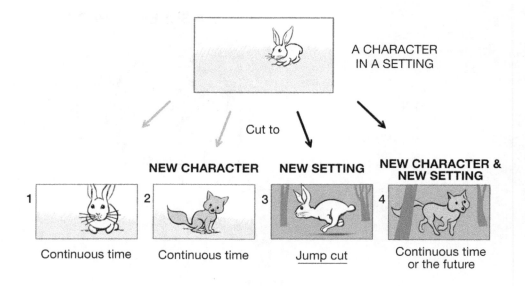

Figure 6.2 Shots can be juxtaposed in four basic ways: the subject changes, the setting changes, both change, or neither changes.

2. The cut is to a new character, the fox, in the same setting, the field. We infer that time is continuous.
3. The cut is from the rabbit in the field to the same rabbit, but it's now in the forest. We are confused because this jump cut is discontinuous in time and space. The rabbit has been transported instantaneously from the field to the forest.
4. The cut is from the rabbit in the field to the fox in the forest. We infer that time is continuous, and there is no jump cut because the fox is a different character.

Continuity editing avoids jump cuts because it is unrealistic when a character jumps instantaneously from one position in space and time to another. Directors sometimes use jump cuts in spite of this drawback in order to quicken the pace of the storytelling, help describe the mental state of a character, or emphasize the urgency of a character's actions. But when they are overused they undermine the reality of the space and time of the story.

The Beta Effect and Shot Contrast

The illusion of motion that results from playing slightly different still images in sequence makes both live action films and animation possible. We don't perceive on-screen images as a sequence of stills, but as a single continuous moving image. This psychological phenomenon is sometimes called the *beta effect*. The illusion of movement that is created from still images can be in any direction, including toward and away from viewers. It can also make objects seem to rotate or transform.

The beta effect occurs naturally from the images contained in one continuous shot, but it also occurs when two separate but visually similar shots are joined. Juxtaposed shots may be similar for several reasons, including what the subjects of the shots are, their shapes and positions, and their apparent size within the frame. When a beta effect occurs at a cut, it's usually unintentional and misleading to viewers. If care isn't taken when designing shots and cuts, beta effects will be created that are seen as jumps, pops, turns, and transformations (Figure 6.3).

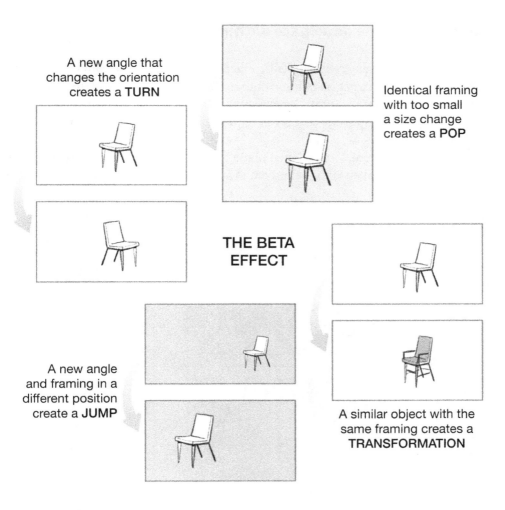

Figure 6.3 The beta effect occurs at a cut when there is an important similarity between the two juxtaposed shots. The characters or objects involved can appear to jump, pop, rotate, or transform.

Shot Contrast Eliminates the Beta Effect

Shot contrast is a measure of how visually different two images are from each other. Shot contrast enables a viewer to quickly see that a new shot is not a continuation of the previous shot, and this helps make a cut clear and smooth. The degree of shot contrast between two images can be evaluated to ensure that nothing is so similar in the two compositions that it might mislead viewers when a cut is made. Figure 6.4 illustrates shot contrast using two abstract compositions. Because the compositions are so different in their lines, shapes, and tones, a viewer does not try to mentally join one to the other.

Continuous Time and Space within a Scene

Good shot contrast generally results in a better cut, but an important exception to this is required when a cut is made to another shot of the same subject. In these cases the camera operator must frame the two shots to *match* certain elements—especially the subject's position—while making sure to have shot contrast in other aspects of the two compositions.

Within a single scene a cut is often made from a shot of a character to a shot of the same character taken with the camera in a new position. This is most often done

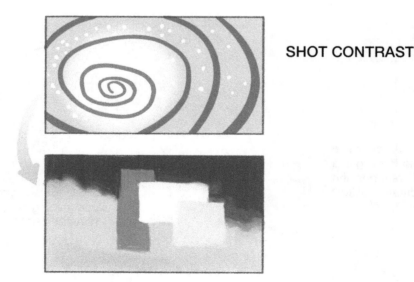

SHOT CONTRAST

Figure 6.4 Shot contrast makes it easy to see that two shots are of different subjects and are not different angles on the same subject. This prevents the beta effect from occurring.

to see the character in a closer shot. The two shots of the same character (or object) have to be carefully designed so that they do not introduce the beta effect because they do not match properly.

The Match Cut

If a character appears in two successive shots and time is continuous, then a *match cut* is the normal method of cutting because it maintains spatial continuity and prevents a beta effect from being created. A match cut shows the same characters continuing their action in a different shot size, usually closer but sometimes from farther away. The two shots are designed to match both the character's position on the screen and the direction of the character's look, but the second shot slightly changes the camera angle so that it is more frontal. Figure 6.5 illustrates a cut to the same subject without a match cut and with a match cut. If the camera is carefully positioned to achieve these goals the shots will cut together well, meaning that there will be no beta effect. Match cuts are looked at in more detail in Chapter 7.

Screen Geography

Screen geography means the left-and-right placement of characters and objects on the screen as established when they are first shown. Once a shot has introduced where things are in terms of the left and right of the two-dimensional screen, continuity editing aims to maintain consistent screen geography so that viewers can

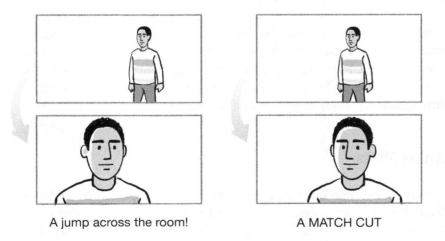

| A jump across the room! | A MATCH CUT |

Figure 6.5 A match cut prevents a character from seeming to suddenly jump across the screen.

The camera can make
characters switch sides!

CONSISTENT SCREEN
GEOGRAPHY

Figure 6.6 When characters remain on their own side of the screen from shot to shot they do not seem to trade places when cuts are made.

easily keep their bearings. In this way viewers can quickly understand each new shot within the framework they have become familiar with. A sudden flipping of established screen geography can create confusion for viewers because they momentarily lose their orientation when characters suddenly switch positions (Figure 6.6). There are ways to reset screen geography, and they are described in Chapter 8.

Opposed Looks (Eyeline Match)

Two separate shots of two characters can show them both looking in the same screen direction, or the shots can show them with *opposed looks*. If one character has a left look and the other has a right look, viewers understand that this means they are looking at each other. When two characters have the *same* look viewers interpret this as both characters looking at the same off-screen person or thing (Figure 6.7).

Matching Shots

Conversations are often shot using close-ups and over-shoulder shots. When a film is edited, there are very often cuts back and forth between these shots. Each pair of close-ups or over-shoulder shots should be *mirrored* in their compositions. If they are not mirrored, differences in size and placement can create a beta effect that appears as a distracting bounce. Pairs of mirrored shots are called *matching shots*

Both are looking at something off-camera

They are looking at each other

Figure 6.7 When separate shots of two characters show them with the same look, viewers understand them to both be looking at the same off-screen character or object in that direction. Characters with opposed looks appear to be looking at each other.

Unmatched shots may bounce!

MATCHING SHOTS

Figure 6.8 Repeated cuts between reverse angles of two characters having a conversation may create a visual bounce if the shots don't match.

(Figure 6.8). Since the bounce does not arise unless there are *several* cuts back and forth, matching shots are not necessary when each shot is on the screen just once or twice during a brief verbal exchange. This topic is explored further in Chapter 8.

Continuity of Screen Motion

When something is in motion on the screen it has a screen direction. The two most important directions are left and right, but travel can also be up, down, or directly into or out of the screen. To maintain continuity a person or vehicle that is seen moving left or right should not normally be seen in the next shot going in the opposite direction (Figure 6.9). There are some exceptions to this and there are ways to change the screen direction. These are examined in Chapter 8.

Three Kinds of Jump Cuts

When continuity editing is not followed, jump cuts occur. A jump cut suddenly moves a character ahead in time (or occasionally backward in time). The character is also in a new position in space, sometimes close by and sometimes far away.

Jump cuts are abrupt and obvious. The farther away the new setting seems, the more abrupt the jump cut is because there is no explanation of how the character arrived there. Jump cuts disrupt the continuity of time and space in the narrative

A change of direction?　　　CONTINUITY OF SCREEN MOTION

Figure 6.9 Continuity of screen motion means maintaining the direction of travel to the left or right of the screen. Unexplained direction changes can create momentary confusion for viewers.

and can make a story seem more urgent but sometimes less realistic. There are other options for time compression, but jump cuts are sometimes a good choice.

Even though jump cuts break continuity editing, some directors use them frequently. In addition to speeding up the pace of storytelling, they can be dramatic or funny. A jump cut can show that a character is in a hurry, very busy, or on a mission. A jump cut might even show that characters are doing the opposite of what they said they'd do. If jump cuts are used too frequently they may undermine the verisimilitude of the film.

A Jump Cut within a Single Shot

Any activity that is covered in a *single shot* can be made more urgent, and the time it takes to achieve it can be compressed, by discarding some of the middle pieces of one continuously recorded shot. A series of *jump cuts within a single shot* is sometimes used to show quickly the steps someone takes as the person gets dressed, prepares food, or builds something (Figure 6.10). The pace is fast and the look is choppy. It is used for comedy as well as drama. Jump cuts within a scene are an alternative to a montage for telling part of a story quickly.

SINGLE-SHOT JUMP CUTS

Cut out some footage

Cut out some footage

Figure 6.10 Single-shot jump cuts are created by omitting pieces of continuous action. A character will make small abrupt jumps in space and this will give the impression that the character is in a hurry or on a mission.

A Jump Cut within a Scene

Action within one scene can also be sped up by using jump cuts between shots. A *jump cut within a scene* is usually a cut to a new angle on the same character now doing something different in a different spot within the same setting just seconds or minutes into the future. The character has jumped a small amount in time and space. The pace and intensity of the storytelling is increased, but time within the scene seems almost continuous because the jumps in time and space are quite short and we do not feel that much of the story has been skipped. A series of such jump cuts is similar to a montage, the difference being that the same character is in every shot.

Within a single scene one or more jump cuts can be made to show a character doing different but related things, such as working on a project, or talking on the phone and then hurrying out the door (Figure 6.11). This compresses time and creates a sense of urgency. This type of jump cut is not as jarring if there is substantial shot contrast. One example is a wide shot of a plane landing headed screen right in a wide shot being followed by the same plane in a tight shot moving left as it pulls up to the terminal gate. The strong shot contrast makes this jump cut work well.

A jump cut backward in time within a scene "presses rewind" to replay an event from a different angle, sometimes several times. It is most often used for explosions, car crashes, or shootings. Some of the shots may be in slow motion.

SAME-SCENE JUMP CUTS

Figure 6.11 A same-scene jump cut is a small jump in time and space that shows the same character performing a new action a moment later in a place near where the character was last seen. A same-scene jump cut is abrupt, but it advances the story very quickly.

NEW-SCENE JUMP CUTS

ABRUPT

URGENT

DELAYED
RECOGNITION

Figure 6.12 A jump cut to a new scene is the most abrupt kind because the distance in time and space is greatest. The jump cut can show urgency, resolve, or comedy. A jump cut is less noticeable if the character is not recognized immediately.

A Jump Cut to a New Scene

If the character who is shown in the very last shot of one scene appears immediately in the first shot of the following scene, this is a *jump cut to a new scene*. This is an especially noticeable jump cut because the character's instantaneous arrival in the new setting makes the character appear to have jumped far in time and space. A new-scene jump cut continues the story abruptly and often urgently in a new setting. Occasionally the jump cut may not register as such. This can occur because the character is not immediately recognized in the new setting due to the camera angle or the lighting, and this small delay can be enough to convey a time interval between the two scenes and preserve continuity. Figure 6.12 illustrates three varieties of a jump cut between scenes.

Avoiding Jump Cuts

Continuity editing avoids jump cuts by not creating hard cuts to the same subject ahead in time. If the script requires that the same subject appear at the end of one scene and the beginning of the next, the jump cut can be avoided by creating a time transition at the start of the second scene. The secret of transitions is to start a shot

AVOIDING JUMP CUTS

Figure 6.13 A jump cut can be avoided by using an in-camera transition so that the second shot begins without the character. The character can make an immediate entrance or be revealed in several ways using an in-camera transition.

with something hidden and then reveal it. The simplest time transition at a scene break is created by briefly hiding the character who is in both shots. This brief suggestion of time passage often serves to put enough distance between the scenes. Figure 6.13 provides a preview of several in-camera transition techniques. These techniques are described in more detail in Chapter 10.

7

Storytelling Cuts and Film Grammar

Film grammar is the term given to the ideas and techniques that are used to maintain continuity of time and space. It was developed early in the history of film, and because it works so well it's the standard for film storytelling. When continuity editing is used, the story flows naturally and viewers are not conscious of the editing. Continuity editing would not be needed if cuts were never made, but cuts cannot be avoided, for both practical and storytelling reasons. A typical film has hundreds of cuts. The length of time each piece is on the screen varies, but on average it is only five or six seconds, so hundreds of cuts are necessary.

Reasons for Cutting

Every cut is used to show a dramatic beat that advances the story in the best way possible. Often there is a purely storytelling reason for a cut:

- The current shot does not show enough detail or have enough emphasis.
- The next beat in a scene cannot be seen in the current shot.
- The story travels instantaneously to a new setting where a new scene begins.
- Time must be compressed.
- A new shot is needed to create a meaningful juxtaposition of images.

Cuts are also often made for a number of practical reasons:

- The scene only exists as an imaginary on-screen combination of separate pieces, such as live action, animation, or even pieces of more than one set that will seem to be in one place when the story is told on the screen.
- The scene takes place in a busy and complex setting, such as a sporting event, a nightclub or a trading floor. Once the setting has been established, the action can continue in simpler shots that avoid angles which would show complicated background action.
- The scene must create the illusion of realistic action when the stunt being shown is too dangerous or is impossible to do in one shot, or when the action must be divided between actors and stunt performers.
- There is a need to reduce the cost of special effects and visual effects (VFX) by limiting the shots in which they occur.

The Art of Cinematic Storytelling. Kelly Gordon Brine, Oxford University Press (2020). © Oxford University Press.
DOI: 10.1093/oso/9780190054328.001.0001.

Avoiding Beta Effects When Cutting

The illusion of movement in film appears when slightly different images play in sequence. This movement is a result of the beta effect, and when it's created by playing thousands of frames of continuously recorded film footage, the motion appears fluid and lifelike.

Unfortunately the beta effect can also be created unintentionally when adjacent shots have visual similarities even though they are not part of the same continuously recorded film footage. Beta movement created unintentionally at a cut may make something on the screen appear to jump, pop, turn, or transform, and this distracts attention from a film's story. The beta effect happens because viewers' minds instinctively try to understand the images in the juxtaposed shots as continuous footage from a single shot. Figure 7.1 shows some ways in which two juxtaposed shots can have too many similarities in their compositions.

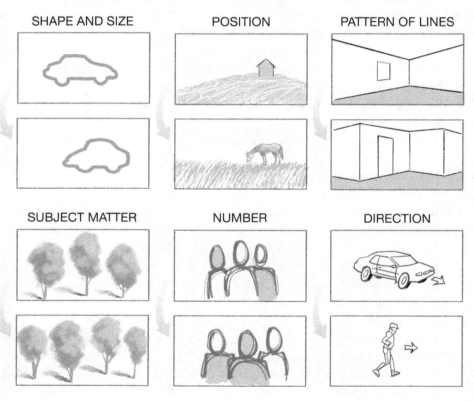

VISUAL SIMILARITIES THAT CAUSE POOR SHOT CONTRAST

SHAPE AND SIZE   POSITION   PATTERN OF LINES

SUBJECT MATTER   NUMBER   DIRECTION

Figure 7.1 A cut can join shots that are too similar and create a distracting beta effect. Some common types of visual similarity that should be avoided when cutting are shown.

Although it might seem that the more similarities there are between two images, the smoother the cut from one to the other should be, the beta effect shows that the opposite is true: the smoothest cuts are between shots that have very *dissimilar* designs. The most important method for preventing beta effects from occurring is by making use of shot contrast. Shot contrast helps viewers effortlessly see that a new shot is of something completely different from the shot that preceded it.

How to Create Shot Contrast

Shot contrast can be created in many ways, and several methods are often combined. The most important ways of creating contrast are listed below roughly in order of usefulness. These types of contrast are illustrated in Figure 7.2.

- Wide and close shots
- The position of the subject on the left or right side of the frame
- Movement to the left and right
- The number of people or things
- Movement toward and away from the camera
- People and objects
- Contrasting abstract patterns
- Interiors and exteriors
- Being in motion or at rest
- The direction of diagonal lines
- The overall brightness or darkness of the image
- Differences in color and texture

The Match Cut

Shot contrast is important for creating smooth cuts, but there are times when it must be partially overridden. These occasions are (1) when cutting to another shot of the same person or thing, (2) when two characters are talking to each other, and (3) in order for the direction in which characters are looking and moving to remain constant from shot to shot.

Often a story requires a cut in continuous time to a closer shot of the character in the current shot. A story beat may require emphasizing the character's action or reaction to events, or a closer view may be needed to highlight an important detail. A *match cut* is the best way to cut closer while maintaining continuity. A match cut is most commonly used to cut closer, but it can also be used to cut to a wider shot (Figure 7.3). The term *match* is used because the subject of the two shots is framed to appear in the same position on the screen in both shots.

CREATING SHOT CONTRAST

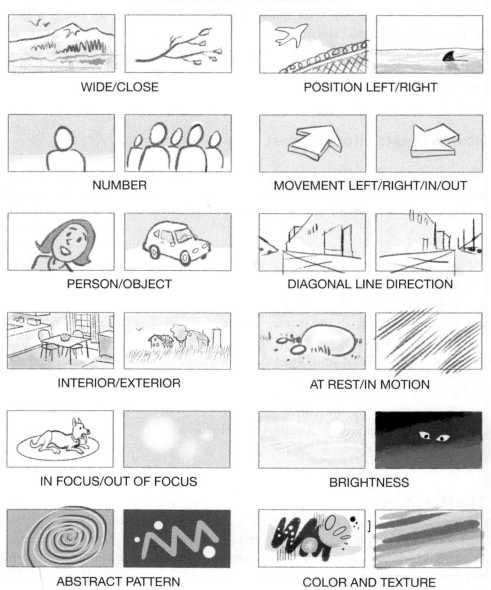

WIDE/CLOSE   POSITION LEFT/RIGHT

NUMBER   MOVEMENT LEFT/RIGHT/IN/OUT

PERSON/OBJECT   DIAGONAL LINE DIRECTION

INTERIOR/EXTERIOR   AT REST/IN MOTION

IN FOCUS/OUT OF FOCUS   BRIGHTNESS

ABSTRACT PATTERN   COLOR AND TEXTURE

Figure 7.2 There are many ways to create contrast between juxtaposed shots to avoid the beta effect when cutting.

In a match cut the camera angle is changed by about thirty degrees. The closer of the two shots is the more frontal view. The direction in which the character is facing is preserved, so a character's nose continues to point in the same general left or right direction in the second shot as in the first. Something to be careful

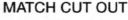

Figure 7.3 A match cut is a cut to the same subject from a different distance and at a different angle. It requires matching the screen position and the screen direction of the look or movement.

about is to make sure that no foreground object such as a bottle or vase jumps from one side of the screen to the other at the cut. To avoid this the item may have to be removed from the closer shot. Figure 7.4 illustrates the five elements of a good match cut.

Usually the two shots that will form a match cut are not created at the same time using two cameras, but rather by moving a single camera and having the actor repeat the action. The 30-degree angle change helps to hide the small differences between the two shots. There may be slight differences in the actor's action and in the details of the actor's hair and clothing. Because the camera angle of the second shot is different, what's in the background changes, and this creates shot contrast that helps make the cut smoother and the new shot more interesting. An angle change greater than 30 degrees makes the second shot too different from the first in its perspective, and makes the cut seem less natural. An angle change of less than 30 degrees creates shots that are too similar and may introduce a beta effect. Figure 7.5 illustrates some potential errors in creating a match cut.

A match can be made smoother by using action to bridge the two shots. A simple action that begins in the first shot can be completed in the second, uniting the shots. The action is a diversion that holds the audience's interest while the cut is made. Examples of actions often used to bridge a match cut are sitting down, standing up, putting on or taking off a jacket or other article of clothing, or raising a glass or a cigarette. The shots are trimmed so that approximately one-third of the action is shown in the first shot and two-thirds in the second.

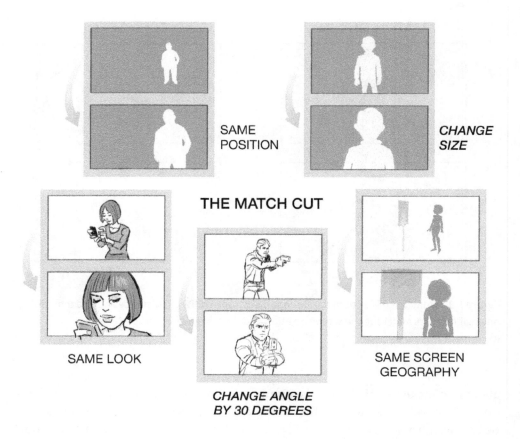

Figure 7.4 To create a good match cut requires similarity in three elements and differences in two.

Graphic Match Cuts

Sometimes the term *match cut* is used to describe a cut or dissolve that has a *graphic match*. To create a graphic match, two adjacent shots are designed to have a substantial similarity in their shapes, colors, or movement, and usually they are joined using a dissolve. The subjects of the shots are both centered. The intention of a graphic match is often to create a smooth and visually interesting time transition. One spinning or round object may dissolve into another, or a lit match may dissolve into a blazing sun.

A graphic match can also be used to propel the story by greatly compressing the time during which a project is accomplished. Imagine a shot of an inventor or architect sketching an idea on paper or building a model, or finding inspiration in the form of an object, and there being a graphic match from this image to a shot of the actual machine or building now fully constructed. Some filmmakers don't use graphic matches because they can seem contrived. In this book the term *match cut* is never used in reference to graphic matches.

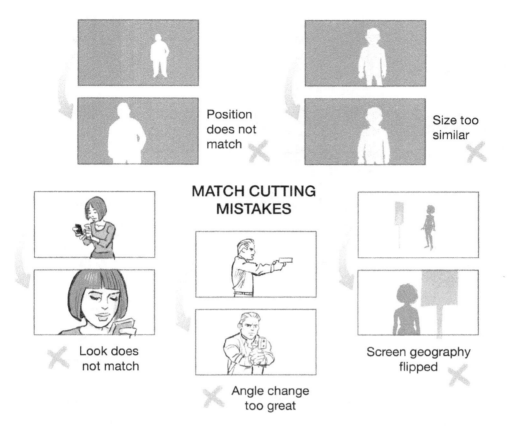

Figure 7.5 A poorly done match cut can cause an unintended jump, pop, or turn.

The Punch In

When a closer shot is needed, an alternative to a match cut is a *punch in*. The camera is not moved when creating a punch in. Instead, either two cameras with different lens lengths are positioned side by side to record simultaneously, or the action is performed twice and recorded the second time with a longer lens on the same single camera. The subject is framed in exactly the same position in both shots (Figure 7.6). Sometimes an additional punch in follows the first, so that the same subject is seen in three successive shots, each tighter than the one that precedes it. This can make a situation seem more tense.

A punch in is sometimes called a jump cut because it may seem like the camera has jumped closer to the subject or like the subject has jumped toward the camera. Unlike actual jump cuts, the punch in does not jump in time or space and therefore does not break continuity editing.

The lack of an angle change means that there is less shot contrast between the two juxtaposed shots of a punch in, so the cut is more noticeable. The second shot always

Figure 7.6 A punch in is a magnified shot from the same camera position. It can create a feeling of urgency, danger, or surveillance. A wipe will make the cut smoother. Two punch ins can be done in quick succession for greater emphasis.

looks like a blowup of the first one because the perspective and the background are identical. To mask this similarity and produce a smoother cut, a person or vehicle can wipe the frame in the foreground at the start of the second shot.

If a very high resolution camera has been used, punch ins can be created during editing. This is because high-resolution footage allows considerable enlargement of a shot before noticeable graininess is introduced. An editor can create a punch in when needed for isolation and emphasis or to show greater detail; this is helpful if there is no closer shot available.

A punch in is sometimes someone's POV. In these cases it is appropriate that both shots be from the same position since they both record the same observer's angle on the action. A punch in can also be used to create a feeling of urgency or danger, or to give the impression that the character seen in the shot is on a mission. When a group is walking toward the camera, a punch in can be used to isolate and highlight selected characters in close-ups and two shots. This works well for both a moving camera and a stationary one.

Reverse Angles

Storytelling often requires pairs of shots with angles that are opposite or almost opposite each other. These are called *reverse angles*. They are used for such purposes as showing what a character is looking at, covering conversation between two characters, and showing the continuing movement of something that has passed close to the camera, such as a person, a vehicle, a thrown object, or a spaceship.

An imaginary line can be drawn between an observer and what the person is looking at, between two people talking to each other, or along the path that a person or object travels. Reverse angles look best if they keep the same angle to this imaginary line in both directions. Usually this angle is quite small because the camera is set close to the line. This makes a POV seem more convincing, makes a conversation more subjective and intense, and ensures that movement is more exciting because it comes close to the camera (Figure 7.7).

The difference in the angles of two reverse-angle shots is usually a little less than 180 degrees; otherwise the subject will seem to be looking straight at or moving

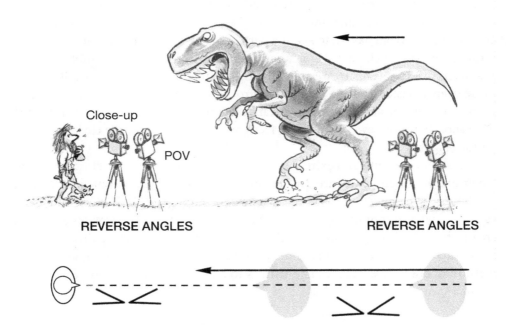

Figure 7.7 Reverse angles have views that are almost 180 degrees opposite each other. They are usually used for conversation, to pair an observer with the observer's POV, or to show a person, vehicle, or object travel close to, pass, and then move away from the camera.

straight toward the camera and then straight away from it. As an example, shots of a car driving past are usually recorded with the camera positioned beside the road, not from a position on the road. Reverse angles are composed so that one has the center of interest a little to the right of frame and the other has it a little to the left. Sometimes reverse angles are exactly 180 degrees opposite each other. In this case each shot is a *dead reverse* of the other. Dead reverses are most commonly used when a pair of shots lead and follow a moving character.

Entrances and Exits

The terms *entrance* and *exit* are used in two different ways. The first use is when they describe the arrivals and departures of characters in scenes. But these terms are also used to describe movement into and out of individual shots even when a character remains in a scene throughout. For example, a character who is visible in a wide shot in a scene may reach toward a bookshelf. A closer shot of the bookshelf follows and the character's hand enters this shot to grab a book. Her hand now exits this close shot. A cut back to the wide shot shows that she is now holding the book.

An exit or entrance can be used to avoid a jump cut at a scene break or within a scene because it implies that time has moved ahead at least slightly. An entrance can also be used to avoid having to shoot a perfect match cut. A *clean entrance* (or exit) is one in which the character is at some point completely out of the shot. Giving a character a clean entrance or exit can be useful in editing. For example, if a cut is made from a master shot of a man at a control panel to a close-up of a button that he presses, a clean entrance of his hand means that the position of the man's hand in the wide shot does not have to match perfectly with its position in the close-up of the button (Figure 7.8).

Characters entering and exiting scenes can be important to the story, but even when entrances and exits are not essential the addition of an entrance or exit can help convey a feeling that time has passed. They also add action and visual variety to what might otherwise be a static scene. Note that entrances and exits are often made through doors, but they can also be made from behind anything large, such as walls, crates, machinery, or bushes. Another common and useful method of creating entrances and exits is to have characters simply step into or out of a shot.

Cutting When Traveling with Characters

A moving subject should be framed to stay quite stable in size and position within the frame, which means that the camera must move at a similar speed. Doing so makes cuts between the various moving shots smoother. The character may be moving by

A CLEAN
ENTRANCE OR
EXIT AVOIDS A
MATCH CUT

Figure 7.8 A difficult match cut can be avoided when cutting to a close shot if a clean entrance is made in the close shot.

any means, on foot, on a bicycle, on a motorcycle, and so on. A scene can begin or end with a character and the camera both in motion, provided that the character is kept at a fairly constant size in the shot. A moving character can be covered from these angles:

- The camera is the moving POV of the moving character.
- The camera moves backward as it leads the approaching character.
- The camera follows the moving character, and is therefore able to hold both the character and the character's POV in the same shot.
- The camera tracks alongside the moving character (but is often angled backward slightly to avoid a flat profile).
- The camera tracks alongside the character at a rear three-quarter angle. This shows a piece of the character's POV and can show the character's face as the character looks left and right.

Smooth cuts can be made between a moving character and the character's moving POV, as well as between the dead reverse shots that lead and follow the character (Figure 7.9). A cut to or from a shot that follows or leads a character to a *tracking* shot alongside the character is smoother if cuts are made at points when the foreground briefly hides the character in the tracking shot.

Cuts can easily be made among moving shots of the characters in a group who are moving together. Characters who require a close-up or a two-shot can be shot as

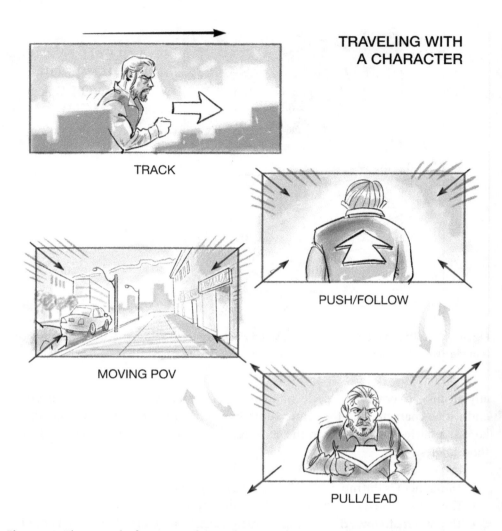

Figure 7.9 These are the four types of shots that travel with a character: tracking, following, leading, and showing the character's POV.

punch ins. These cuts work well if the group moves as a unit and the members maintain their spatial relationships to each other, just as they would in a car, or on a train, a plane, or a ship.

An interesting variation on moving shots is to have the actor stand on the same dolly as the camera. This technique is used to portray characters who are in shock about something they have just learned. The actor is framed from the waist up, and the camera is either in front of or behind the actor on the dolly. Because the actor is not walking, the actor's upper body is largely motionless as it travels on the dolly with the camera. The character seems to be floating in a trance.

Cutting between Stationary and Traveling Shots

A shot that travels with a character can keep that character framed at a constant size and in a fixed position. Only the background moves in this type of shot. Scenes can start or end with such a shot, with the camera either leading or following the character. What requires more planning are cuts between shots of the same character when one of the shots is stationary (and objective) and the other is traveling with the character (and subjective).

The Camera Starts and Stops When the Character Does

The most straightforward way to switch between stationary and traveling coverage is to avoid a cut and simply start or stop moving the camera when the character starts or stops moving. There are several variations on this. One is for a stationary frontal shot of the character to pan 180 degrees as the character starts to walk, and then fall in behind. Several of these techniques are discussed in Chapter 12.

Cutting from a Stationary to a Traveling Shot

A common and effective way to cut from an objective stationary shot of someone walking to a subjective traveling shot of the same character is to let the character exit the stationary shot close to the camera and cut to a leading shot (Figure 7.10). This cut is an opportunity to move time ahead slightly and pick up the character continuing to walk in a different setting nearby.

There are other ways of switching from stationary to traveling coverage of a moving character. They are all based on making the character disappear briefly, either at the end of the first shot or the beginning of the second. Several common techniques are described here and illustrated in Figure 7.11.

1. In a wide stationary shot the character disappears behind something or goes through a door. Cut to a shot that leads the character.
2. In a wide stationary shot the character walks in a direction that angles away from the camera. As the character crosses the center of the frame, a cut is made to a moving shot that leads the character. A pedestrian can optionally be used to begin the second shot to make the cut smoother or move the character ahead on the journey.
3. The character walks toward the stationary camera and exits frame beside it. Cut to a shot in which the camera is following the moving character.

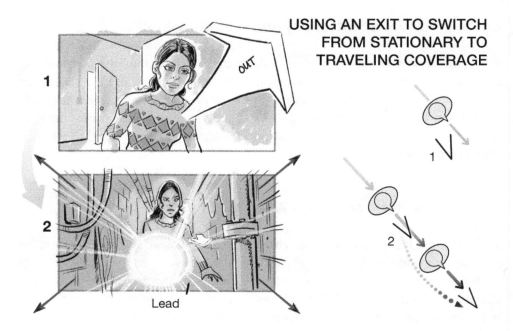

Figure 7.10 If a character exits a stationary shot close to the camera, the shot that follows can be a traveling shot that leads or follows the character.

4. The character approaches the camera but is wiped. Cut to a shot that follows the character.
5. The character walks across the frame (or diagonally toward or away from the camera) in a wide stationary shot or a pan. Cut to a tracking shot of the character that begins with a foreground object momentarily obscuring the character until the camera passes it.

Ways to Cut from a Traveling to a Stationary Shot

A cut is often made to switch from a shot that is traveling with a moving character to a stationary shot of the character continuing on the journey. This is a switch from subjective to objective coverage. It can be used to establish or re-establish the setting of a scene, it can be a second character's POV, or it can move the character ahead in time and space on the journey. Once again the trick is to make the character disappear briefly, either at the end of the first shot or the beginning of the second. The techniques described below and illustrated in Figure 7.12 use a walking character as an example, but they can be applied to anything that's traveling.

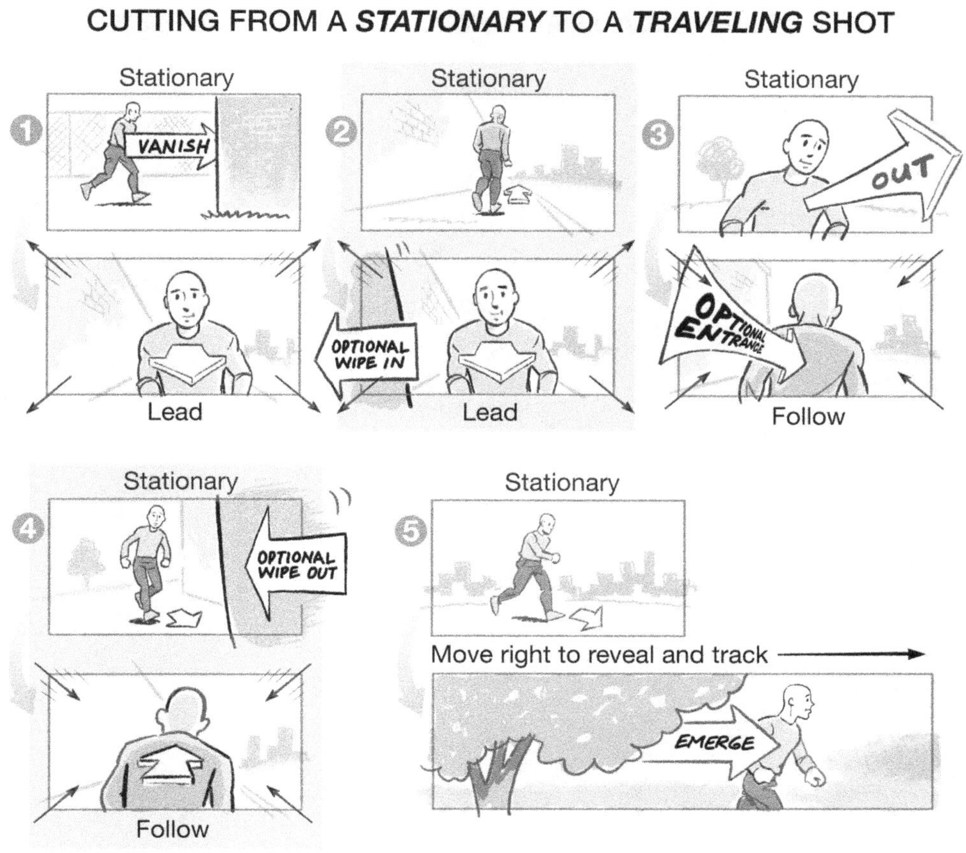

CUTTING FROM A *STATIONARY* TO A *TRAVELING* SHOT

Figure 7.11 These are five useful ways to cut from a stationary-camera shot of a traveling character to a traveling-camera shot.

1. The camera is leading the character. Cut to a wide empty stationary shot in which the character comes through a door or steps out from behind an object such as a wall, a vehicle, or foliage.
2. The camera is leading the character. Cut to an empty stationary shot that the character enters by stepping into the frame.
3. The camera is leading the character and now the character exits the shot. Cut to a wide, stationary, reverse-angle shot of the character moving away.
4. The camera is following the character. Cut to a stationary shot that begins with a wipe that reveals the moving character.
5. The camera is tracking the character but now the view becomes blocked by a foreground object such as a wall, foliage, or a vehicle. Cut to a wider stationary shot of the character approaching.

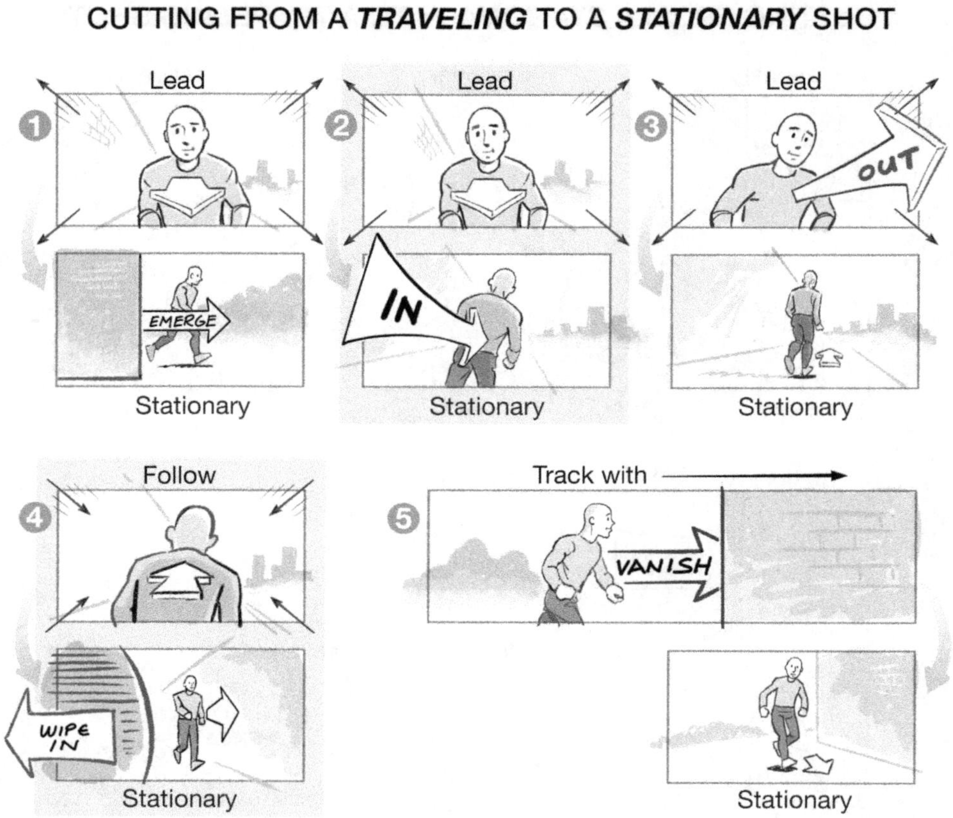

CUTTING FROM A *TRAVELING* TO A *STATIONARY* SHOT

Figure 7.12   These are five useful ways to cut from a traveling-camera shot of a moving character to a stationary-camera shot

Motivating and Hiding Cuts

Cuts are usually needed every few seconds, but they can be jarring. As we've seen, shot contrast is one important way to make cuts smoother. There are several additional techniques that help make cuts less noticeable. Motivating a cut dramatically means making viewers curious to see what's next, and this desire is satisfied by what's shown in the following shot. One example is the desire to see the interior of a building when shown an image of the exterior. Bridging a cut with action that starts in the first shot and continues in the second unifies the two shots and makes the cut stand out less. A cut can be hidden by creating a visual distraction that takes viewers' minds away from the cut, which is not unlike the way a magician diverts the audience's attention so they don't notice the sleight of hand that's taking place.

Ways of Motivating a Cut Dramatically

- Viewers want to see how someone is reacting to what just happened.
- A character looks off-screen and viewers want to see what the character sees.
- An off-screen sound makes us want to see what caused it.
- An object or a shadow falls into the frame and we want to see what caused it.

Using Action That Bridges a Cut

- A match cut can show an action that spans two shots. Usually one-third of the action is shown in the first shot and the remaining two-thirds in the second shot. This is cutting on action and it makes a cut very smooth. The action can be as simple as a character raising a phone or sitting down.

Using Action to Distract Attention from a Cut

- A character or a vehicle exits the shot or the scene.
- A cut can be helped by an actor making any small movement.
- Cut as something wipes the frame.
- Cut at the instant something that is very visual happens, such as the firing of a weapon, an explosion, a door being closed, or lights going out.
- Begin the second shot with the movement and mystery of a reveal.
- Begin the second shot with a visually dramatic event, such as an explosion.

Additional Techniques to Distract Attention from a Cut

- Use a sharp or loud noise created by someone shouting, playing an instrument, using a power tool, or slamming a door. The sound can be used to end a shot or begin the next shot.
- If a character has several lines of dialogue, a cut can be made between two lines. The dialogue bridges the cut, and the new angle can add dramatic emphasis to the second line.
- Music, sound effects, or dialogue from the following scene begins a few seconds early, making viewers interested in seeing the next scene. This sound prelap is called a J-cut.
- Alternate between left and right centers of interest in successive shots to distract viewers by making them look back and forth at the "tennis match" of shots.

Avoiding Cuts

Sometimes certain cuts can be avoided, and the result can be a more fluid and cinematic sequence.

Panning

Panning and tilting can keep a character in frame, and thus a cut may not be necessary. Visual variety can be added by the character coming diagonally closer or moving diagonally farther from the camera during the pan. A pan can be used to frame a walking character who joins a second character in what becomes a two-shot. A pan can also be made from characters to their POV, if adding a small delay in seeing what a character sees suits the storytelling.

A short pan from a close-up of one character to another who is nearby is occasionally filmed. This small move may be motivated by a line of dialogue or a look. The motivation may also be a story's need to show the second character's reaction to the first character, or when both characters are watching the same character or event and the reactions of both characters are needed. This technique avoids the necessity of a cut as well as the time needed to move the camera and adjust the lighting for the second close-up. A single camera position that is used for close-ups of characters standing or seated in a row is sometimes called a swingle. The camera *swings* from one character to another and frames each in a *single*. The close-ups may be used with or without the pans.

Rack Focus from One Character or Object to Another

A change to what's in focus can be used to make viewers pay attention to something else in the same shot. This is a rack focus. It allows an additional beat to be played in the same shot, thus avoiding a cut.

An Invisible Cut Using a Wipe and a Reveal

An invisible cut is created by using a dissolve to unite two almost identical images. This creates the illusion that two shots are one continuous shot. In most cases the cut occurs when a pillar or tree crosses the frame in the foreground as the camera passes nearby while it tracks a character. In order to make the dissolve less noticeable, two very similar dark foreground objects with minimal detail are typically used. Some other methods are to use a totally dark section of a cave or a corridor, or to have smoke or fog fill the frame and briefly block the camera's view.

When creating an invisible cut using two tracking shots, the first shot tracks the traveling character until the person disappears behind a dark foreground object that completely wipes the frame and ends the shot. The second shot begins with its view entirely blocked by a similar dark foreground object. The camera moves sideways off this object to reveal the moving character, and the shot almost immediately becomes a tracking shot. The two shots are dissolved together to create what appears to be a single tracking shot whose view is momentarily obscured when it passes what appears to be a single foreground pillar or tree (Figure 7.13).

The invisible cut technique can accomplish these additional goals while it hides a cut:

- Change the shot size of a character who is being tracked.
- Shorten or lengthen a character's journey.
- Cheat to make two separate sets seem like they are one.
- Join a drone or crane shot to a Steadicam shot to give the appearance of a single camera move (by using an object, smoke, or fog for the dissolve).

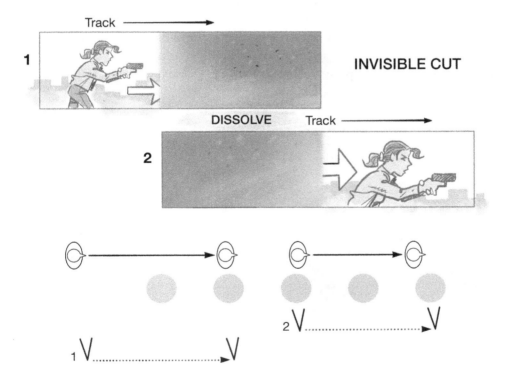

Figure 7.13 Most invisible cuts are made by dissolving two shots that pass similar foreground objects to create the illusion of one shot that passes one foreground object. This technique can compress or extend space and time, change sets, or move to a different shot.

- Join a shot of a character walking directly toward and almost into the camera with a shot of that character walking away from the camera.

An invisible cut can also be used to create the illusion of the camera passing through a ceiling. The shot created in the lower room consists of the camera rising until its view is blocked by a dark object positioned near the ceiling. The shot created in the upper room starts at the floor with the camera's view initially blocked by a dark object resting on the floor; as the camera rises the room is revealed. A quick dissolve unites the shots created separately in the two rooms, and the dark object is understood to be the floor between the two rooms. The upper room could be anywhere at all and still seem on film to be located in a room that's directly above the lower room.

Swish or Whip Pans

A swish pan (or whip pan) is a fast pan from one character to another. It simulates the visual experience of glancing quickly from one person to another. A swish pan can be created as a single rapid pan from one character to another, or it can be created from two separate shots. When created from two shots, the first is a rapid pan off one character, and the second is a rapid pan onto a second character. The two characters can be on the same set or on different sets. A quick dissolve of the two swishes unites them in what appears to be one continuous fast pan, and the result is an invisible cut. Swish pans can show a frenetic pace of action as well as urgency and conflict (Figure 7.14).

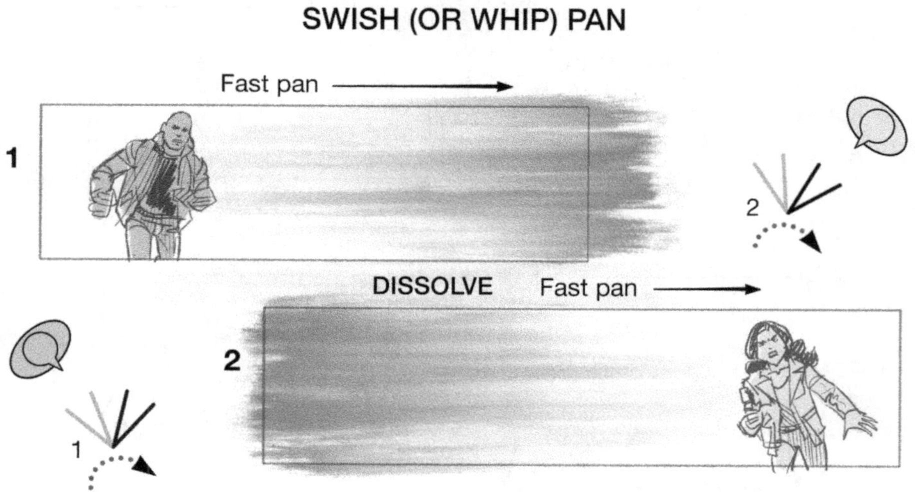

SWISH (OR WHIP) PAN

Figure 7.14 A swish pan simulates the effect of moving one's eyes rapidly from one character to another. It is created by dissolving a shot that holds a character in frame before panning away quickly with one that pans quickly before landing on a second character.

Long Takes

A long take is a carefully planned and choreographed shot that lasts much longer than a typical shot and avoids many cuts. It covers many beats that would typically be shown using several shots. When it's done well a long take is exciting, realistic, immersive, and cinematic. Long takes are sometimes used to follow a character through a busy environment such as a battlefield, a restaurant kitchen, a crowded hallway, or a market. Sometimes what seems like a long take is actually created by using shorter shots that are joined using invisible cuts.

The main drawback of a long take is that it is difficult to do well because so much has to happen perfectly, including the timing of all the action and dialogue, and the framing of the shot throughout. A long take is difficult to cut away from, and there may not be other shots available that cover the scene, so a director may be stuck with the long take for its entire length, even if it's flawed. When a scene is covered in a more standard way by using several shots, the director and editor have more storytelling options for the drama and the pacing.

8

3D Spatial Continuity and 2D Screen Geography

When a scene begins in a new setting, viewers expect to understand the space just as they would understand it if they had stepped into it. If the images they see seem to give contradictory information about where things are situated in space, and how the action is unfolding, viewers become momentarily confused. During the fraction of a second in which viewers work to reorient themselves in a film's space, they are distracted from the story. Although their confusion may be brief, this situation is not good for the storytelling. For this reason it's usually important for a filmmaker to present space clearly by not cutting to shots that contradict viewers' understanding of the space and what's in it. If there are such cuts, it should be for a good storytelling reason.

Juxtaposition Implies a Context in Space and Time

When we see two juxtaposed shots, we assume that they are connected in space and time unless something in the shots suggests otherwise. If we see a shot of a man walking in the woods and then a shot of woman walking in the woods we will assume that it's the same woods, at the same time, and that they are probably not far from each other. We will be surprised if any of these assumptions turn out to be false.

Imagine a shot of a cat that is followed by a shot of a woman (Figure 8.1). Because the cat is looking up and to the right and the woman is looking down and to the left, we infer a spatial relationship that assumes they are looking at each other. We would not draw this conclusion if the shots had very different backgrounds. If nothing obviously flags the shots as being in different settings, our minds automatically create a spatial and temporal context that unites the two images in one place and time. If a third shot followed and showed us that the cat and the woman are in different rooms, or even in the same room but facing away from each other, we'd be surprised.

Misdirection

Good direction normally strives to make it easy to understand the spatial reality of a film, but sometimes directors intentionally mislead viewers to surprise them.

The Art of Cinematic Storytelling. Kelly Gordon Brine, Oxford University Press (2020). © Oxford University Press.
DOI: 10.1093/oso/9780190054328.001.0001.

Juxtaposed shots can create meaningful connections in space, in time, and in the story

Figure 8.1 When we see two juxtaposed shots we infer that the images are connected in space, time, and the story unless something tells us otherwise.

Imagine a scene in which someone is being held hostage in a house that we haven't seen the exterior of. In the scene that follows we see the SWAT team arrive outside a house. We assume that the hostage will soon be liberated, and we're surprised when it turns out that the SWAT team is at the wrong house. This technique is called *misdirection.*

Sometimes a scene ends with two characters talking, and what at first seems like the final reaction shot of one character turns out to be that character in a new setting. For example, imagine a manager telling an employee, "Your presentation will be to a group of 100 executives." The cut that follows is to the employee's shocked reaction. But viewers soon see that the employee is now in front of that very group, looking nervous as he's about to start his speech. It takes viewers a moment to realize that this is the first shot of a new scene that has moved us ahead in time. This technique makes viewers feel the employee's shock and nervousness more vividly. This type of intentional misdirection is an exception to the usual goal of presenting time and space clearly to viewers.

Misdirection can also be used in ways that don't involve space and time. For example, by visually emphasizing misleading information while downplaying actual clues the audience can be led to believe that an innocent person has committed a crime. Leading viewers down the wrong path increases their shock when the real criminal is revealed.

What Is 3D Spatial Continuity?

Three-dimensional space is the real space in which a film was shot. *Spatial continuity* means making sure that characters and objects don't change their positions, eyelines, or actions in real three-dimensional space from one shot to the next without an explanation or some indication that time has passed. An example of no spatial continuity is a character standing at one spot in a room in one shot but standing in a different spot in the next shot. Breaking spatial continuity in this way creates jump cuts.

Unfortunately even if spatial continuity is maintained while recording several shots, these shots may not cut together well unless the camera has been positioned with a view to creating consistent *screen geography*, which is very important to continuity editing.

What Is 2D Screen Geography?

2D screen geography is concerned with characters' positions, looks, and movement in terms of the left and the right of the two-dimensional screen. Screen geography provides a simple framework that makes it easy to understand where things are even though the camera moves to a new position with every cut. If screen geography is consistent, it's easier for viewers to understand characters' positions, looks, and movement. When 2D screen geography is not consistent from shot to shot, it makes characters jump, turn, trade places, and look in the wrong direction.

The left and right of the screen are important for four types of information that are important for maintaining continuity:

- The *position* of the subject, especially with respect to which side of the frame the person is on
- The *ordering* of people and objects across the screen
- Whether a character is *looking left* or *right*, no matter how slightly
- The *left or right direction of movement* of a character, animal, vehicle, or other object, no matter how slight the angle is

For something to be on the left or the right of the screen means that it is at least slightly more on one side than the other. Similarly a look or movement to the left or the right can be quite small yet still be significant for editing purposes. Movement and looks to the left and right can be at any diagonal angle to the camera. A character could be looking or walking at an angle that is only very slightly toward the right or the left side of the camera lens. Similarly a character could be walking almost directly away from the camera and be moving only slightly to the right or the left of the frame. Even though screen geography is two-dimensional, if it's presented consistently it makes the three-dimensional space of a scene much easier to under-stand, just as a two-dimensional map can clarify spatial relationships in the real world. A map is a projection of three-dimensional space onto a flat surface, and so is an image on a movie screen. When screen geography is suddenly reversed it causes confusion for viewers that is similar to the confusion that results from rotating a map 180 degrees while studying it, or looking at a map in a mirror.

Keeping Things on Their Side of the Screen

An imaginary line can be drawn between two actors or objects who will appear in a shot together. This line is an important spatial reference if more than one shot will be taken, and it's often called the *axis*. This line is the basis of the spatial relation-ship between the two actors, and it's the basis of their screen geography. The axis is a useful tool when deciding where to put the camera. Two characters may be looking at and talking to each other, or there may be more action such as walking toward each other, throwing a ball, shooting, or throwing punches. If this is the case the axis may be called the *axis of action*.

It becomes important to think about the axis when the camera is moved to a new position to take a second shot of the same actors. When an observer looks at two people standing and talking to each other, one is on the left and one is on the right. If the observer walks to a new vantage point, from that new position the people being observed may keep their left and right positions, or from the observer's new position they may have traded sides. To the observer the change of sides seems natural be-cause it came about gradually during his or her walk to a new position. But in film a cut to a shot that has a radically different view is instantaneous and comes without a warning or an explanation.

A cut that flips what's seen on the left and right parallels the effect of blindfolding an observer, walking the person to a very different vantage point, and removing the blindfold. The angle change would be momentarily confusing to the observer. It would be the most confusing if the left-right orientation of two characters were ex-actly opposite what it was before the move: the two characters would appear to have traded places. The confusion that such a new view would cause could be avoided by choosing a new position for the blindfolded observer (or the camera) that does not cross the axis and therefore does not make the two characters switch sides (Figure 8.2). Cuts can be made between these shots without confusing viewers.

Shots taken from one side of the axis all share the same geography, and they form a family of related shots. When a director chooses to position the camera on the far side of the axis it's called *crossing the axis*, and it flips screen geography by introducing an unrelated shot that's not a member of the family.

As noted, when a cut is made to a shot that puts characters or objects on the sides opposite those where they were last seen, it's confusing. The storyboard panels on the left side of Figure 8.3 illustrate screen geography that is consistent, while those on the

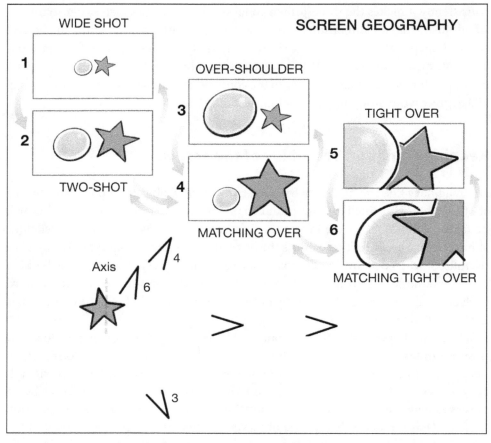

Figure 8.2 Screen geography is clear when objects do not switch their positions from shot to shot. In this example the egg is on the left side and the star is on the right side in all shots.

right illustrate inconsistent and confusing screen geography because the characters trade sides because the camera crossed the axis to create the wide shot.

Points of View, Eyelines, and Matching

An *eyeline* is an imaginary line that starts at a character's eyes and runs directly to what the person is looking at, much like a camera's line of sight. This line may run in any direction, and what's most important for continuity editing is whether it's running toward the right or the left side of the frame. If the eyeline runs toward the right, the character has a *right look*, and if it runs toward the left the character has a *left look*. Eyelines change whenever a character looks from one thing to another, or moves to a new position. Each new eyeline establishes new screen geography because a new axis between the character and what is being observed is created. The term *eyeline match* is used to describe keeping the camera on one side of the axis

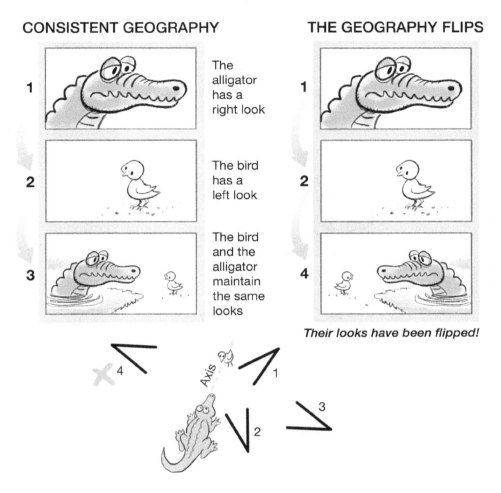

CONSISTENT GEOGRAPHY

THE GEOGRAPHY FLIPS

1 — The alligator has a right look

2 — The bird has a left look

3 — The bird and the alligator maintain the same looks

Their looks have been flipped!

Figure 8.3 The storyboard panels on the left keep the alligator and the bird on their own sides of the screen in all three shots. The panels on the right show that a camera position on the far side of the axis makes the animals trade sides.

in order to keep the character and what's observed on opposite sides of the screen (Figure 8.4).

Most POVs are straightforward, but they may be cheated to a slightly different angle in order to show a more attractive background or to set up a shot such as one in which the observer walks into her own POV. The shot may even be designed to begin with what seems like the character's POV, but then the camera begins to pan, as though the character is scanning what's in view. After a rotation of 90 degrees viewers are mildly surprised when the pan lands on a profile of the observer. This may seem like a strange technique, but viewers accept it.

Although a character's eyeline often comes quite close to the lens, actors are seldom directed to look directly into the camera lens. A direct look into the lens is

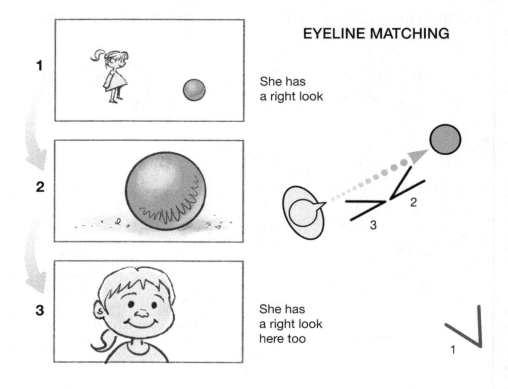

Figure 8.4 An observer and what is observed should stay on opposite sides of the screen when cutting. The observer's look should be in the same screen direction in all shots. Choosing camera positions on only one side of the eyeline is the key.

appropriate when a character is looking into a camera, microscope, or rifle sights. It is also occasionally used when a character is looking at a computer screen. Some directors have actors look into the lens during interrogation scenes or to convey the very subjective view of a semiconscious patient being asked questions by a doctor.

Occasionally actors are directed to look straight into the lens to address the audience. This is called *breaking the fourth wall*. It's done in mockumentaries and cinéma vérité. Naturally looking into the lens is the standard for newscasters, hosts, and narrators.

Tie-Up Shots

Story beats can often be conveyed more effectively by using cuts to new angles and tighter shot sizes. Because closer shots have a more restricted view, the spatial connection between characters and objects can unfortunately be lost. By including a piece of one of the elements in the foreground a *tie-up shot* can strengthen both

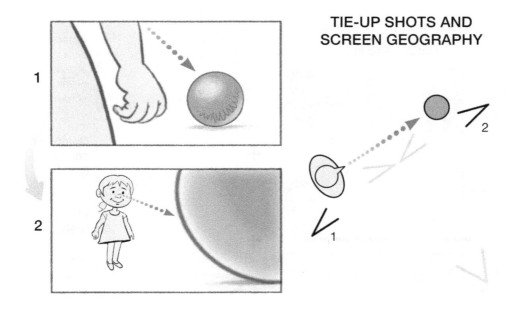

Figure 8.5 A tie-up shot unites things both in space and psychologically. Tie-up shots over both characters or objects must be on the same side of the axis between them.

spatial and psychological connections (Figure 8.5). A tie-up shot must maintain the left-right orientation of the shot it follows. An over-shoulder shot is a very common tie-up shot. Another type of tie-up occurs when a character who is leaving crosses through the shot of a character who remains.

If two characters are not actually in the same space, a *composite* (or composited) shot can be created. Composite shots have many uses, and creating tie-up shots is an important one. Sometimes part of a shot is digitally generated animation of a creature or an environment. Composite shots are also used when it would be dangerous for an actor to be filmed in a real location, such as dangling from a cliff or witnessing an explosion.

To create a composite shot, a green screen is set up behind the actor and a shot is recorded of the character's action. A separate shot is created of what must be seen in the shot with the character, for example such things as a dinosaur, a wild animal, or a spaceship. The two images are combined during editing. The green that surrounds the actor is replaced by the contents of the second shot, and the resulting composite shot creates the illusion that the elements are together in one space (Figure 8.6).

Sometimes there are more than two layers to a composite shot. Often the top layer is an actor shot against a green screen, the middle layer is computer animation with a transparent background, and the lowest layer is a *plate shot* of a real or animated VFX background that contains no characters or action. These shots must all be created

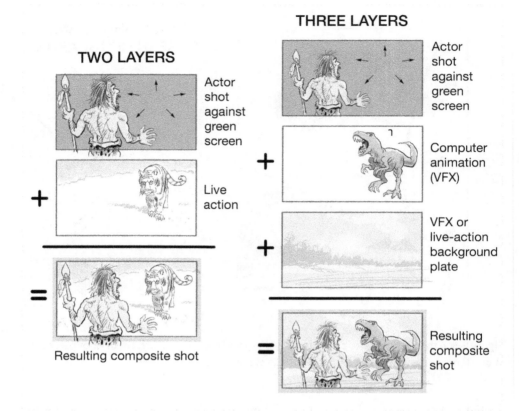

Figure 8.6 Compositing is combining several source images to produce a combined image. Often one or more layers are digitally generated animated.

either with the camera *locked* to prevent movement, or using *motion-control* so that camera movement is synchronized in all layers.

Opposed Looks and Eyeline Match

If two shots that play in succession show two characters with opposed looks, then viewers assume that they are looking at each other. The angle of their looks can range from very close to the camera lens right through to a rear three-quarter angle, but the angle should be the same for both characters. Opposed looks are also usually used for characters on the phone to each other, even though they cannot see each other and could be looking in any direction. This convention makes the cuts look better and provides viewers with clear screen geography.

As noted, an imaginary line can be drawn between two characters who are looking at and talking to each other. If the camera never crosses this line, or axis, then these characters will have opposed looks in all of their shots. If two characters are seen in

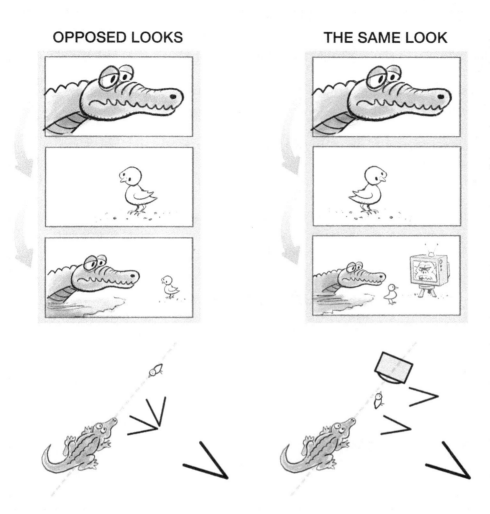

Figure 8.7 When two characters shown in separate shots have opposed looks, they are assumed to be looking at each other. If they have the same look, they are assumed to both be looking at a third person or an object.

separate shots and their looks have the same *screen* direction, viewers assume that they are not looking at each other but are both looking at the same person or thing (Figure 8.7).

Matching Shots for Dialogue

In film it's standard to shoot two characters who are talking to each other in a pair of mirrored shots. Making the shots mirror each other makes the cuts look smoother. Mirrored shots are called *matching shots*. Matching shots may be of seated or standing characters, and they may be face to face or shoulder to shoulder. Matching shots may be clean or dirty. A dirty shot contains a piece of the closer character in the shot, usually a shoulder and often a piece of the back of the closer character's head.

The characteristics of matching shots are illustrated in Figure 8.8, and are described here:

- The screen positions of the two characters are mirrored on the left and the right of frame.
- The characters' looks mirror each other, with one looking screen left and the other looking right.
- The characters have an equivalent amount of look-space.
- Both characters must have the same apparent head size on the screen, even if in life one character has a larger head.

MATCHING SHOTS

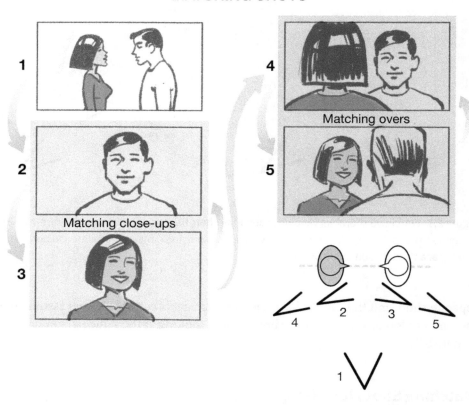

Figure 8.8 Matching shots are used for conversation that lasts longer than two or three lines. The geometrical similarity of the mirrored design of matching shots eliminates the beta effect that results from mismatched shots.

- The angle formed by the camera's line of sight and the axis between the characters must be the same for both characters.
- If the shots are over-shoulders, the framing with the pieces of shoulder and the sides of the faces must approximately mirror each other.
- The camera height for both shots is usually slightly below the eye level of the shorter person. Using other heights is discussed in Chapter 15.

Matching is important for dialogue because there are usually many cuts back and forth between dialogue shots, and if the shots are not mirrored, a distracting bounce is produced as a beta effect. If two characters have only a brief exchange involving just a line or two of dialogue, matching shots are not critical, but for longer dialogue they are. If two sizes of matching shots are recorded, the cuts between them should be mainly between matching pairs of one shot size at a time. If multiple cuts are made between shots of different sizes, this will also create a bounce.

When Dialogue Shots Don't Match

Figure 8.9 illustrates the problems that can arise when shots don't match because of incorrect camera positioning. The camera may be on the wrong side of the axis, at the wrong angle, or at the wrong distance.

Short-Sided Matching Shots

In order to create balanced compositions, shots of people are usually framed to have look-space in the direction in which characters are looking. Short-sided matching shots are like classic matching shots in all respects except that the two characters are not given enough look-space. Some directors frame dialogue shots this way, with the aim of making conversation seem more intense, intimate, or confrontational (Figure 8.10).

Matching Shots for Two Side-by-Side Characters

If two characters have dialogue while they stand or sit shoulder to shoulder, their shots should match. While it's true that their eyes and noses will both point left in some shots and right in others, what is most important is the psychological connection between them, not what which way their noses point in the shots. The coverage is similar for characters seated side by side in cars. A two-shot and two over-shoulder shots are illustrated in Figure 8.11.

WHEN SHOTS DON'T MATCH

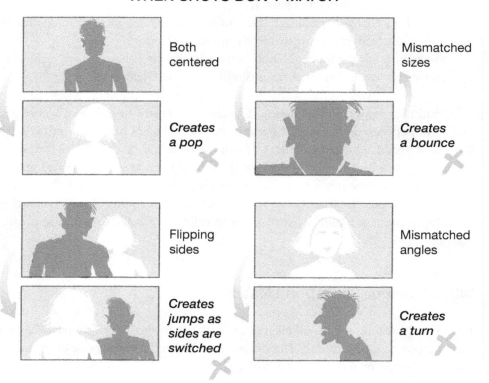

Both centered

Creates a pop

Flipping sides

Creates jumps as sides are switched

Mismatched sizes

Creates a bounce

Mismatched angles

Creates a turn

Figure 8.9 When dialogue shots don't match and shots are intercut several times, several kinds of beta effects can arise.

Continuity of Screen Motion

Keeping the direction of movement of characters and vehicles is important for screen geography. The path that something travels along is called the *axis of action*. The camera may be positioned anywhere on either side of the axis or even on the axis itself. Depending on where the camera is placed, a walking character may appear to be moving toward the left or the right of the screen. If the camera is positioned on the axis with its line of sight pointed directly along the axis, the character will be seen moving either directly toward or directly away from viewers in a neutral direction (Figure 8.12).

The position of the camera may make the axis of action be at a diagonal to the camera, so that a character may appear to move to the left or right while at the same time moving closer to or farther from the camera. If the camera is at a high or low angle, the character will also move up or down within the frame while traveling left or right across it.

CLASSIC MATCHING SHOTS   **SHORT-SIDED MATCHING SHOTS**

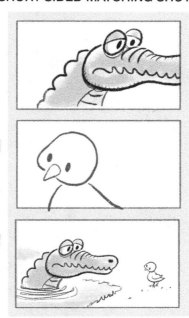

Figure 8.10 Short-sided shots reduce characters' look-space and crowd them toward the edge of the frame in the direction in which they are looking.

Keeping something moving in the same left or right screen direction from shot to shot is called *continuity of screen motion*. Continuity of screen motion applies to everything that moves, whether people, animals, vehicles, or objects. Even if something is moving diagonally toward or away from the camera and because of this the amount of left or right movement across the screen is small, flipping the screen direction of movement between right and left will still be confusing for viewers. If something that's moving actually makes a turn, then this change of direction should be shown on the screen.

Suppose that a man who is walking along a path is filmed in two shots, as shown in Figure 8.13. The camera could be positioned twice on the same side of the path or once on each side. If both positions are on the same side, the man will move across the frame in the same direction in both shots. If the camera positions are on opposite sides of the path, the man will move in opposite directions in the two shots. When these shots are cut together, the direction change will imply that the man has turned around. Whenever the camera is moved across the axis of action, the direction of travel is flipped.

In film on-screen movement to the left and right is much more important than movement up and down. A low-angle shot of a rocket blasting off often shows it arcing

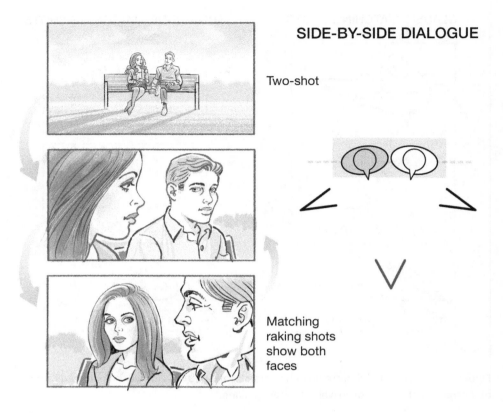

SIDE-BY-SIDE DIALOGUE

Two-shot

Matching
raking shots
show both
faces

Figure 8.11 Matching shots of two characters seated shoulder to shoulder must be taken from one side of the axis that connects them, even though their noses point in opposite directions in the two-shots.

slightly to the right as it heads upward. An effective shot to follow this one is a high angle looking down at the rocket with the earth below it. In this shot the rocket should appear to continue moving right in the frame, but because it's a high-angle shot, the camera can be positioned so that the rocket appears to move downward in the frame (Figure 8.14). For continuity it's more important to show that the rocket continues moving right than it is to show it moving upward on the screen. Viewers do not find it odd that the rocket moves downward on the screen. This is also true of shots of such things as a person climbing a staircase, or something being thrown out a window.

Even though continuity of screen motion may seem restrictive, it is important for clear storytelling. Limiting camera positions to one side of the line still allows for visual variety in the shots. One way to create interesting visual variety when shooting a traveling character is to alternate between shots that have the character moving diagonally toward and away from the camera. In all of these shots the character continues in the same screen direction. Another way of looking at this is that

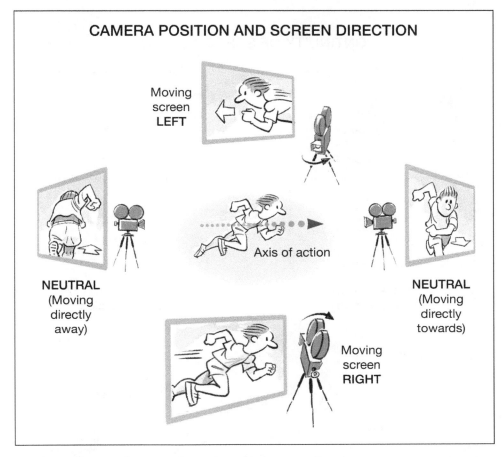

CAMERA POSITION AND SCREEN DIRECTION

Moving screen LEFT

Axis of action

NEUTRAL (Moving directly away)

NEUTRAL (Moving directly towards)

Moving screen RIGHT

Figure 8.12 Camera placement determines whether a traveling character appears to move to the left, the right, into, or out of the screen.

the camera alternates between shots that show the character approaching and ones that watch the character moving away.

Crossing the Axis but Preserving Continuity

Keeping the axis in mind and not positioning the camera on the other side of it is a convenient way of avoiding continuity problems. But the current axis will disappear and a new one will be created whenever an actor moves to a new position or looks in a different direction, and also whenever a new scene begins that has no known or important geographical relationship with what has just been seen. While a particular axis is active, there are several techniques for moving the camera to the other side of the current axis without breaking continuity.

CONTINUITY OF SCREEN MOTION

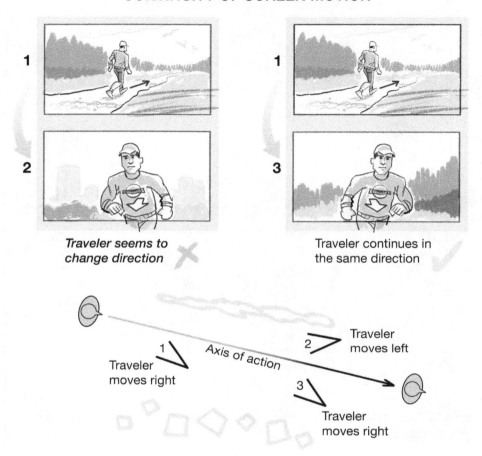

Figure 8.13 A moving character follows the axis of action. The camera position determines the direction of movement as it appears on the screen. If the camera crosses the axis, movement in the shot will be in the opposite screen direction.

Using a Neutral Shot to Bridge a Direction Change

Two shots from opposite sides of the axis can be bridged by using a neutral shot between them. Another way to describe this is that the camera is allowed to cross the line of action if it stops to take a shot along the axis. An example of this technique is illustrated in Figure 8.15 and described below:

- A character is seen moving left or right at any angle.
- In a neutral shot the character moves either directly toward or directly away from the camera exactly on its line of sight.

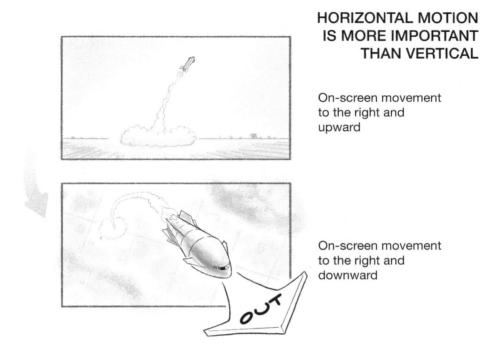

HORIZONTAL MOTION IS MORE IMPORTANT THAN VERTICAL

On-screen movement to the right and upward

On-screen movement to the right and downward

Figure 8.14 The upward or downward component of movement in a shot can change without affecting continuity as long as the movement in both shots is in the same left or right screen direction

- The character is now seen moving in the screen direction opposite that of the first shot.

Another example uses a neutral shot to change the look of a character who is using a computer. In the first shot the character has a right look to the computer screen. The second shot is either the character with a neutral look seen over the top edge of the computer screen, or is a neutral angle from directly behind the character's back. In the final shot the character has a left look to the screen.

Dollying Sideways across the Axis

As the camera is recording a shot it can dolly sideways to a new position that is on the other side of the axis. This flips the screen geography but does so in the gradual and understandable way that an observer in the room would experience while walking to a new position. This is most often used to slide the camera behind one character's head during a conversation: an over-shoulder shot on one side becomes an over-shoulder shot on the other side. This technique is often used

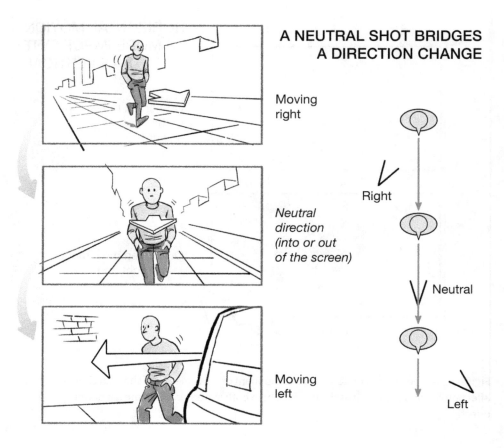

Figure 8.15 A neutral shot can be used as a bridge between shots with screen motion in opposite directions.

at the moment when there is a shocking dramatic turn to the conversation. It is also employed when the camera is moved sideways across a road or sidewalk as a car or character approaches, whether for visual interest or to set up the axis for the next shot.

Using a Large Object as a Landmark in Both Shots

A large object can serve as a point of reference for viewers to help them quickly understand that the axis has been crossed. Some examples of landmarks that can be used are escalators, gangways to planes and ships, architectural elements, and fences. The visual landmark must appear as a significant part of both shots to make the geography clear.

Using Strong Shot Contrast

Strong shot contrast helps to mask a screen direction change. For example, a long shot of two people seated on the porch of a farmhouse can be followed by a two-shot over them from behind. In a similar manner more shot contrast helps the cut when a character changes direction while moving through a doorway.

Cutting to a Something That Erases the Current Geography

Although screen geography is important, it is quickly forgotten when the story cuts away to other action elsewhere. When the story returns to characters who haven't been seen in the last few shots, they can be given new camera angles that set up new screen geography. Here are some examples:

- Cut to another character in the scene and then cut to that character's POV, which sets up a new axis.
- Cut to a wide shot of the scene that establishes new geography from a new angle.
- Use a cutaway to something nearby that's relevant to the story or the setting, and then return to the scene at a new angle.
- Cut in to show something such as hands writing or preparing food, or reaching to pick up a phone, and tilt up to the character at a new angle.
- Pan the arrival or passing of a waiter, coworker, or pedestrian. The shot lands on the scene at a new angle. This provides an opportunity to move the story ahead by a few minutes.
- Use a wipe to introduce a new shot at a new angle. This also provides an opportunity to move the story ahead by a few minutes.

Cutting to an Exterior or to a Concurrent Scene

Cutting away from a scene for a moment enables a new angle and a new axis to be established when the story returns to the scene. Several examples of this technique are described here:

- Cut to a view of the action framed in a window, or framed under an archway or through trees, and so on.
- Use a cutaway shot of something outside that is relevant to the story, such as train wheels spinning.
- Cut to a cityscape or view out the window of a car or train as the surroundings race by to show time passage.
- Cut to a concurrent scene with parallel action, and then return to the original scene.

Screen Geography That Spans Scenes

It can be important to a story to have screen geography that spans and spatially unites two or more scenes. Some common reasons for doing this are described below and illustrated in Figure 8.16:

- People who are traveling to meet each other (or who have parted) should travel in opposite screen directions.
- When one character is pursuing another, they will both head in the same screen direction.

Figure 8.16 Viewers understand a story more easily when screen geography supports the story's logic, even when the action is taking place in separate places.

- Opposing forces in conflict, such as military forces or police and criminals, will move in opposite directions on the screen.
- Phone conversations are usually shot with opposed looks.
- Characters headed from one well-known location to another will move in a screen direction that corresponds to east and west on a map.

Intentionally Flipping Screen Geography

Occasionally directors and editors flip the direction of a character's on-screen movement because they believe it creates a better shot or a better cut. When the axis is flipped for a moving character, a match cut is used to position the moving character at exactly the same point in the frame at the instant the cut is made. The two shots have opposed directions of travel, different camera angles, and different shots sizes. This direction-changing cut works best when the story beat at that point is less about trying to reach a destination and more about what the character is doing while walking, such as thinking or having a conversation.

Sometimes a cut is made to a driver who is facing the opposite direction to the direction of movement of his or her vehicle in the previous shot. For example, a motorboat that is seen in a medium wide shot headed screen right may be followed by a close-up of the skipper now headed screen left, and this cut generally works. But it could be argued that continuity of screen motion doesn't apply to these situations, since in the first shot the motorboat itself is really the character, while in the second shot the skipper is the character, and the direction of the boat's movement is not relevant because the camera is on the boat and shares the skipper's frame of reference. In other words, the skipper is not moving relative to the boat and the camera. Similarly a cut from the exterior of a moving car, train, or plane could show a passenger facing any direction.

Sometimes screen geography has to be flipped as a matter of necessity because of the physical limitations of the set. At other times an axis flip can be used dramatically to graphically underscore a story beat. Some directors are more concerned with screen geography than others. But even directors who frequently cross the axis still have continuity editing in mind much of the time. The following lists are examples of situations where screen geography must be flipped, either because of physical restrictions or to help dramatize the story.

When Screen Geography Has to Be Flipped

- A character enters a doorway, and limitations imposed by the architecture make it necessary to shoot from the opposite side of the axis as the action continues on the other side of the doorway.
- Over-shoulder shots taken when a couple is slow dancing or during a prolonged hug can never be matching shots.

- Narrow passageways in caves, tunnels, staircases, and submarines limit the possible camera angles and often necessitate axis crosses.

When Flipping Screen Geography Helps the Story

- When characters hear something that turns their world upside down, an axis flip can help communicate this moment to viewers.
- Flipping a character's screen direction can help show graphically that the character is lost.
- A shot of a car driving and exiting the frame can cut to a closer shot of the car now stopped and facing the other way. This shows that the trip is over, perhaps having ended suddenly due to a problem such as car trouble.
- A cut from a running character to another shot of the same character, now motionless and facing the other way, suggests time passage, and could suggest exhaustion or an injury.
- A cut to a wide shot of a scene that flips the established screen geography can suggest that it's an unknown observer's POV.

9

Compressing, Expanding, and Ending Scenes

A movie usually tells a story that takes place over days, months, or years. Compressing a story into an hour or two of screen time requires techniques that move time ahead in ways that seem natural. Most of the jumps in time occur between scenes, but even though the time in each individual scene seems continuous, it is often shortened. This chapter looks at techniques for compressing and expanding time within a scene, ways of expanding time when required, and techniques for ending scenes. We'll look at techniques to move time ahead between scenes in Chapter 10.

Compressing Time within a Scene

Time within a scene is often compressed in small ways to cut out what's unimportant, boring, or repetitive.

Showing Work That Has Been Accomplished

One useful way to greatly reduce the time needed to show the work that a character has completed is to start a shot with the camera scanning over what has been accomplished. The camera pans, tilts, or moves over the what's been done until it lands on the character continuing with the work or taking a break (Figure 9.1). This technique can also be used to show the aftermath of a disaster or any number of other events. For example, the camera could start on packed boxes, empty liquor bottles, discarded clothing, or chopped vegetables to quickly tell the story of what activity the person that the shot lands on has been doing. Action can be added to the camera move by starting the shot at the moment something relevant hits the ground in front of the camera, such as a shovelful of dirt landing on a pile. The camera tilts up to find a worker digging a hole.

Another useful way of showing that someone has been doing something for a period of time is to have the camera start close on a foreground wall and dolly or pan off it to reveal the character. Any of these techniques can be used either to start a scene or to compress time midway through a scene.

The Art of Cinematic Storytelling. Kelly Gordon Brine, Oxford University Press (2020). © Oxford University Press.
DOI: 10.1093/oso/9780190054328.001.0001.

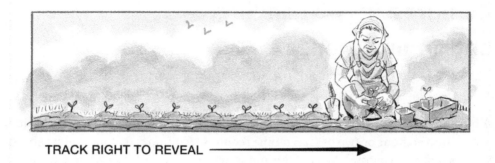

TRACK RIGHT TO REVEAL ⟶

Figure 9.1 The camera can move over the evidence that shows that an activity is underway until it finds the character involved. This quickly tells the story without devoting much screen time to mundane activity.

Eliminating the Middle of the Action

Time can be compressed for an activity by cutting it into parts. One example is a person answering a phone. The character hears it ring from the opposite side of the room and we see the character exit the shot. We cut to a close shot of the phone and see a hand reach in to pick it up. We tilt up with the hand as it raises the phone to the character's ear, and we now see the character again in close-up. These two shots in combination can be much shorter than a single shot that pans the character to the phone and shows the action in its entirety. Imagine a shot of a character opening a tool box that's followed by a close-up of wood being drilled in the middle or near the end of some carpentry work. Another example is seeing a shot of a man cooking, then cutting to a close shot of a plate of food, which now tilts up to reveal the seated man as he begins to eat his meal.

Watching a character walk for several minutes would be boring. The travel time can be greatly reduced by cutting the journey into three pieces. A woman could be shown exiting a shot close to the camera as she starts her journey. Next she could be shown walking part way along her journey in a wide shot, possibly entering this middle shot by emerging from behind something, or we could instead see her walking and then disappearing around a corner, through a door, or next to the camera. Entering or exiting the middle shot helps convey the passage of time. The woman could be seen once again entering the third shot as she arrives at her destination. These three shots could compress a walk of many minutes into a few seconds.

Setting Up Action That Continues

Ending a scene with a wide shot of the activity that a group or character is participating in leaves us with the feeling that what is going on will continue. This will help convince us that any changes we see if the story returns to this setting are reasonable.

Montages for Quick Storytelling

A montage is a sequence of images on one theme that work together to tell a story quickly. It can start a new scene by establishing many elements of a setting, including the time of day, the weather, the mood of the locale, or the activities that are going on there. It can also quickly tell a story much like a picture book of a trip, a wedding, a project, training, or any other event or undertaking.

Cutting Away and Returning

If we cut from a shot of one activity to a different activity, we can return to the first one at a point a few minutes into the future. A *cutaway* is a brief cut to someone or something else in the scene that is not in the current shot. It can even be to a re-establishing exterior shot of the outside of the building the scene is in, or a wide view of part of the scene that is visible through a window. When a cut is made back inside, time may have moved ahead. Cutting to another scene and then back to the first scene at a later point in time is another way to compress time. If students are getting started decorating a high school gym for a dance, and we crosscut with the action in other scenes, we can soon be in the gym as the finishing touches are applied even though only a few minutes have elapsed.

Jump-Cutting Ahead in Time

A jump cut is a cut to the same character, usually seconds or minutes into the future. A character who is searching desperately for something in an office or apartment could be shown in a series of jump cuts both to emphasize the urgency of the search and to compress time.

Expanding Time within a Scene

In film events are usually shortened, but sometimes an event that happens quickly deserves to be on the screen longer to emphasize how shocking, interesting, or beautiful it is.

Slow Motion

The most effective method to expand time is slow motion: it can extend a run, a jump, a fall, an explosion, a crash, or any other action. A slow-motion reaction shot has more significance and intensity. Slow motion can run at various speeds, and the high-speed footage from which it's created can be ramped down from normal speed to slow motion and back up again as desired. Slow motion shots can transform otherwise ordinary and fast-paced shots into something subjective and poetic, and can create feelings of wonder, time standing still, hopelessness, tragedy, or destiny.

Replaying an Event

Repeating the same action using multiple shots from various angles makes an event more dramatic and more important. This technique is sometimes used to show an explosion, a fight, something smashing on the floor, a car crash, or a character being shot. The action is usually performed just once while being shot with several cameras.

Signaling the End of a Scene

The task of starting a new scene falls mainly on the first shot of the new scene. The script limits the shot possibilities that can signal the end of a scene, but a suggestion that a new scene is coming makes its introduction smoother. Sometimes a visual signal suggests that a scene is ending. Sometimes an auditory clue indicates that a new scene is coming. Ways that scenes can end and the arrival of the next scene can be heralded are listed here, and several of them are illustrated in Figure 9.2.

- A sound prelap consisting of dialogue, sound effects, or music from the scene that is about to begin is heard before the current scene has ended.
- A close-up, sometimes with a push in, is a reaction shot to events as a scene ends.
- A character or vehicle exits the shot.
- A wipe by a foreground person or vehicle "closes the curtains" on the scene.
- A door closes: this could be an exterior or interior door, a closet, a cupboard, a hatch, a gate, or an elevator or a garage door.
- A character or vehicle travels deep into the shot.
- Dramatic action occurs, such as an explosion, a glass smashing against a wall, or a gun being fired.
- A shot goes out of focus, or a character who is in focus exits or walks out to leave an image that is entirely out of focus.
- The lights go off.
- A character walks straight toward the camera and blocks its view.
- The camera moves backward (and sometimes up) to widen the shot and leave the characters in their environment or at the mercy of their environment.

A few editing-room transitions are used occasionally and usually indicate a greater disconnection between scenes:

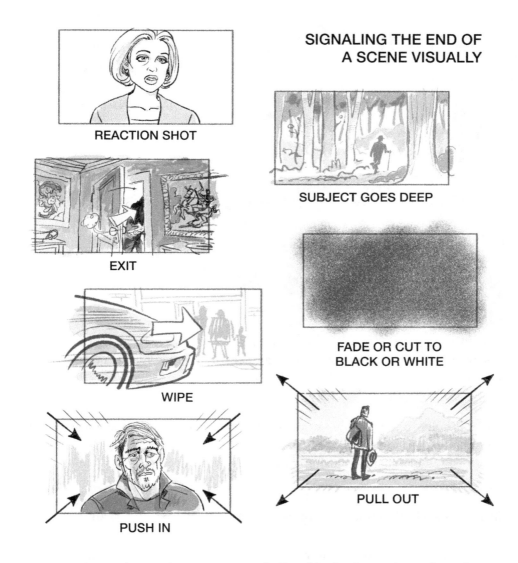

REACTION SHOT

SIGNALING THE END OF
A SCENE VISUALLY

SUBJECT GOES DEEP

EXIT

FADE OR CUT TO
BLACK OR WHITE

WIPE

PULL OUT

PUSH IN

Figure 9.2 These techniques have in common a feeling of finality that can be used to make a cut to a new scene seem more natural by visually suggesting that the current scene is ending. But with the exception of cuts and fades, they can also be used elsewhere in a scene.

- A *fade to black* signals the end of a movie or of a significant time period.
- A *cut to black* abruptly signals that something important or final has just happened, such as a character losing consciousness. The next scene can fade in or it can start suddenly.
- A *fade to white* can begin on something bright that ends the scene, such as the sun, the desert, a fire, or an explosion. A fade to white can also begin on a close-up of someone witnessing destruction. Fading to white can be used to signify that an ill or injured character has died or is ascending to a higher plane of existence.

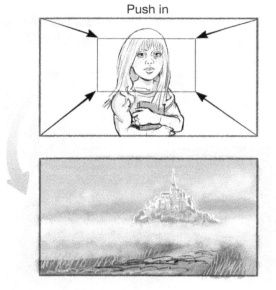

Push in

SIGNALING A
FLASHBACK OR
A TRIP INTO THE
IMAGINATION

Figure 9.3 A push in to a character can emphasize a reaction, but it can also signal that the next scene is within a character's memories or imagination. This is especially true if the push is to an extreme close-up, or if the two juxtaposed shots are dissolved.

- A *dissolve* to the first shot of the next scene usually signifies that a significant amount of time has passed.
- The POV of a character losing conscience can go out of focus

Starting a Flashback or Entering Someone's Imagination

A new scene may occur within a character's memories, dreams, or imagination. Usually the character sees or hears something that triggers a journey into the character's own thoughts. This fact is signaled to viewers by slowly pushing into the character's reaction shot (Figure 9.3). An alternative way of signaling that the next scene is in the character's mind is to have the character back away from something in shock; this either dissolves to the character's flashback, or it fades to white. Now the flashback fades in. A scene set in a character's mind often ends when a voice or a noise (such as a phone or doorbell) brings the character back to the present and we return to the close-up.

10

Beginning Scenes and Using Transitions

A new scene begins when a story's action continues in a new setting. Time may be continuous, or it may be reset to a new point in the future or the past. Even when time is continuous with the previous scene, the sudden arrival of a new scene may seem too abrupt. When a new scene makes a sudden jump in space and time it's usually better to make it seem smooth and natural through the application of an appropriate visual technique, or to divert the audience's attention from the cut by using a brief distraction.

Sometimes as a new scene begins it's obvious that the action of the story in the new scene is continuous in time and space, such as when a character is shown entering a building and the new scene shows the character arriving somewhere inside. But a new scene often brings about a greater change in time and space, and in these cases transitions are used to bridge the discontinuities.

Most frequently-used transitions are created within a scene's first shot by using camera movement or by the movement of something in front of the camera. Unfortunately if such in-camera transitions are not built into shots as they are being recorded, there is no opportunity to create them afterward during editing. It's often a good idea to incorporate in-camera transitions into any shot that is likely to begin a scene. During editing that part of the shot may or may not be used, but it's good insurance. One great advantage of building an in-camera transition into a shot is that there it will provide good shot contrast with the last shot of the previous scene. As this chapter explores the ways in which new scenes start, particular attention will be paid to in-camera transitions. Figure 10.1 shows a schematic overview of the ways in which a new scene can be introduced.

Cuts to the Past, Present, and Future

A Scene Begins in Continuous Time or with Parallel Action

When a new scene begins, viewers assume that time is continuous or parallel unless something tells them otherwise. New scenes in continuous time and those that are intercut with ongoing parallel action in neighboring scenes often begin with hard cuts. Sometimes a quick wipe is used to help clarify that a scene change is happening as well as to provide shot contrast. Other types of transitions generally suggest a longer gap in time between the two scenes and would fight the goal of showing continuous or parallel action. When cross cutting is done between two settings, it confirms that events are happening in parallel.

The Art of Cinematic Storytelling. Kelly Gordon Brine, Oxford University Press (2020). © Oxford University Press.
DOI: 10.1093/oso/9780190054328.001.0001.

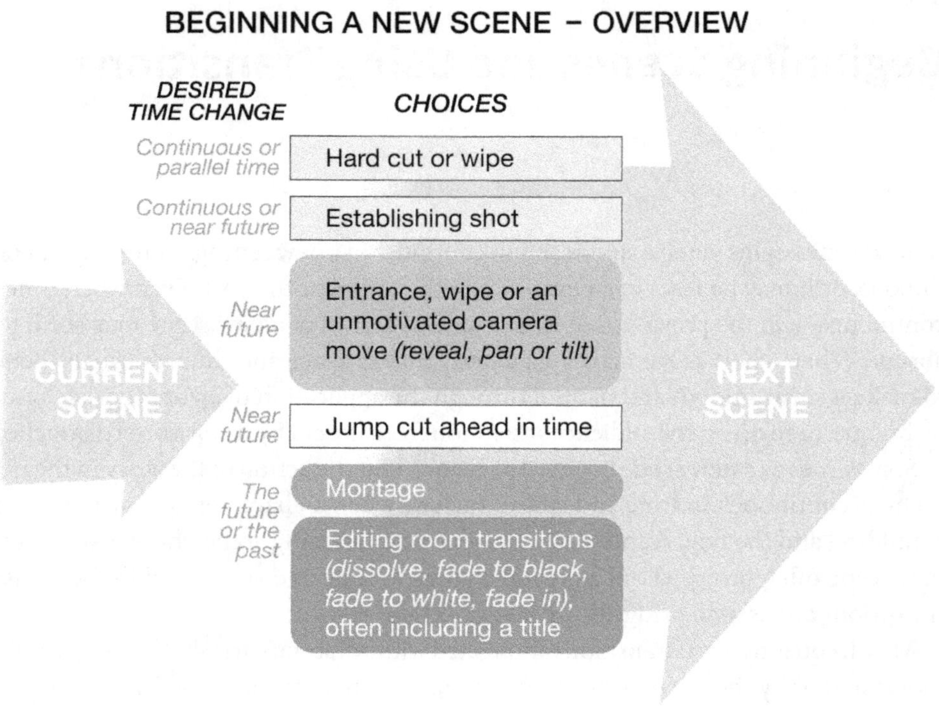

BEGINNING A NEW SCENE – OVERVIEW

Figure 10.1 How a scene begins suggests how time has changed. This overview summarizes which techniques are commonly employed to signal the time difference as a new scene begins.

Moving Time Ahead by Seconds, Minutes, or Hours

A new scene may move the story into the future by seconds, minutes, or hours. Which transition technique to use to accomplish this depends on how much the clock has moved ahead, how far away the new setting is, and whether the setting has been shown in an earlier scene.

Visualizing is the best way to choose from among several transition techniques. This involves imagining the shots and transitions in sequence and evaluating them. What do various types of transitions seem to say about the time and place of the new scene? With practice it is possible to greatly improve your skill at this. Common time techniques that gracefully signal that time has advanced as the story continues in a new setting include the following:

- Establishing shots
- Wipes, entrances, reveals, and other in-camera transitions
- Shots that show a change in the time of day or the weather
- Human activity that indicates the time of day. Having a meal, commuting, arriving at an office building or at home, pursuing a leisure activity, and preparing for bed all tell us what time it is.

Moving Even Further into the Future or the Past

Common techniques that signal a change of time and place into the more distant future or past include these:

- Separating two scenes by placing a scene between them
- Fading to white or black and then fading into a new shot
- Using text overlaid on an establishing shot to state precisely where and when the scene takes place, such as "Six weeks earlier" or "Two years later"
- Showing a different season either through the weather or through the celebration of an event such as Thanksgiving
- Beginning a scene with a montage that establishes a new setting or a season, or tells a story
- Using architecture, fashion, vehicles, technology, or furniture to establish a different time period

A Jump Cut to a New Scene

A jump cut to a new scene is a cut from a character in one setting to the same character in a new setting. A jump cut is abrupt, but it is the fastest way to move the story forward. Jump cuts compress time and space in a way that is similar to montage, although montages do not usually show the same character in every shot. A jump cut creates a sense of urgency that adds excitement to a story. It often suggests that the character is in a hurry or on a mission, but it breaks continuity editing. Jump cuts can lose their effectiveness and make the storytelling seem choppy if they are overused.

A jump cut is less noticeable if there is good shot contrast. This is because the shot contrast makes viewers take a moment longer to recognize that the same character is in the new shot, and this slight delay can be long enough to create a feeling of time having passed. Notable examples of this are cuts to characters' hands, their back, the back of their head, or their silhouette. The cut will also not seem like a jump cut if the character is not immediately recognized in a long shot or as part of a crowd. Anything that creates a delay in recognizing the character reduces the abruptness of a jump cut and helps to maintain continuity editing.

A Juxtaposition That Links Two Scenes

Sometimes a scene begins with an image that relates to what was said or done in the final shot of the previous scene. Such juxtapositions can be used for humor, irony, or pathos, or to advance the story. The connection in meaning ties the two scenes together and distracts attention from the fact that a new scene is starting, making the cut seem more natural. Here are a few examples of the use of such juxtapositions:

- Someone or something that is mentioned or is on a character's mind at the end of one scene is shown in the first shot of the following scene.
- A character's mood at the end of one scene is underscored by the mood of the first image of the next scene, such as crashing waves, the sun rising, taillights out of focus, drums being played, or something being smashed.
- A cut from a funeral to a shot of a place associated with the deceased, such as a room, an empty chair, tools, or a musical instrument.
- One character says, "Let's go fishing." The second character replies in a close-up, "I hate fishing." Viewers soon realize that the second character's close-up is in a fishing boat.
- A scene ends with dialogue or an event, and the next scene begins with people laughing about something unrelated: it seems to be in response even though it is not.
- A question is asked or a comment is made at the end of a scene and the next scene starts with a shot that is a humorous or serious response to what was just said (Figure 10.2).

USING JUXTAPOSITION

A scene ends with a comment

OUR SECURITY IS STATE OF THE ART!

The next scene begins with an image that contradicts it

Figure 10.2 A question that is asked or a comment that is made at the end of a scene can be answered seriously, humorously, or ironically by the juxtaposed image or dialogue that begins the following scene.

A Hard Cut to a Character's Action

A hard cut is a cut to a new scene without a transition or an entrance. A hard cut works best when there is strong shot contrast with the last shot of the previous scene. The action of the scene hits the ground running, and suggests continuous time with the previous scene. Using an entrance or a transition, or even having the character turn to the camera, makes a smoother cut, but this is not always the right choice. For instance, a hard cut to a specific character may be effective because that character is linked to the action or the dialogue at the end of the previous scene. Recall that a hard cut to a character in motion toward or away from a camera whose movement is synchronized with the character cuts just as well as would a cut to a stationary character shot by a stationary camera. This is because the character remains at a constant size and in a constant position within the frame (Figure 10.3).

Sometimes a new scene continues the story of a character in a setting where the story left the person a scene or two earlier. A hard cut is often made to such a character whose action is ongoing, since the character and the setting are already

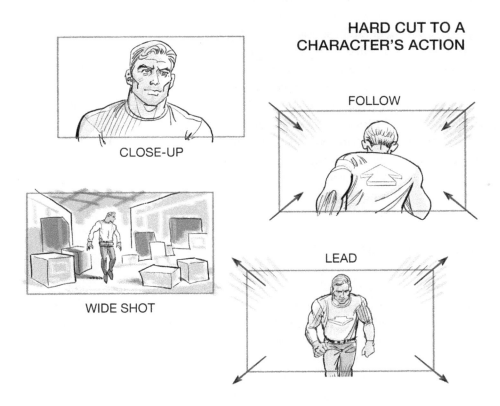

Figure 10.3 A hard cut directly to a character's action starts a scene more subjectively and more urgently.

familiar to viewers. Even if the first shot of the new scene is not very wide, the presence of this character and a few characteristic elements of the setting are often enough to make it clear that we're picking up this character's continuing story. Beginning a scene with a hard cut to a character can give a feeling of subjectivity, intensity, and urgency, and a feeling that not much time has passed since we last saw this character.

An Establishing Shot

The most straightforward way to show that a new scene is starting is to use an establishing shot. An establishing shot that introduces a new setting is most important when the setting is seen for the first time, especially if it is a complex or unusual environment. It's common for an establishing shot to incorporate a pan or a tilt because these movements are able to show settings more immersively and in more detail, as well as creating better separation from the previous scene. Sometimes a montage of wide establishing shots and close shots of details is used for an even fuller introduction of the new scene's characteristics.

An establishing shot can show the elements and mood of the new setting, as well as provide an overview of the spatial relationships of buildings, people, vehicles, and objects. It may help establish the time of day, weather, or season. Sometimes an interior scene is preceded by an establishing shot of the exterior of the structure in which the scene takes place. The scene continues within the house, office building, factory, car, boat, plane, spaceship, or other structure whose exterior was just shown. Sometimes interior scenes are cheated in the sense that they are shot on sets in studios far from the locations where their exterior shots are recorded.

An economical exterior establishing shot can be created for a story that is set in the past. By keeping the background of a city street in soft focus, all the clues that would indicate that the movie was shot today are blurry: only some foreground period set dressing is needed.

A Hard Cut to Close Action

A scene can start dramatically on a close shot of something unexpected happening. The action is often threatening, violent, or mysterious, but could be as simple as a cork popping out of a bottle (Figure 10.4). Answers to questions about where we are and what's happening are provided in the shots that follow. Here are some examples:

- A gun is fired in a close-up, or an axe strikes a tree trunk.
- Boots enter the frame, a tire rolls into frame, a shovel hits the dirt, a dart hits a dartboard, a tomato splats on a poster, a basketball lands in a hoop, or a bottle explodes against a door.

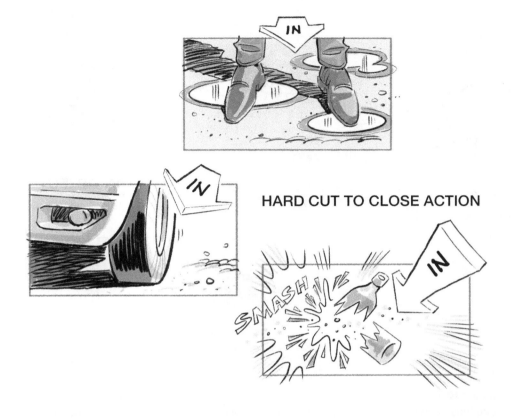

HARD CUT TO CLOSE ACTION

Figure 10.4 A shot of sudden close action starts a scene dramatically, diverts attention from the cut that is being made to a new time and place, and provides good shot contrast.

- A piece of crumpled paper lands in a wastepaper basket, clothing lands on the floor, or drops of water or blood drip into a puddle on the ground.

A Hard Cut to a Close-Up of an Object

A close-up of an object can begin a new scene (Figure 10.5). Often a hand will enter the shot to pick up the object. The object in the close-up is often quite significant to the story. It may be a tool, a letter, flowers, a gun, a clue to a crime, or something interesting that is characteristic of the locale for the purpose of helping to establish the new setting. Often the fact that this type of object would not be found in the setting of the previous scene signals the start of a new scene.

A close-up of an object often cuts well with the shot that precedes it because it creates contrast with any wide shot or any shot of people. A cut to a close object can also be intriguing and attractive, which helps break the hold of the previous scene on viewers' thoughts. Sometimes a scene begins close on a foreground object and

HARD CUT TO AN OBJECT

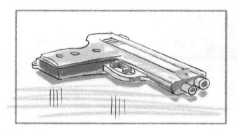

Figure 10.5 Starting a scene close on an object provides shot contrast, signals a new setting and thus a new scene, and may create a mood of mystery or intrigue. The object shown is often important to the story.

then rack-focuses to a character who now becomes visible in the background. This is especially effective if there is a connection in meaning between the object and the character, but it may also simply serve to get the scene started.

An Off-Screen Look or a POV

A scene may begin with a close shot of a character looking at something off-screen, and this shot is followed by the character's POV. A new scene may also begin by showing the POV first and then the character. Beginning a scene with a POV may help provide shot contrast, and may prevent a jump cut that would occur if the character were shown first. A POV can be virtually anything, including a computer screen, a television, or the view through binoculars, rifle sights, or a microscope.

When a POV is used to open a scene, it is usually but not always clean, meaning it does not contain any part of the head or shoulder of the character whose POV it is. At first it seems like an establishing shot and not anyone's POV, but a separate shot of the observer follows (Figure 10.6).

Figure 10.6 When a scene starts with a POV, it is usually clean and seems like an establishing shot, but is shown to have been a POV when a cut is made to the observer.

There are several ways to start with a clean POV, but then incorporate the observer into the same single shot. Three methods involving a pan, an entrance, and a pull are illustrated in Figure 10.7.

A scene can begin with the observer already in his own POV. This can be extended quite cinematically by having the actor turn to the camera and approach it, perhaps delivering a line to as-yet-unseen characters as he does so. The camera pulls backward in response, and this pulls two other characters in from the sides. Now the dialogue continues among these three characters, who are covered in several additional shots. This scenario is illustrated in Figure 10.8.

A scene can begin with a shot that is understood as a character's POV even though it is not close to the character's true visual angle. The most common use of this is a shot that begins close on a character's hands and tilts up to find the character in close-up. The character may be preparing food, using a tool, pouring a drink, tapping on a mobile phone, fidgeting nervously, or writing a letter (Figure 10.9). Such a shot creates a transition because its action and mysterious nature help stop viewers from thinking about the previous scene. This technique also suggests that time has passed.

Rack Focus between Characters and Their POV

A scene can begin with a single shot in which a rack focus changes what's in focus between an observer and what's observed. Either the POV or the observer is in focus at

A DIRTY POV THAT BEGINS CLEAN

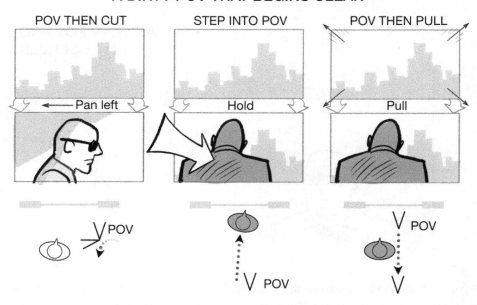

POV THEN CUT
Pan left

STEP INTO POV
Hold

POV THEN PULL
Pull

POV

POV

POV

POV

Figure 10.7 A shot that begins as a clean POV can be made to include the observer a moment later by having the character enter or by using a pan or a pull to reveal the character.

Hold then pull

Lead

START WITH OBSERVER IN HIS OWN POV, THEN LEAD

POV

Figure 10.8 A scene can begin on a character's back as he stands in his own POV. Now he turns and delivers a line as he approaches the camera, which pulls back to reveal the two characters he has begun a conversation with.

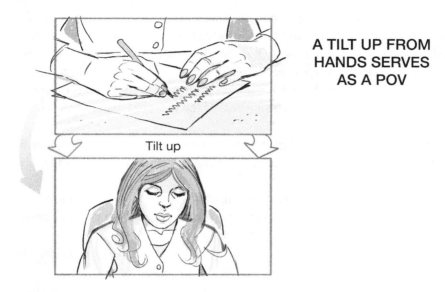

A TILT UP FROM
HANDS SERVES
AS A POV

Tilt up

Figure 10.9 Scenes often begin with a cinematic tilt up from a character's hands. The angle serves as the character's POV even though it is not the character's true POV.

the beginning of the shot; a rack focus shifts the focus to the other element of the shot, and only one element is in focus at a time. The lens length, aperture size, and distances must be adjusted to achieve a shallow depth of field for this to be possible.

It is also possible to do a rack focus with either the POV or the observer seen only as a reflection in a window. These shots can be surprising, moody, mysterious, and artistic. To make a rack focus that uses a reflection work, the key is to remember that what is seen through the glass must not be as bright as what is reflected, because otherwise the reflection will be washed out by the brightness behind the glass. Which side of the window is best for camera placement will therefore depend on whether it's day or night and whether what is seen through the glass is more brightly lit than what is on the camera's side of the glass.

An Entrance

Beginning a scene with an entrance is often effective. The action is engaging and creates a diversion that helps to hide the cut. Tighter shots of an entrance, as well as entrances made from right beside the camera, are usually more interesting and dramatic than entrances in wide shots. An entrance can be made through a doorway, around a corner, from behind an object, or by simply stepping in front of the camera.

An entrance often suggests that time has passed. Because scenes often end on a character, a scene that starts without a character visible often provides better shot contrast than one in which a character is already present. If the character was recently seen elsewhere, an entrance will help prevent viewers from wondering how the character got to this new setting so quickly, and it prevents a jump cut if the character was in the shot that ended the previous scene (Figure 10.10). A related technique is to have the character exit the earlier shot. Now when we cut to a shot of the character in a new setting, there is no jump cut and we already know that the character was headed somewhere. Which technique to choose often depends on whether the earlier scene should end on the story beat of the character reacting psychologically to events or taking action.

Entrances are effective for starting scenes in film, just as they are in theater. Some of the many types of entrances are listed below, and a few are illustrated in Figure 10.11.

- Doors in buildings, elevators, and vehicles account for most entrances.
- A character can enter a shot from around a corner, or from behind a fence, a machine, vegetation, or other obstruction.
- A character can step into the shot from just out of frame at any angle. The character may turn into profile or toward the camera to be identified.
- A character can step into the frame near the camera in profile, and the camera can immediately pan with her as she takes a few steps to her destination.

ADDING AN ENTRANCE
TO AVOID A JUMP CUT

Figure 10.10 Sometimes a character is in the last shot of a scene and must also be in the first shot of the next scene. Adding an entrance to the second shot is one easy option to avoid a jump cut. An alternative is to add an exit to the earlier shot.

ENTRANCES

Figure 10.11 Scenes often begin with an entrance, which may be through a door, from off camera, or from behind an object. Wider shots of entrances establish a new scene's setting, while closer shots are more dramatic and subjective.

- A character can arrive head first at the top of a ladder or out of a hole.
- A character can arrive feet first down a ladder or staircase.
- A character can step out of the shadows, fog, haze, or smoke.
- A vehicle or a person can become visible rising up over the crest of a hill.
- The camera can already be tracking left or right when a vehicle or a person enters moving in the same direction but a little faster. Now the camera adjusts its speed to move with the character.
- A spaceship, the head of a dinosaur, a construction elevator, or something falling can enter a shot from the top of the frame.

Using Action or Light to Reveal the Scene

An entrance is an effective way to begin a scene, but often an entrance is not possible because the story requires that a character already be there. A substitute for an entrance is a *reveal*. A reveal is usually created in one of these two ways: either what's blocking the camera's view moves out of the way, or the camera moves to find the character. A third type of reveal occurs when a character is already visible in the shot but is not identifiable because her face is hidden or is not illuminated. In these cases the character is revealed when she changes position or the lighting changes. The movement that creates a reveal can be visually interesting, and the delay in showing a character is mysterious and creates separation in time and space from the previous scene. Reveals often begin with an image that provides good shot contrast.

A Wipe In Starts the Scene

A wipe is created by a person, vehicle or object crossing through the frame close to the camera as a shot is being recorded. What crosses is close enough to the camera to momentarily block its view. A *wipe in* begins with a character or object already moving across the screen and quickly exiting as though a curtain has been opened. A *wipe out* ends a shot when a person or object enters the frame and starts to cross it, blocking the view as curtains would. Most wipes are created using vehicles or extras. Digital wipes can also be created. A digital wipe looks something like a windshield wiper blade that changes the image as it crosses the frame. Digital wipes seem artificial and are seldom used.

Wipes created in-camera are an extremely useful and effective transition technique that looks natural, adds visual interest, and guarantees shot contrast. A wipe like this can introduce a new scene, compress time, and show that an environment is busy). Wipes give the impression that a small amount of time has gone by since the previous scene ended (Figure 10.12).

An Element of the Scene That Blocks the View Is Moved

A scene can begin with something stationary blocking the camera's view, and it is quickly moved out of the way, often by a character, to reveal the scene. It might be a vehicle that is driven away, a curtain that is pulled to the side, or a cupboard door that swings open. A reveal differs from a wipe. A wipe is generally something that is already in motion and seen only fleetingly, is not in itself particularly important to the story, and is added to the shot only as a transition. Its movement is not controlled by a character. A reveal, on the other hand, is often created when a character or extra moves something. The object is more clearly seen than an object that wipes the frame, and it may not entirely leave the shot. Reveals provide good shot contrast. Here are some examples of reveals:

- A van, truck, or bus drives out of frame, revealing the passenger who has just disembarked.
- The camera sits in darkness inside a fridge, cupboard, closet, safe, van, or car trunk. As the door swings open, it reveals the character.
- Someone's back is completely blocking the lens, but as the character walks deep the scene is revealed.

WIPE REVEALS

Figure 10.12 Wipes are often added to start shots that begin scenes. Wipes make cuts smoother, suggest a busy environment, and compress time. Extras and vehicles are usually used.

A Hidden Face Is Revealed Using Action or Light

A character whose face is obscured may be in a shot from its beginning. In this case a reveal is whatever action allows viewers to see the character's face. It might be that a character lowers something to reveal a face, or by lighting a match the character reveals a face. This type of reveal begins with the question of the mysterious figure's identity, but the question is quickly answered. This is enough to interest and distract viewers, and this diversion helps get the new scene started. A few examples are illustrated in Figure 10.13. Here are some additional examples:

- Binoculars are lowered or an umbrella is raised, revealing a face.
- A mask, hood, or bag comes off someone's head.
- Someone lying in bed turns to face the camera.
- A breeze blows laundry hanging on a clothesline, revealing a face.
- A shadowy figure steps into the light of a streetlamp.
- Curtains or shutters are opened, illuminating the room.
- A car arrives and its headlights illuminate a character.

ACTION REVEALS A CHARACTER'S IDENTITY

EMERGE FROM SILHOUETTE
OR STEP INTO THE LIGHT

TURN TO CAMERA

UNCOVER
FACE

Figure 10.13 A new scene may begin with a shot of a character who cannot be identified. A character's identity can be revealed by action in many ways, including the ones shown.

Pan with Something That Does a Handoff Reveal

A *handoff reveal* is created using an extra's motion to motivate the camera to pan until it finds the character who starts the scene. The extra plays someone whom one would expect to find in this type of environment. Pedestrians, waiters, workers, cyclists, and paramedics with gurneys can be used to create handoffs. The handoff begins with the camera panning the extra, who is walking diagonally closer to the camera. When the extra is quite close to the camera and the camera's angle is in line with the important character who starts the scene, the camera stops panning and holds this angle, letting the extra leave the frame. Now the character the camera was seeking is in the shot and the scene's action begins. The dialogue may already have started. Beginning a scene this way provides a time transition, shot contrast, a pan of the setting, and some relevant action in what might otherwise be a static dialogue scene.

An Unmotivated Camera Reveals the Scene

Unmotivated camera moves are often useful for starting scenes. Since their use is almost entirely limited to shots that open scenes, they are understood by viewers to be signaling the beginning of a new scene. They often begin with a somewhat abstract composition that helps disconnect the storytelling from the previous scene, and their motion helps introduce and ease viewers into the environment of the scene that is starting. Unmotivated camera moves also create visual interest through their motion, which is helpful when a scene has little action. They typically create shot contrast that cuts well with the last shot of the previous scene.

The Camera Tilts to Reveal

A tilt that opens a scene begins as a well-composed angle looking up or down, and when the move ends, it attractively frames the characters and their action. A *tilt up* often starts as a close-up of an object. In a tilt up the initial image frequently begins to tell the story of the scene. The shot may start close on something such as a letter, hands, food, work in progress, a murder victim, a gun, a smashed dish, scattered clothing, a campfire, hands on a keyboard, reflections on wet pavement, or anything else that is relevant to the story at that point or helps describe the scene's setting.

The image that is framed at the start of a *tilt down* is usually visually interesting, but often it does not yet convey a story beat. The shot may begin as a low-angle view of treetops, a building, a rocket, clouds, or an interesting ceiling or chandelier, and the tilt down finds the characters in the scene as their action begins or is already underway (Figure 10.14).

The Camera Pans to Reveal

A scene can begin with a pan across an exterior or interior setting that stops when it finds the character who begins the scene. The pan must be well composed at both ends. The shot establishes the setting and the mood and may provide some backstory, or it may offer clues that start viewers guessing what the camera will find. These clues might suggest a party that has ended, a murder scene, a bedroom scene, or the current progress of work that is underway. Using a pan to transition to a new scene makes a clean break from the previous scene and begins the new scene at a slow pace that often suggests a distance in time and space. Figure 10.15 shows two examples of pans that could introduce scenes.

TILT UP OR DOWN TO REVEAL

Figure 10.14 A tilt up or down can create an effective in-camera transition as it introduces a new time and place in an attractive and intriguing way before finding the action as a scene begins.

The Camera Moves Off Foreground to Reveal

Having foreground blocking the camera's view and moving off it is another useful in-camera transition that helps separate scenes in time and space. It also provides good shot contrast. At the start what is blocking the camera's view is often something dark or plain and uninteresting. As the camera moves off the foreground, it reveals the characters in the scene. What's in the foreground may be a wall, a pillar, a piece of furniture, a tree trunk, foliage, or a vehicle (Figure 10.16). A variation on this technique is to begin with a wide establishing shot, and as the camera dollies

PAN LEFT OR RIGHT TO REVEAL

Figure 10.15 A pan can create a separation in time and space from the previous scene. It often establishes the setting, shows evidence of recent events, or provides backstory before finding the action as a scene begins. The pan may begin on the shadow or a reflection of the characters.

DOLLY OFF FOREGROUND TO REVEAL →

Figure 10.16 An time transition can be created by dollying, panning, or booming up off plain or dark foreground to find the action as a scene begins. This also provides excellent shot contrast.

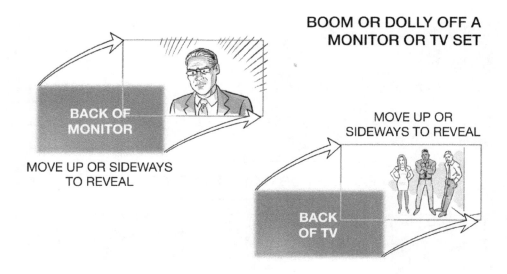

BOOM OR DOLLY OFF A MONITOR OR TV SET

BACK OF MONITOR

MOVE UP OR SIDEWAYS TO REVEAL

MOVE UP OR SIDEWAYS TO REVEAL

BACK OF TV

Figure 10.17 The camera can begin a scene by dollying off the back of a foreground monitor or television set to reveal a character studying the screen. It provides a transition as well as excellent shot contrast.

sideways it unexpectedly discovers a character near the camera in a close-up or medium shot.

Moving off foreground is a frequently used transition that is similar in effect to a curtain being pulled open. Often the dialogue of the characters is heard before they are seen, or if the move is off the back of a television set, the broadcast is heard. It's a convenient way to create a transition when other options are limited. When there is no foreground object available to dolly off, such as in a corridor, a substitute is to start with the camera looking directly at a plain nearby wall, and then to pan 90 degrees to find the action.

A similar reveal can be created by booming up or down off something in the foreground. This is effective if the characters are looking at the object that the camera was behind, such as a television screen or monitor (Figure 10.17). At other times this technique may serve simply to create separation from the previous scene, or be used because other transition options are limited. Some additional examples of reveals created by the camera moving off a foreground object are listed below.

- Dolly off the back of a crime board in a police station.
- Dolly off the back of technical equipment.
- Dolly off a tombstone or statue.
- Dolly off a person's back, the back of the head, or a high-backed chair.
- Crane down from a chandelier, neon sign, or branches.
- Dolly across the bedsheets covering a reclining figure until a face is revealed.

The Camera Is Pulled Backward to Reveal

The camera can start on something that is isolated and highlighted by the composition, but its significance is not yet clear. Now as the camera is pulled backward to take in more at the edges of the frame, the significance of what was shown is understood in its context. Such a shot often begins close on food, tools, money, cards, weapons, equipment, or maps. Hands may reach in to the shot as the camera pulls back to a wider shot. Often the dialogue of the characters is heard before they are seen. This technique also works when the shot begins with a clean POV of something of interest, such as a military objective, a piece of art, or a safe (Figure 10.18).

Figure 10.18 A scene can begin with a shot that isolates and highlights something that is not fully understood. The camera almost immediately moves backward to reveal more, and the significance of the initial image is now understood.

A pull-out reveal may also start with one character already in the frame. As the camera moves backward it pulls other characters into the shot, reveals an unexpected setting, or reveals something funny or tragic lying at the character's feet.

One common use of this transition is to begin a scene in which people do not move much, such as when they are seated and having a conversation. The visual changes that are created by the camera's movement help compensate for the lack of action in the scene. Revealing the characters by pulling out also makes it seem like the action of the scene is well underway. A pull out provides good shot contrast. Some additional examples are listed below:

- Pull out from a person in a chair to reveal his interrogator facing him.
- Pull out from a shot of the casket with flowers on the lid to reveal the mourners at the gravesite.
- Pull straight up from a body on the ground to reveal several detectives discussing the crime.

Other Ways to Open a Scene

There are a few additional ways to begin scenes that might be considered more abstract than the ones mentioned so far. They are not used as often but they can be useful.

Begin the Scene out of Focus

A scene can begin with an image that is out of focus, creating a mood of mystery. A character may already be in the shot and be brought into focus, or walk toward the camera and come into focus. Alternatively, a character can step into this shot in the focal plane. These techniques clearly signal a new scene, provide a time transition, and provide good shot contrast. Some examples of when focus could be used to start a scene are listed here:

- A shot of a scene such as people dancing in a club is out of focus, and a character steps into the shot in focus close to the camera.
- An out-of-focus close-up of a character's face is brought into focus as the character wakes up or regains consciousness.
- A character's out-of-focus POV is brought into focus as the person regains consciousness.
- A shot can follow a character while keeping what's ahead out of focus. This may show that a character is in his own world or make the scene's beginning more suspenseful.

Swish Pan from One Scene to the Next

A swish or whip pan is created by merging two quick panning shots with a dissolve. It's rapid blurred movement off one character and onto another can be used to connect two scenes in time and meaning. The action seems to be happening at the same instant, and it creates a feeling of urgency and excitement.

A Graphic Match between Scenes

A graphic match is the technique of beginning a new scene with an image that is graphically similar to the image in the last shot of the previous scene. A dissolve unites these two images. The graphic match connects the scenes visually and often in meaning. Most directors seldom use graphic matches except to create invisible cuts. Here are some examples of the use of graphic matches to begin scenes:

- A child's pinwheel fan dissolves to a waterwheel that the observer is inspired to build.
- A shot of water flowing dissolves to another shot of water flowing, but this one is in the setting of a new scene.

Editing-Room Effects as Transitions

There are many editing-room transitions that are almost never used in films and television, perhaps because they are essentially two-dimensional. These have names such as *ripple, flash, push, uncover*, and *page turn*, and they are more commonly used in PowerPoint and Keynote presentations. But there are two effective and important editing-room transitions that are commonly used: dissolves and fades. These techniques are illustrated in Figure 10.19, and their storytelling uses are described below:

- *Dissolve*: A significant amount of time has passed. The longer the dissolve, the longer the time. A flashback or dream is beginning. (A dissolve is also sometimes used as a last resort to hide a lack of shot contrast between juxtaposed shots.)
- *Fade to black*: A character is falling asleep. This transition gives a sense of closure when an important part of a story is ending. It is often used at the end of a movie.
- *Fade in from black*: This is often used as a movie begins, or to introduce a scene set in the distant past or the future. Text is overlaid to identify the time and place.

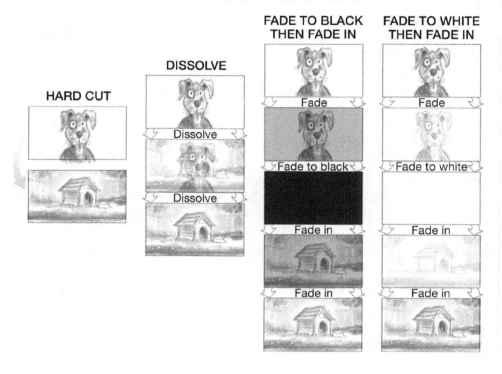

Figure 10.19 The most commonly used editing-room transitions are fading to black or white, fading in from black or white, and dissolving.

- *Fade to white*: This does not give the sense of closure that a fade to black does. It ends a scene with more uncertainty. It may emphasize the destruction of a powerful explosion or the close-up reaction of a witness to destruction, or indicate that a character dies or ascends to a higher plane of existence.
- *Fade in from white*: This is necessary if the previous scene faded to white.
- *Cut to black*: This gives a feeling of great finality to a chapter of a story.

11

Scenes with Stationary Action

Stories often contain scenes in which a single character is stationary for a period of time while on the phone, working at a desk, reading, eating, or sleeping, and so on. This chapter looks at ways to enhance the storytelling when shooting a character who is largely stationary. Shot size, angles, camera movement, and important compositional techniques can all be used to heighten the drama. POVs and reaction shots are often especially important when a scene has little action, and these are explored.

The Setting and the Mood

Tableau Shots

The rectangular opening in a theater's wall through which a stage production is seen is called the *proscenium*. It's bounded by the stage floor, a wall on each side, and an arch or lintel across the top. The audience watches stage performances through this "window." In film a *tableau shot* frames action in a way that mimics the audience's view through the proscenium. Tableau shots are wide, stationary, and often framed to be aligned squarely with the walls of the set. A tableau shot may show the action of an entire scene without a cut. More descriptive angles and closer shots that isolate, emphasize, and heighten the action and emotion of the scene are not used.

A tableau shot is carefully designed, and is not unlike a painting that has come to life. The absence of cuts makes the action seamless, and the careful composition can be appealing. The major disadvantage is that because other angles and shot sizes are not used, the visual storytelling is constrained to being a play-like presentation of the action that always favors the single camera. This imposes constraints similar to those imposed by a theater stage. Most directors do not use tableau shots, probably because of their artificial style and their many limitations. A tableau shot makes a scene with limited action more monotonous.

Establishing Shots

A stationary character and the setting of a scene can be introduced together in a wide establishing shot. Establishing shots may be long shots, but for interiors they are closer because of the limitations of room size. An establishing shot that begins with a pan or tilt will provide welcome visual variety to a static scene. Establishing shots are objective shots that show spatial relationships, often suggesting the story

The Art of Cinematic Storytelling. Kelly Gordon Brine, Oxford University Press (2020). © Oxford University Press.
DOI: 10.1093/oso/9780190054328.001.0001.

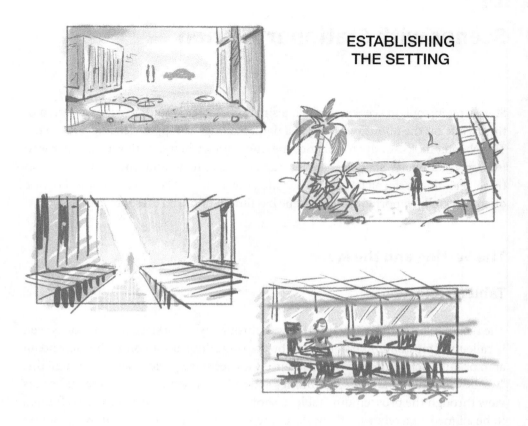

ESTABLISHING THE SETTING

Figure 11.1 An establishing shot is often used to begin a scene. The emphasis is on the setting, the mood, and spatial relationships. The shot can be stationary or involve a pan or a tilt.

relationship of the characters with their environment. The mood is created through lighting, composition, and the details of the set (Figure 11.1).

Unlike a tableau shot, an establishing shot does not have to be composed to be able to show the action of an entire scene, because additional shots are created as needed. It is standard to cut from a wide establishing shot to closer shots that emphasize the action and emotions of the characters.

Re-establishing Shots

A re-establishing shot is a reminder of what the setting is and sometimes a reminder of the setting's spatial relationships. It may be the same establishing shot that was used earlier in the scene, or a new one. It provides a visual break from close shots when there is little action. The angle chosen for the re-establishing shot may be effective for emphasizing the current drama, perhaps by underscoring a character's

**REESTABLISHING
SHOTS**

THROUGH A WINDOW

A FRAME WITHIN A FRAME

FROM A DIFFERENT HEIGHT

PARTLY HIDDEN BY
PEOPLE OR OBJECTS

Figure 11.2 Re-establishing shots remind the audience of the setting and of spatial relationships. The composition of the shot is an opportunity to graphically reinforce a story beat.

isolation, conflict, predicament, or weakness. Some options are high angles, framing the character in a doorway or from outside through a window, or partially obscuring the character by using foreground (Figure 11.2).

Wide Shots

A wide shot is generally what would be the viewpoint of an objective observer. Wide shots are not generally as wide as establishing shots, but they are often wide enough to show characters as full figures. A wide shot can establish a character's spatial relationships with other characters, the architecture, and important props. Because cuts from one wide shot to another lack shot contrast, a wide shot is normally followed by a closer and more subjective shot of the action. A wide shot often serves as a master shot for an entire scene.

From time to time a wide master shot may be reintroduced in an edited sequence. This may serve as a reminder of the scene's spatial relationships, it may re-establish who or what is nearby, or it may illustrate a dramatic beat such as a standoff or the fact that a character is isolated. Reusing a master shot can also be a way to "press reset" on a scene, and this provides the opportunity to once again gradually build the tension of the scene by cutting to tighter and tighter shots.

A wide shot can be brought to life and made more visually interesting by very slowly dollying the camera sideways throughout the scene (Figure 11.3). This commonly used technique is ideal for adding visual interest to static scenes involving stationary characters who are seated in restaurants, hospital rooms, offices, and homes. The slow movement makes the shot more cinematic, three-dimensional, and immersive.

A slow sideways dolly can create a feeling of tension, conflict, or danger, and it may act like a darkening sky that foreshadows drama ahead. Such a shot can be made more immersive if as the camera slowly creeps sideways it passes foreground objects such as pillars, plants, people, equipment, blinds, or fencing. These objects appear to move slowly across the screen in the direction opposite that of the camera's movement. The shot may begin with a transition if it starts

Figure 11.3 A static scene can be heightened dramatically and made immersive by slowly moving the camera sideways past foreground in a wide shot. A transition can be added by starting on a foreground object.

on a foreground object and moves off it to reveal the scene. Another option is for the camera to gradually tighten a wide shot as it very slowly moves directly toward a character throughout a scene. This is likely to create a feeling of foreboding, suggesting that the character is under pressure or in danger even if they do not yet know it.

How to Make a Character Seem Important

Scenes are written so that the drama builds as they progress. Shots and cuts should be designed to heighten the drama. Several ways to make a character more important are illustrated in Figure 11.4 and are described below.

Figure 11.4 A character can be made to seem more important to the story by match cutting, zooming, pushing closer, wrapping the character, or tilting from the hands to the face.

Match Cut

A match cut shifts viewers' attention from the setting to the character and the character's action. It is the fastest and most common way to create more subjective coverage of a character.

Punch In

A punch in is an emphatic cut to a magnified view of the character with the camera on exactly the same line of sight. It seems less natural than a match cut, but it is more intense and suspenseful.

Tilt Up

A tilt up from what a character's hands are doing can start a scene or be used mid-scene. It has the advantage of combining a description of what a character is doing with that character's close-up in a single cinematic shot. Sometimes a movement can motivate the tilt up, for instance a fork being used to raise food to the character's mouth, or a phone being raised to the character's ear. A tilt can also begin elsewhere on the figure, such as on the feet.

Push In

A push in is slower than a match cut and puts more emphasis on the character's psychology and reaction to events. It is generally used only at important moments when a character has an idea, an insight, or is deeply affected by events, and the camera does not usually push for long. The push is normally done slowly but may be done quickly if the character is shocked.

Zoom In

A quick, short zoom in is occasionally used instead of a push to accentuate a startled reaction to events. Another use is to quickly zoom from a wide shot to a medium shot to place a character in the geography. An example is a quick zoom from a wide shot of building to a sniper on the roof or on a balcony. Zooms stand out because they seem less natural than camera movement. Some directors never use zooms except as a minor adjustment to the framing hidden in a panning shot.

Wrap

A *wrap* is created by rotating the camera part way around a character. The lens constantly points inward at the character like a satellite orbiting the Earth. A wrap is an effective way of prolonging and intensifying a character's reaction to something of great importance. It can also suggest a confused, bewildered, or uncertain state of mind, or that the character is reacting and considering alternatives. As the camera wraps, it should cross the character's eyeline just before it comes to rest.

A Character Looks at Something Nearby

There are several ways to show that a character looks at something nearby and reacts. Cuts or camera moves can be used. Pans and tilts are more fluid and cinematic than cuts, and their slower pace can increase the feeling of mystery and suspenseful. When choosing from several options for a combination of a look, a POV, and a reaction, there is no substitute for imagining several alternatives and gauging your own reactions in order to determine which one best suits the story beats.

Cutting to a POV of Something Nearby

A character's POV can be shown before cutting to the character's close-up—viewers understand the relationship regardless of the order of the two shots. Often a true POV of something that is nearby and lower down (such as a desk drawer or what is being held in the hands) makes a less attractive composition than a POV angle that is cheated by lowering and angling the camera a little, so this is preferred. A character's close-up reaction can be seen in a side shot instead of a frontal one if the character turns in the camera's direction to react, look around, or exit. Figure 11.5 illustrates three different POV sequences.

If characters are at some distance from what they are looking at, the story may require that they approach it. This can be done by panning them in their reaction shot. The camera may have to be pulled back as the pan is done to widen the shot so that both the character and what the person is looking at can be framed at the end of the shot. An alternative is to simply pull back and not pan at all; this is a more subjective approach because the camera moves with the character.

Connecting a POV to the Observer in One Shot

Sometimes what is being looked at is quite close, and in these cases it may be better to show both the observer and what is being observed in the same shot. The beats of

A CLEAN
POV AND A
CLOSE-UP

**VARIATIONS ON A POV OF
SOMETHING NEARBY**

A LOOK, A CLEAN
POV AND A REACTION

WIDE
EYELINES

Figure 11.5 A POV sequence can begin with either the observer or what is being observed. A POV of a low object can be cheated by using a more attractive angle. A profile reaction shot allows the character to look or exit near the camera. A reaction can be shown in a close-up.

a character looking at something close by and reacting can be combined in several ways. Figure 11.6 illustrates the four techniques described below:

- Start close on the character's hands. Tilt up from this false POV to the character's face for a reaction. This shot can be frontal or in profile.
- Pan a short distance from the observer in profile to what is being looked at, or vice versa.
- An object is near the camera, and the observer is deeper. Rack focus from one to the other in either order.

Figure 11.6 An observer and a POV can be combined by panning, tilting, or using a rack focus.

A Character Looks at Something in the Distance

The combination of a character looking at something in the distance and reacting to it can be done in various ways. Several options are listed below, and Figure 11.7 illustrates three of them.

- Start with the observer's medium close-up looking off-screen, cut to the reverse angle of what the character is looking at, and then return to the observer for a close-up reaction shot. The character may exit this shot headed toward what was seen.
- Start with a shot over the character's shoulder to what he is looking at, then cut to his close-up for a reaction.
- Start on the point of view and pan to find the character in profile.

CLOSE-UP

A DISTANT POV AND
A REACTION

OVER-SHOULDER

CLEAN POV

PAN TO REVEAL

REVERSE

Figure 11.7 These are three common approaches to showing characters and their distant POV in one or two shots.

A Stationary Character Watches Something Pass

To fully tell the story of a character watching a car (or anything else) go by requires four shots and five cuts. Pieces of the shots are intercut with each other. The first shot begins with the character in medium close-up looking off-camera at what's approaching, turning his head in sync with what he's watching (Figure 11.8). The second shot is the character's panning POV of the approaching car. We cut back to the first shot as the man tightens his look to the camera because the car is about to pass him. In the continuation of the car shot previously shown we pan with the car as it passes and starts to move away. The medium shot of the character is now used for the third time to show his eyes sweep past the lens as he turns his head to watch the car zoom away.

To make the scene more real, an over-shoulder is now used to tie the character to the car as it drives farther away. For continuity, this shot has to be taken over the character's right shoulder to maintain the right look that he had at the end of the first shot. The final shot is the character's close-up reaction shot to what he's just seen.

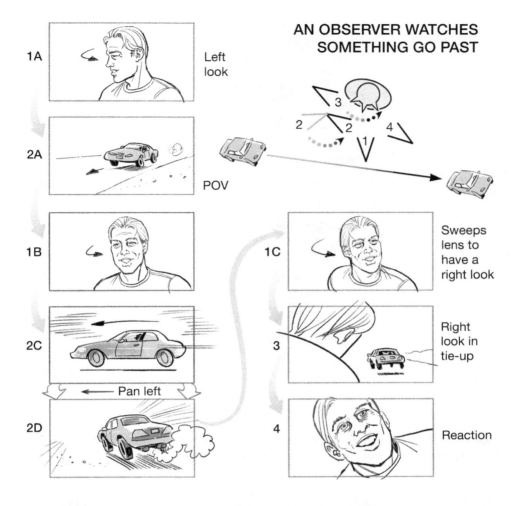

Figure 11.8 This sequence illustrates a stationary observer watching a car go past. Note that the observer has a left look at first, but his gaze sweeps past the lens as the car drives by, and the observer has a right look from this point onward.

Note that the axis that is important for the continuity of these shots is *not* the line the car drives along: it's the line from the character to the car, which changes as the car moves. This line sweeps past the camera as the car goes past and the character turns his head in sync with it.

Using a False POV

There are many occasions in stories when characters must be shown picking up an object with their hands. Often the sequence begins with a character looking off-screen at something and exiting the frame. Figure 11.9 picks up the story with a shot

USING A FALSE POV

Tilt up with

Figure 11.9 What seems like a character's POV can in fact be a reverse angle. As the character's hand reaches into this shot and raises the item to her face, the camera tilts with it.

that serves as the character's POV, but it is actually a different angle that is set up to show her hand reach in, grasp the phone, and raise it to her ear.

Sometimes the action of picking something up is shown in a sequence that dispenses with the character's look and POV. A scene can begin this way, with a hand reaching in to grab an object that is framed in a close shot. This approach is also sometimes used mid-scene to compress time.

A Character Stands Up or Sits Down

There are several options for showing a character sit down. The action can play and the scene can continue in a wide shot, especially if the character is uncomfortable in the setting. A close shot can tilt or move down to continue subjective coverage in the same shot size. If the choice is made to go from wide to close, or from close to wide, a match cut can be used. In these cases the action of sitting provides a cutting point and bridges the cut, hiding it. Figure 11.10 illustrates tilting and using a match cut to cut closer as a character sits down.

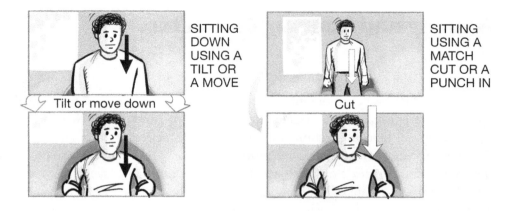

Figure 11.10 Sitting down can be shown in three ways: as a wide shot, in a closer shot that tilts or moves down as the character sits, or as a match cut. If a cut is used, the sitting action that bridges the cut helps to hide it.

Figure 11.11 Standing up can be shown in three ways: as a wide shot, in a closer shot that tilts or moves up as the character stands, or as a match cut. If a cut is used, the standing action that bridges the cut helps to hide it.

There are similar options for showing a character standing up. A wide shot can show the action in its entirety, especially if the character is going to walk closer to the camera. A close shot can tilt or move up to continue subjective coverage in the same shot size. A match cut from a close shot to a wide shot can be made as the character stands. Figure 11.11 illustrates both tilting and using a match cut to cut closer as a character stands up.

12

Walking and Running Characters

Just as going for a walk is more interesting than sitting in one place, action makes a scene more engaging both visually and in terms of storytelling. This chapter describes several blocking techniques that affect the storytelling through camera placement and movement relative to a moving character. The same ideas can be applied to a character who is traveling whether walking, running, bicycling, or using any other mode or means of locomotion. Viewers can be made to infer things about traveling characters, such as whether they are strong, weak, safe, threatened, in a hurry, or being watched. Coverage can be objective or subjective. A mood of suspense or heightened intensity can be created. It's always worth considering a range of possibilities for covering a moving character so that the best options are chosen.

The Camera as an Objective Observer

Stationary Wide Shots and Diagonal Walks

A wide shot of a character walking is the viewpoint of an objective observer. It illustrates a character's relationship to the surroundings. This distant perspective is somewhat detached and does not make viewers identify with a character. We may understand a character's current circumstances in a story, but because we are not close to the character and don't accompany the character on the journey, we do not get inside the person's thoughts and feelings. Only through closer shots and camera movement with a character do we begin to experience events with a person.

When characters walk at a right angle to the line of sight of the camera, their size does not change throughout the shot, but the camera can be repositioned so that the character is instead walking at a diagonal to the camera. This will make a character either grow or shrink in apparent size while walking, and the result is a more visually interesting shot that affects the storytelling. If characters grow in the frame, the story becomes more about them, while if they shrink, they become less important and their environment grows in importance. This can be used to switch from objective to more subjective coverage or vice versa without a cut being required (Figure 12.1).

The Art of Cinematic Storytelling. Kelly Gordon Brine, Oxford University Press (2020). © Oxford University Press.
DOI: 10.1093/oso/9780190054328.001.0001.

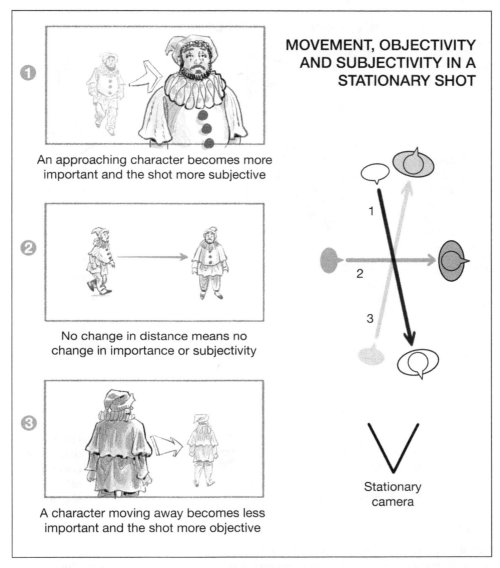

Figure 12.1 In a wide shot a character's movement toward or away from the camera can be used to change the degree of subjectivity or objectivity of a shot.

Pans and Diagonal Walks

Pans are visually interesting because the background and foreground change continuously. A panning shot tends to make viewers feel like objective observers because the camera is not traveling in synchronization with the traveling character, but is only rotating, much like a stationary observer's eyes and head would be. To add storytelling emphasis, the camera position for a pan should be chosen strategically so

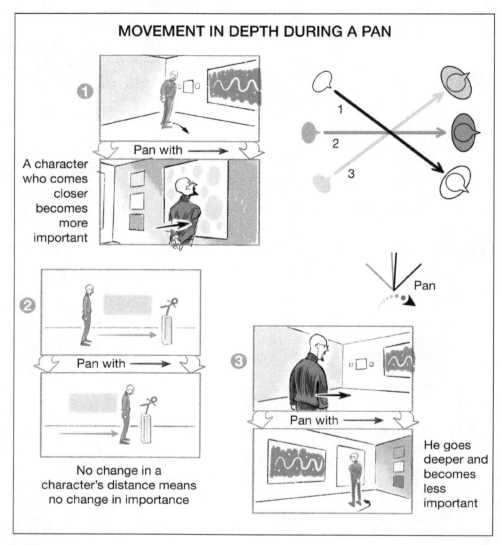

Figure 12.2 A pan can be designed so that a character's walk takes the person closer to or farther from the camera. Coming closer makes the shot more subjective, while moving farther from the camera brings new emphasis to the surroundings.

that the walking character arrives at a position either closer to or farther from the camera, depending on the needs of the story at that point (Figure 12.2).

Low Angles Strengthen Characters

When characters are shot from a low angle as they walk, they seem more in control, more important, more powerful, and possibly more threatening. Whatever mission they are on seems more certain. Perhaps we instinctively feel this way because

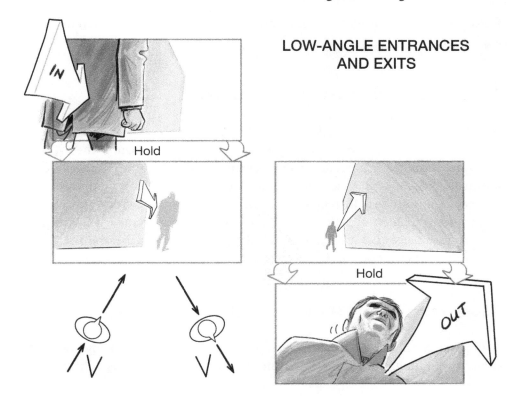

**LOW-ANGLE ENTRANCES
AND EXITS**

Figure 12.3 Low-angle shots make a character seem more powerful, in control, and often more threatening.

a low-angle camera is a child's perspective. A low angle also emphasizes the height of background buildings and trees, making us feel small, while at the same time creating a more dramatic composition. It also isolates the character to some degree because less is seen of any distracting elements that are nearby, which might include people, vehicles, technology, or signage. A character is shown entering and exiting two low-angle shots in Figure 12.3.

High Angles Immerse or Weaken a Character

A high-angle shot can be used to make a traveling character seem weak, to clarify the action from a descriptive angle, or to establish a setting. A high-angle shot is often used to make a character seem weak or lost by making the environment seem dominant and threatening. If a character is trying to accomplish something, the outcome will seem less certain. Examples of when a high angle of a person walking might be appropriate are crowded environments, such as a busy train station or a market, as well as large, unusual, or isolated environments, such as an abandoned factory or a forest. A balcony, rooftop, drone, or crane may be used to create a high angle shot.

The Screen Direction of a Character's Travel

A character's on-screen direction of travel has a psychological effect on viewers. What is most important to storytelling is that in general movement to the left of the screen seems more negative and uncertain, while movement to the right seems more positive and certain. Movement up and down has a similar but less significant effect. Movement upward usually seems more positive and movement downward seems more negative. Often other considerations are more important when designing shots and sequences, but it is always worthwhile to consider whether the direction of on-screen movement can be chosen to graphically reinforce the story (Figure 12.4).

A Long-Lens Shot of a Moving Character Is Subjective

A long lens can be used to create a subjective shot of a character moving toward the camera even though the camera does not travel with the character (Figure 12.5).

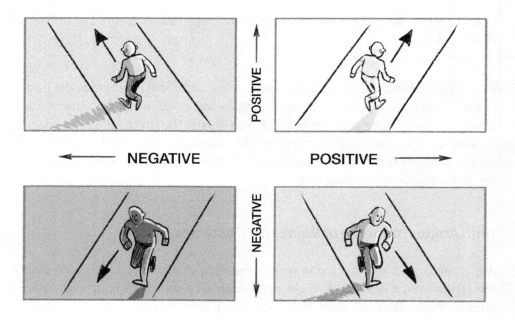

Figure 12.4 The direction of on-screen movement has a psychological effect on viewers. Movement to the left seems more negative, while movement to the right seems positive. Movement up and down has a similar but less pronounced effect.

Figure 12.5 A long-lens shot isolates and slows the progress of an approaching character. Although the camera does not move, the shot seems subjective nonetheless because the character appears to maintain almost the same distance from the camera.

A long-lens shot usually frames a character fairly tightly. A moving character's size changes slowly, so the fact that the camera is not actually moving with a character is less noticeable. The subjectivity of such a shot is enhanced because the depth of field is limited, which means that the foreground and background are in soft focus and the character is more isolated. The effect can be dreamlike.

Long-lens shots down city sidewalks are often used, and blurry cars and pedestrians cross the shot at various depths for visual interest and verisimilitude. A long-lens shot can be used to make crossing a busy street seem more dangerous because the flattened perspective creates the illusion that vehicles are closer to a character than they actually are.

The Camera Travels with the Character

A camera that travels with a character creates subjective shots in which viewers feel that they are accompanying the character and seeing the world through the character's eyes. The camera movement is generally simple and is synchronized with the character's movements.

Tracking Beside a Character

A tracking shot is taken from a camera that holds a moving character in view while it travels laterally beside a character. Usually the camera is angled slightly back to see more of the character's face than would be seen in a strict profile. Often there is foreground between the camera and the character, and this foreground adds visual interest and makes the shot more three-dimensional and immersive. What's visible in the foreground may be vegetation, shelves, tools, industrial equipment, parked cars, or a fence. Because they do not travel along exactly the same axis as the character who is being tracked, tracking shots are not quite as subjective as shots that lead and follow a character. Figure 12.6 illustrates a tracking shot.

A tracking shot can begin with a character's entrance, or an instant before a stationary character starts to move. Another option is for the camera to already be in motion but with its view blocked by something in the foreground, such as a wall or a vehicle. As the camera reaches the end of the obstruction, it discovers the character already in motion at the same speed as the camera, and the shot continues.

When a character walks through a doorway it is sometimes possible to track the movement through a parallel doorway. This option is not often found on real sets, but in the studio a set can easily be constructed to make this possible. The tracking shot that can be created is visually interesting and cinematic as it seamlessly takes a character from one room to another. Viewers don't seem to mind the artificiality of this technique. When such a shot is not possible a character can instead be followed or led, or the action can be cut into two shots.

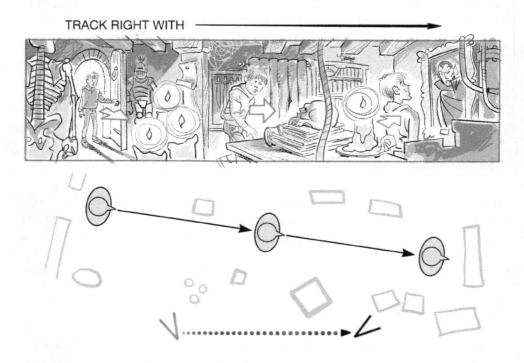

Figure 12.6 A tracking shot is subjective and immersive because the camera moves with the character and foreground objects cross the frame.

Leading and Following a Character

Shots that lead and follow a character are the most effective at making us feel that we are in the company of the character. Usually these two shots are used in combination, and the character's very subjective moving POV is often added to this set (Figure 12.7). These three shots can be used for any type of travel, including walking, running, cycling, crawling, and climbing. Although the leading and following shots may be full shots, they are usually tighter to increase the level of subjectivity.

A shot that leads a character is often created with the camera moving slightly more slowly than the character so that the character gradually grows in size. So, for instance, if the shot starts as a full shot it may end as a medium shot. This adds visual variety to the shot at the same time as it increases the subjectivity and dramatic intensity of the shot. A following shot is more constant in its framing unless the character stops, at which point the camera may continue forward a little to tighten the shot and end as an over-shoulder shot.

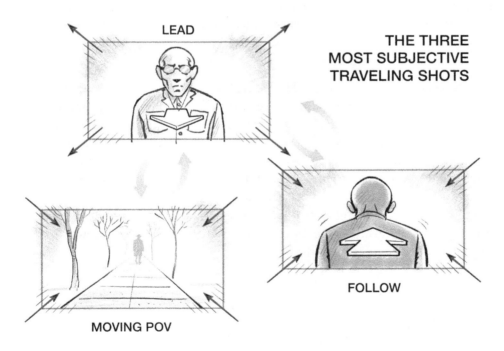

Figure 12.7 Traveling with a character can require a shot that leads the character, one that follows the character, and a moving POV. Short scenes may be covered using only the leading and following shot, only the leading and moving POV shot, or only the following shot.

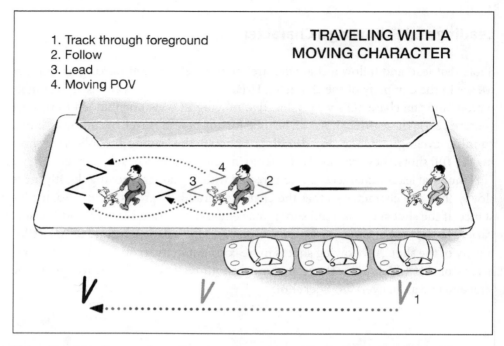

1. Track through foreground
2. Follow
3. Lead
4. Moving POV

TRAVELING WITH A MOVING CHARACTER

Figure 12.8 This diagram shows the camera's movements for the four subjective traveling shots. Traveling with a character can require all four kinds of shots, but short scenes may need fewer.

Both leading and following shots are typically taken from a slightly low angle in order to make the composition more attractive and the character more important. Leading and following shots cut with each other well as dead reverses, and the leading shot and the moving POV cut well with each other if the camera was moved at the same speed. A cut between a following shot and a moving POV does not work well because the shots are both looking forward and this creates a visual jump. Sometimes the only shot that is needed is the following shot, and the character typically looks to the side at some point, or stops and turns so viewers will know who it is. Figure 12.8 illustrates the movement of a character along a sidewalk and the movement of the four cameras that record subjective coverage.

The Camera Stops or Starts with a Traveling Character

This section presents ways of starting and stopping the camera's movement as a character starts to walk or stops walking. These techniques reduce cuts and are more cinematic than using several shots to cover the same action.

A Stationary Shot Becomes a Subjective Moving Shot

A character can start to travel in a shot, and the camera can begin to move in unison with that character, either leading or following. For instance, a character can start to walk toward the camera and this motivates the camera to begin to move backward in sync with the character. The shot stays subjective as we accompany the character on the journey. Note that a shot seems more natural if the camera anticipates a character's starting and stopping. The operator can start or stop the camera move an instant before the character starts or stops to avoid the camera seeming to be delayed and out of sync with the character's action (Figure 12.9).

Pan with and Then Travel with a Character

Another way to switch from a stationary shot to a moving shot is to pan with a character as the character approaches and passes the camera. As the character passes, the camera starts to follow. This turns an objective shot into a subjective shot (Figure 12.10).

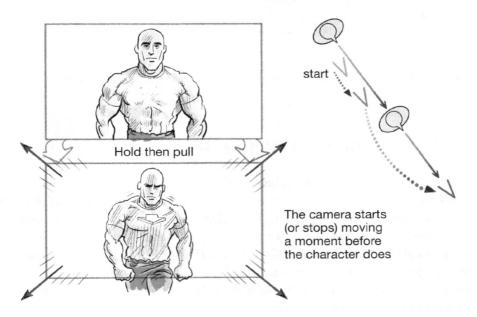

THE CAMERA ANTICIPATES A CHARACTER'S MOVEMENT

Hold then pull

start

The camera starts (or stops) moving a moment before the character does

Figure 12.9 A stationary shot can become a traveling shot and vice versa. The camera operator anticipates the actor's movement.

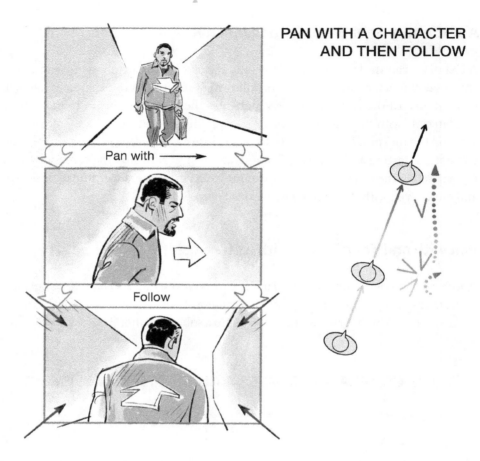

Figure 12.10 A stationary shot of a moving character can pan with and then follow that character as subjective coverage begins.

The Character Walks into a Moving POV

A scene can begin in a suspenseful way with a shot that is a character's moving POV before we have even seen the character. At first it's a mystery whose POV it is. The motion of the shot and the initial lack of a clear subject provide good shot contrast. Our curiosity is satisfied when after a moment the character steps into the shot and continues to walk as the camera falls in behind (Figure 12.11). In some cases we may not recognize characters when seen from behind, but when characters look to the side or stop and turn, they can be identified. An alternative to this is simply to cut from the shot that follows a character to one that leads.

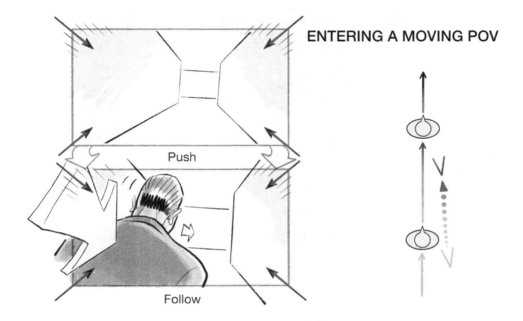

ENTERING A MOVING POV

Push

Follow

Figure 12.11 A sequence of moving shots that cover a moving character can begin with a mysterious moving POV that the character steps into. This technique can be used both to begin a scene and to advance time within a scene.

A Character Stops in a Moving Shot

When a walking character stops, the camera has to stop too. As shown in the maps in Figure 12.12, there are several ways to do this:

1. When the camera is leading a character and the character stops, the camera may stop a little early to allow the character to grow in frame for emphasis. Alternatively the camera can move slightly to one side as it stops, and pan 90 degrees with the character until the character has stopped in a profile close-up.
2. When the camera is leading a character, it can stop and pan the character into an over-shoulder shot as the character stops.
3. When the camera is following a character and the character stops, the camera can continue a little to come closer, and the shot can become an over-shoulder.
4. When the camera is following a character and the character stops, the camera can continue past the character as it wraps to keep the character in frame and lands in a close-up.

A WALKING CHARACTER AND THE CAMERA BOTH STOP

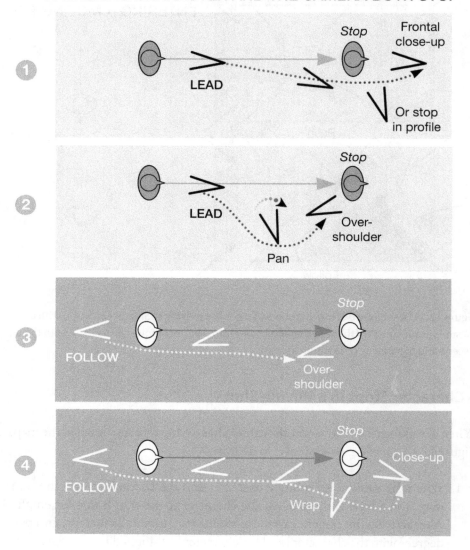

Figure 12.12 A shot that leads a character can (1) stop in a close-up when the character stops, or (2) stop early and from that point pan the character into an over-shoulder. A shot that follows a character can (3) land in an over-shoulder when the character stops, or (4) wrap the character and land in a close-up.

Compressing Travel Time

To keep a story interesting, travel that's longer than a few steps is usually compressed into a much shorter period of time on the screen. This can be accomplished by dividing a trip into several pieces, and then shortening each piece by using entrances and exits of various kinds. Cutaways and crosscuts can also be used. When the story returns to the traveler, the character is much farther along on the journey. Compressing time is almost always good to keep the pace of a story up, although a sequence in which someone is being stalked or chased may be more suspenseful if the travel time is not compressed.

Using a Cutaway

A cutaway in the middle of travel to someone watching or to something character-istic of the setting is an effective way to compress time. When the next shot returns the story to the traveling character, we find them farther along on their journey. To illustrate this, imagine a character walking somewhere outside at night. To move the character farther ahead on the walk, a cutaway to the moon or a stray cat could be used. When seen again, the character can be closer to their destination.

Cutaways make storytelling momentarily less subjective, but this effect can be reduced by connecting the character to the cutaway. For example, the shot of the moon could be connected to the character in several ways. The camera could tilt down to find the character, the character could walk into the shot, or, if there is a cut from the moon back to the character, the person could be looking upward so that we consider the shot of the moon to have been a POV. These techniques maintain the subjectivity of the storytelling while allowing the character to be shown at a point farther along on the journey. As a result, travel time is compressed.

Using Three Stationary Shots

Travel time can be compressed by showing a character exit a setting in one shot and then enter a new setting in the following shot. Entrances and exits can be made through doors or be achieved simply by stepping into or out of the shot (usually right beside the camera). Compressing travel time with two shots works best if the dis-tance covered is small. It can seem like characters have been transported magically if they step out of one environment and directly into another if the new one seems very different and far away. Adding an intermediate shot that shows the character traveling somewhere in the middle of the journey makes the journey seem more real (Figure 12.13).

Using Traveling Shots

A character's journey can be divided into three shots, a stationary one with an exit, a shot that leads the character, and finally a moving POV that the character steps

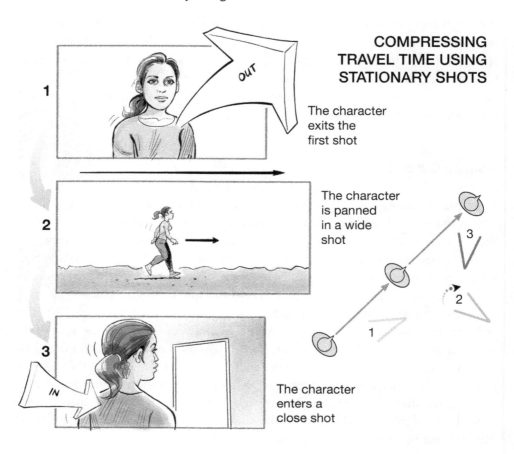

COMPRESSING TRAVEL TIME USING STATIONARY SHOTS

1 — The character exits the first shot

2 — The character is panned in a wide shot

3 — The character enters a close shot

Figure 12.13 Travel time can be compressed by adding exits and entrances to stationary shots. A short trip can be divided into an exit and an entrance, while a longer trip will seem more real if one or more middle shots are added.

into and optionally stops in (Figure 12.14). Using several shots makes time compression possible, and the traveling shots make the storytelling both more subjective and more exciting than would be possible by stationary shots alone.

Using Corners for Entrances and Exits

To compress time, cuts are always required. To avoid jump cuts, a character must be made invisible for a moment, either at the end of the first shot or at the beginning of the second. The character reappears almost immediately, but is farther along in the journey. The character's disappearance can be achieved in a number of ways. The most obvious places for entrances and exits are doorways, but the edge of the frame, large objects, and corners are just as good.

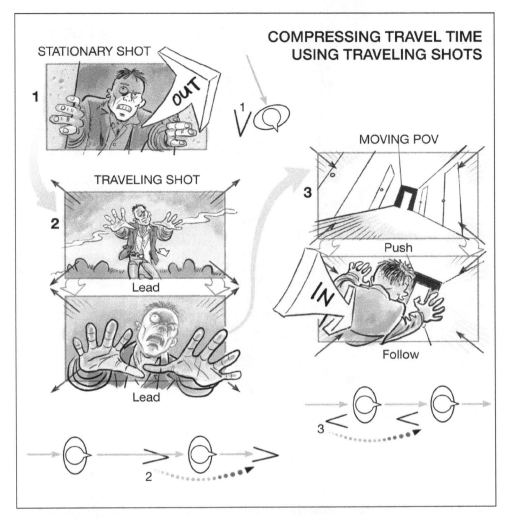

Figure 12.14 Travel time can be compressed and the story can be told more subjectively by using traveling shots.

What is used for an entrance or an exit depends on the location, although the edge of the frame is always available. Things that are often used are walls, vehicles, foliage, machinery, and other large objects such as shipping containers. Figure 12.15 illustrates four ways in which a corner can be used to make a walking character appear or disappear in a sequence of two shots that work together to compress time by seconds or minutes. Note the shot contrast and the continuity of screen motion. These four methods are described below:

1. The character moves away from the camera in a stationary shot. Cut to a stationary shot of the character coming around a corner a few minutes ahead in time.

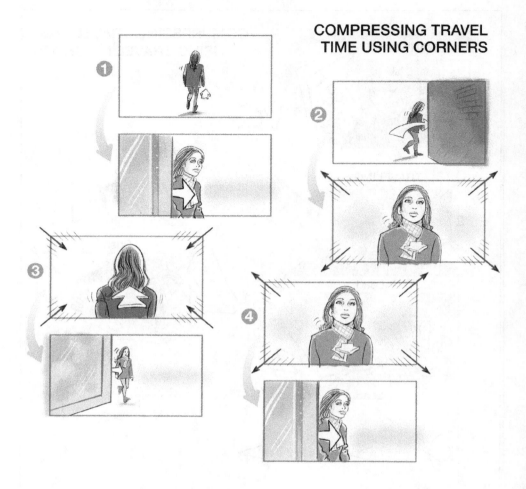

Figure 12.15 Corners can be used both to compress time and to switch between objective and subjective coverage.

2. The character disappears around a corner in a stationary shot. Cut to a subjective moving shot leading the character a few minutes ahead in time.
3. Follow the character. Cut to a stationary shot of the character coming around a corner at a point ahead in time.
4. Lead the character. Cut to a stationary shot of the character coming around a corner a few minutes ahead in time.

Passing through a Doorway

A character may travel through a doorway within a scene or between scenes. Sometimes this is shown in two shots, but the option exists for the camera to follow the character through the door in a very cinematic way. Sometimes following a character is not possible because the exterior door and the interior door are actually parts of two different sets that are cheated to seem like one place.

If a character can continue in the same direction in the second shot, this is better because it maintains clear screen geography. Sometimes a filmmaker may be forced to change a character's direction of movement because there is a wall that makes ideal camera placement impossible. At other times there may be a story reason to change the direction, for instance in order to suggest symbolically that a character has entered a different world. The times when it's most important to maintain continuity of screen motion are when a character is in a hurry, on a mission, or is chasing someone. The two shots should have shot contrast whether the direction of travel changes or not.

A Character Walks in a Park or a Forest

As we have already seen, storytelling is greatly influenced by the shots that are used to show the action. The simple examples that follow illustrate a man walking in a forest as he would be seen in various types of shots. Each one creates a mood and suggests something to viewers about the man's story. Shot design has a remarkably strong influence on how even a simple walk is understood.

The Setting Is What's Most Important

A wide shot establishes a forest in an objective way, and this typically includes something about the time of day and the season. A montage of several shots of the setting would make viewers feel immersed in it, and such a montage could be used to show how dense, rugged, or well tended the forest is, for example, or the arrival of spring. If a small figure of a walker appears in the wide shot, the traveler will seem subordinate to the natural environment. There may be a small feeling of mystery until the walker is identified, but there is no suggestion of anything ominous, and the character of the forest itself is the main story being told (Figure 12.16).

The Environment and the Character Are Both Important

If a scene begins with a stationary full shot, or a cut is made from a wide shot to a full shot, the walker's appearance and behavior will be seen more clearly, and this will make viewers speculate on why he's walking in this setting. A full shot keeps the character and the environment in balance. Ideally the camera is placed so that the walker's path brings him closer to it. Having him grow in size provides visual interest

Figure 12.16 A wide objective shot emphasizes the setting over the character, and may imply that a character is dominated by the natural environment.

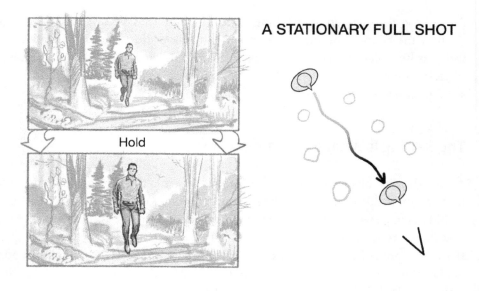

Figure 12.17 A stationary full shot balances the character and the setting. Usually the camera is placed so that the character comes closer and grows in size and importance.

in the shot, as well as making the story become increasingly focused on the character and less on the forest itself (Figure 12.17).

The Character Is in Control

As shown in Figure 12.18, a low-angle stationary shot makes a character seem stronger and more in control, and often happier. If a low angle of a character appears

Figure 12.18 A low-angle shot makes a character seem stronger and more in control.

in a sequence where viewers already know there is a threat, it may suggest that the character is unaware of the threat. A low-angle camera is often positioned so that the character approaches and exits the frame close to the camera. At this point a cut could be made from objective to subjective coverage in which the camera travels with the character.

Someone Is Watching

The camera can move out from behind a tree or other object just far enough to reveal the man walking nearby (Figure 12.19). This technique suggests that it is the POV of someone watching from a hidden vantage point. The shot will often pan with a moving character to keep him in the frame longer. The next cut may show who the observer is, or the person's identity may remain a mystery until later in the story. This type of shot is sometimes used even when there is no observer in order to create a feeling of suspense.

Panning Immerses Viewers More but Remains Objective

A shot that pans to keep a walking character framed is visually interesting and three-dimensional because the foreground and background are both in motion (Figure 12.20). Only the walker maintains a constant position within the frame. A pan holds the promise of something new and surprising being brought into the frame. This feeling of anticipation may have the storytelling effect of suggesting that something significant will happen during the trip. A pan can even suggest that someone is watching, because it seems like the POV of a stationary observer. A pan is much cheaper and easier than tracking and Steadicam shots. But from the perspective of

**MOVE OFF FOREGROUND
TO REVEAL**

Move right ⟶

Figure 12.19 A shot that moves off foreground to reveal a character seems like someone's POV, especially in the middle of a scene. It creates suspense even when no observer is present.

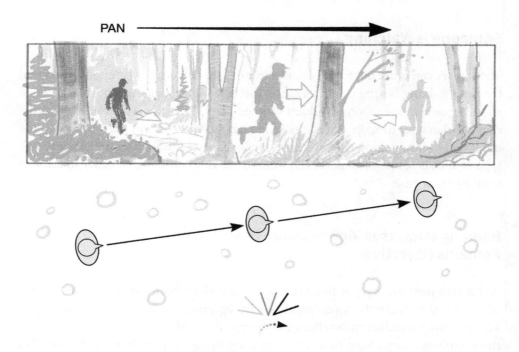

PAN ⟶

Figure 12.20 Panning is attractive and immersive, as well as being easier to create than a tracking shot. Because a pan is the vantage point of a stationary observer, it creates an objective shot.

storytelling, a pan with a moving character is an objective shot, while traveling in sync with a traveling character is a subjective one.

A pan can be set up at any distance using various lens lengths. A longer lens set farther back from the traveler's path will make the trees appear flattened or stacked because the long lens reduces the effects of perspective. All of the trees will seem more similar in size: the foreground trees will seem smaller than they would on a wider lens, while the background trees will seem larger. The forest will appear more dense in both the foreground and the background, and may seem more threatening. With a long lens set back at a greater distance, the foreground trees will cross the frame more slowly because the camera will not have to pan as far or as fast. A long lens creates a more subjective and dreamlike feeling.

A wider lens must be set closer to the path to frame the walker at a suitable size. Because of this the pan will be quicker and the trees will move across the screen more rapidly. There will be fewer foreground trees between the camera and the man because the camera is positioned closer to the path. The camera's position and the pan's faster and greater rotation will also show a broader range of background. The man will grow in size quickly as he comes closer to the camera, and he will quickly diminish in size as he moves away down the path. The size change of the walker and the faster movement of the trees will make the shot seem more agitated, implying that the man is in a hurry.

Tracking Immerses Us in the Environment and Is Subjective

Figure 12.21 shows an example of a shot that tracks the man walking in the forest. A tracking shot moves with the traveler at his speed, and the camera is normally just a little ahead of the character so that the lens is pointed slightly backward at the character. This is to avoid creating a flat profile of the figure, which is less attractive and engaging. As the tracking shot moves along in step with the walker, the trees in the foreground and background march across the screen in the opposite direction while the walker's position remains constant in the frame. A tracking shot often begins with a reveal or ends with a wipe created by a foreground tree. It can also end by turning into an over-shoulder shot when the camera reaches a mysterious observer.

Tracking shots can make viewers feel that they have stepped into the world of the film, and the movement of foreground across the frame makes them the most immersive shots. With this comes a greater feeling of potential danger. A tracking shot is busy and subjective, and is like the view of a fellow traveler on a parallel path.

Traveling with a Character in a Forest

Shots that travel with a character cover the character's journey subjectively. While a tracking shot makes viewers feel that they are also on the journey,

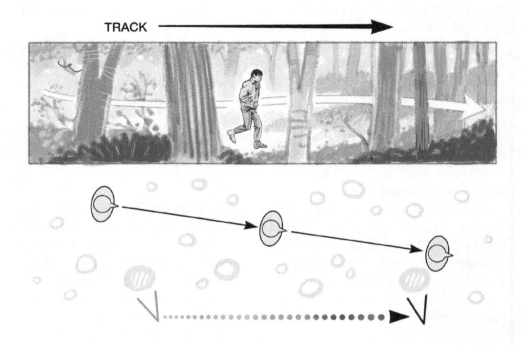

Figure 12.21 A tracking shot is subjective because it travels with a character. The movement of the foreground and background makes the shot immersive. A tracking shot can begin with a reveal and end with a wipe created using a tree or a rock.

leading, following and moving POV shots make viewers truly identify with the character, almost as though each viewer is that character and sees through the character's eyes.

Leading, following, and moving POV shots can unfortunately only be recorded using a handheld camera or a Steadicam because dolly tracks would be visible in the shots (unless the shots are very tight or low-angle). This is because the tracks would have to run along the same path as the walking character. An alternative is to track on the path beside the character with the camera looking forward or back at approximately 45 degrees. These two shots approximate leading and following shots and do not show the dolly tracks. If a Steadicam is not available the character's POV has to be either a handheld moving shot or a stationary shot from a point where the character stops for a moment.

Leading, following, and moving POV shots are shown intercut in Figure 12.22. Note that as the camera records the leading shot, the character is often allowed to slowly catch up to intensify the drama of the shot. Also note that characters can exit a leading shot at some point, and can also enter their moving POV and turn it into a following shot. Adding these elements to the shots provides visual interest and cutting points, as well as opportunities for time compression. A tracking shot could be intercut with these three shots.

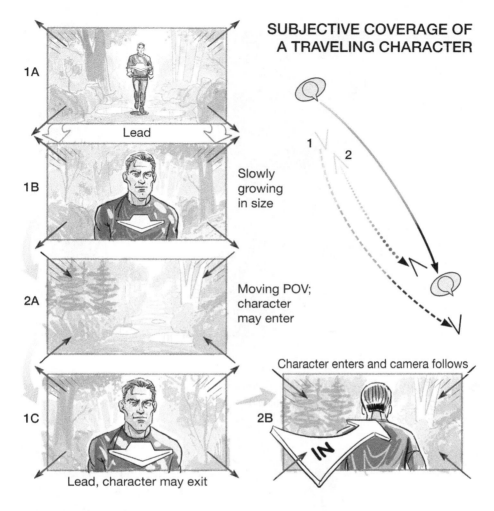

SUBJECTIVE COVERAGE OF
A TRAVELING CHARACTER

1A

Lead

1B

Slowly
growing
in size

2A

Moving POV;
character
may enter

1C

Lead, character may exit

Character enters and camera follows

2B

IN

Figure 12.22 Subjective coverage of a traveling character combines leading and following shots with a moving POV. A tracking shot can also be used.

If a Steadicam is not available, a handheld shot would be too shaky, and a tracking shot is not possible, then the best remaining options for somewhat subjective and immersive coverage are pans and long-lens shots.

A Character Is Not in Control

There are several ways to suggest that a character is not in control. High-angle shots will diminish characters and put them more at the mercy of their environment, especially if the shot is wide (Figure 12.23). The character may seem isolated, lost, weak, helpless, or threatened. A canted shot puts the composition off balance, and can be

HIGH ANGLE

CANTED

Figure 12.23 A high-angle shot can make a character seem weak or vulnerable. A canted shot may add visual interest, or it may foreshadow dangers ahead.

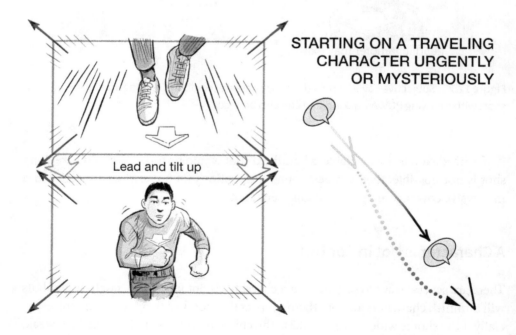

Lead and tilt up

STARTING ON A TRAVELING CHARACTER URGENTLY OR MYSTERIOUSLY

Figure 12.24 A tilt up from the feet is a more mysterious and urgent way to start a shot that leads a character. This shot can also be used as a transition into a scene.

used to show a character's frightened or agitated state of mind. Handheld shots further increase the feeling of danger. High angles, canted shots, and handheld shots can all foreshadow trouble that lies ahead, even for a character who is powerful or evil.

There are additional ways to show that a character has lost control. Pushing the camera toward characters as they run up to it and stop can give a feeling of desperation. The character can be led in a close-up. The character can be followed closely and be seen looking left and right. A tracking shot can show only the legs of a character who is stumbling through thick foliage. Characters can be led using a shot that at first frames only their legs as they walk or run. After a few seconds the camera tilts up to their face (Figure 12.24).

13

Stories about Searching

In many stories a character searches for something or someone. This chapter illustrates one such search and brings together many techniques discussed in earlier chapters. The sequence is designed to show the beats of the story in a dramatic and cinematic way, and continuity editing is used throughout. The actor's movements and the camera positions have been designed to highlight the story beats visually. The search sequence illustrates objective and subjective coverage, reaction shots, entrances and exits, continuity of screen motion, shot contrast, transitions, and the use of cutting points. The techniques that are used here can be applied to many stories involving many types of searches.

An Example of a Story about a Search

In this simple story a woman who is awakened by a noise gets out of bed to investigate. She walks along her hallway to the kitchen, where she discovers a broken dish. She concludes that her cat is to blame and heads back to bed. Even a sequence as simple as this one deserves careful thought to tell the story clearly and to enhance and embellish the drama. Of course there are always many ways to tell the same story, and what's shown here is just one of them.

Some of the shots require more than one panel to illustrate, and these panels are connected with twin arrows as usual. Shots are labeled with shot numbers in the storyboards and on the map at the end of the chapter. Several of these shots with two or three different numbers could be recorded at the same time as one longer shot. Each longer shot would be cut into several pieces to be intercut with other shots during editing. So even though the numbering of the storyboards makes it seem like there are 20 shots, from the point of view of production there are only 13. But I have numbered the shots in this manner to make the relationship between the text and the panels as clear as possible. When reading the descriptions of the action, remember that "left" and "right" always refer to the camera's view, not Mary's.

The Search Storyboard

Our search story begins with shot 1 in Figure 13.1, which is an exterior night shot of Mary's house and which establishes the setting where our story begins. The wind howls and a shadowy figure wipes the frame. The wipe suggests the presence of a menacing character outside, foreshadows future events, and serves as a convenient

The Art of Cinematic Storytelling. Kelly Gordon Brine, Oxford University Press (2020). © Oxford University Press.
DOI: 10.1093/oso/9780190054328.001.0001.

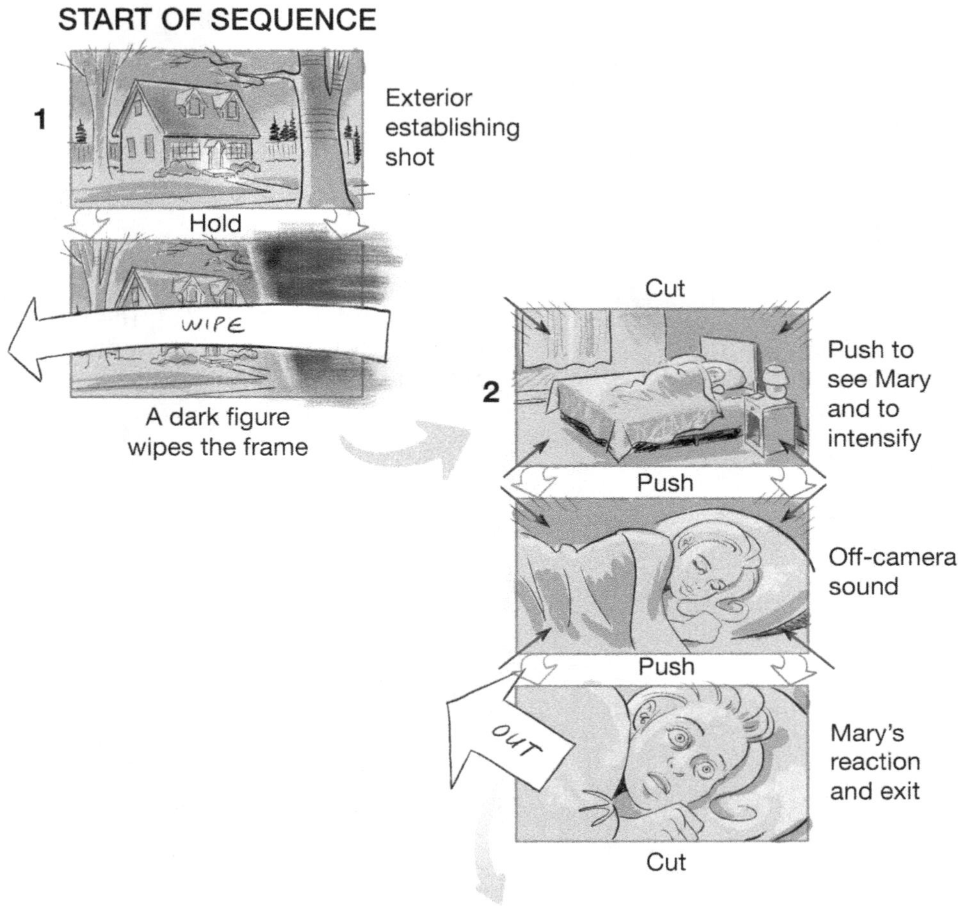

START OF SEQUENCE

1 Exterior
establishing
shot

Hold

WIPE

A dark figure
wipes the frame

Cut

2 Push to
see Mary
and to
intensify

Push

Off-camera
sound

Push

OUT

Mary's
reaction
and exit

Cut

Figure 13.1 The story begins with an exterior establishing shot of Mary's house. We cut inside to Mary's bedroom , where she is awakened by a sound.

cutting point to go inside the house for shot 2. Now we're in Mary's bedroom, and the camera is a little low and pushes slowly toward her bed to find her sleeping. The ominous unmotivated push in that is shot 2 is fine because this is the first shot of a new scene. As we reach Mary's close-up there's an off-screen crash, and she opens her eyes and gets up nervously. She exits the frame to allow us to compress the time it would take her to find her robe. She exits left because this direction gives more of a feeling of moving out of her bed, and it's also more suspenseful if she moves to the left. Her exit is our cutting point.

In Figure 13.2 we cut to Mary in rear three-quarter profile (shot 3) with her robe already almost on, and once it's on she walks deep through the door, stopping to look up and down the hallway. Since she took two steps out of her bedroom headed in a neutral direction, we can cut around 180 degrees to a dead reverse for her close-up (shot 4) as she looks first screen left and then right. We could optionally add Mary's

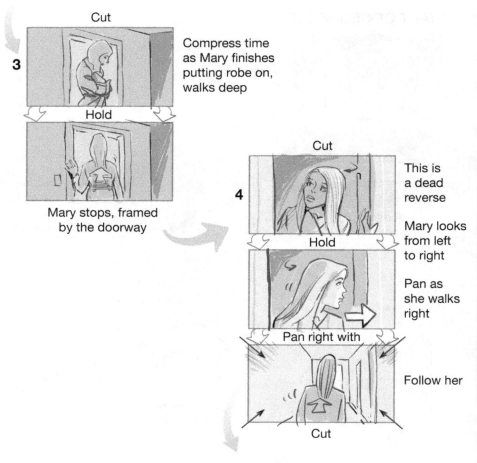

Figure 13.2 Mary gets out of bed, puts her robe on and enters the hall warily.

POV as she looks left, especially if we wish to emphasize her fear. Now Mary sweeps the lens to look right, and rather than cutting to her POV we simply pan right too, motivated by her head turn and her first steps, and we now follow her in a subjective traveling shot in order to explore the hallway with her. We keep Mary centered, as is the standard for shots that lead and follow.

Figure 13.3 begins with a dead reverse (shot 5) of Mary now approaching the camera as it leads her along the hallway. Mary is shown walking along the hall, and we follow close behind. Mary looks left and right nervously as she walks. The dramatic intensity of this shot can be increased by slowing down the camera and allowing Mary to grow a little in the shot as she walks into the unknown.

We can cut to a shot that looks through the open door of a room along the hallway (shot 6). Mary walks past. This shot cuts with better continuity if we maintain a right look by having Mary looking primarily very slightly camera right in shot 5. Shot 6 builds suspense by foreshadowing that Mary is being watched and is at risk, even though no one is watching from this room. In shot 7 we smoothly return to Mary's

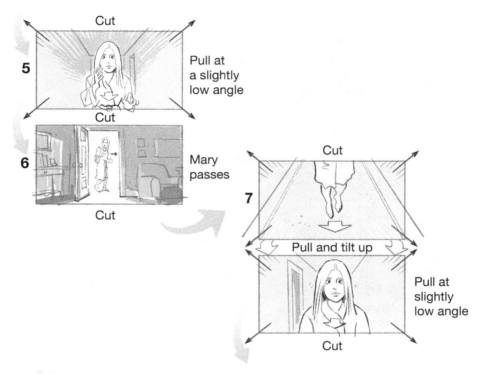

Figure 13.3 Mary starts her search for the cause of the sound she heard. She looks into a second bedroom but sees nothing unusual and continues along the hallway.

subjective coverage by starting on her legs and feet or nervous hands and tilting up to find her face while we continue to lead her.

Figure 13.4 begins with shot 8, and this image of a stuffed bird in a study located off the hallway is a startling cut from shot 7, as well as setting up the pan left. Note that the bird has a left look and is not centered, but is instead a little on the right of frame. This provides shot contrast that creates a better cut with Mary in shot 7. From the bird we pan left to the study door. An unmotivated pan is appropriate here since this shot is almost like the beginning of a new scene because we are in a different space. At the instant the pan reaches the door, Mary opens it: she looks into the study for the cause of the crash she heard. If she has a flashlight she should sweep the room, being sure to shine it directly at the lens to create a lens flare that could be the shot's cutting point.

While Mary is still scanning the study, we cut to shot 9, a low-angle full shot of Mary as seen from the kitchen. This cut signals that her inspection of the study has ended. Just as Mary closes the door a dark blur (which we will discover later was the cat) suddenly crosses close to the camera, perhaps making a noise. On this wipe we punch in to Mary's close-up (shot 10) as she turns her head and reacts to the cat she just heard but did not see. A punch in is more shocking than a match cut, and at any rate the narrow hallway makes a match cut impossible.

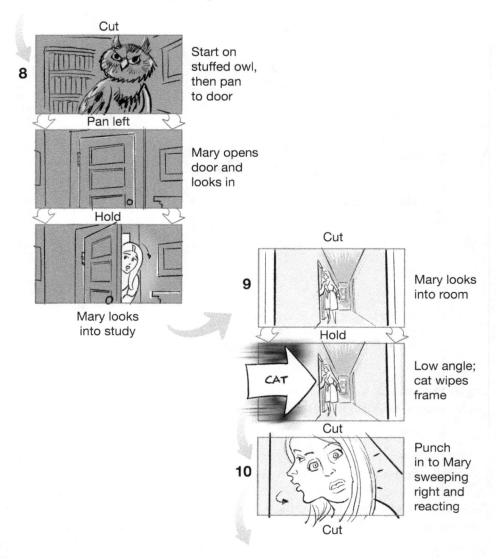

Figure 13.4 Mary opens the door to a dark study and scans the room. As something crosses the lens Mary turns suddenly to face the kitchen at the end of the hallway.

In Figure 13.5 shot 11 is Mary's point of view, and the kitchen at the end of the hall looks empty. Shot 12 is a continuation of shot 10, and Mary is puzzled and frightened as she continues her walk toward the kitchen. She exits right. Shot 13 is a tracking shot of Mary's feet as she walks right and then exits. It emphasizes that she is walking toward something that's uncertain. It also adds visual variety to the hallway shots. Her feet exit and provide a cutting point. If the hallway is too narrow for the camera to take this shot, it could be shot as a cheat in a room that has a matching floor and wall.

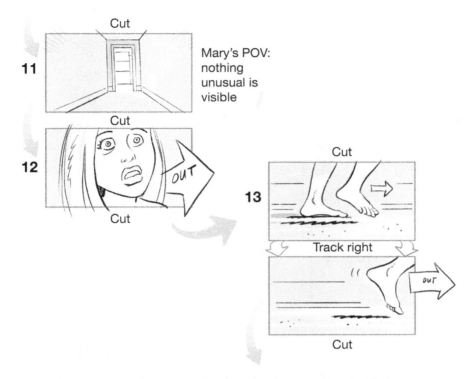

Figure 13.5 Mary sees nothing unusual and cautiously approaches the kitchen.

In Figure 13.6 shot 14 follows Mary as she continues her walk toward the kitchen. Following Mary allows us to see what she sees and to experience events with her. A cut to a dead reverse (shot 15) allows us to see her reactions as we lead her. The camera moves slightly slower than she does to allow her to grow in size to help build the suspense.

The camera stops an instant before Mary does at the entrance to the kitchen (shot 15). She looks down. This motivates a cut to Mary's POV of a shattered cup on the floor (shot 16). The POV should probably be cheated to a more attractive angle than her true POV, and the shot could include her feet. Shot 17 continues Mary's close-up at the end of shot 15 as she thinks about the broken cup. An off-screen meow prompts her to look off-screen camera right.

Mary's look in the last frame of shot 17 in Figure 13.6 motivates the cut to her POV in shot 18 of Figure 13.7. This is Mary's POV of her cat sitting on the kitchen counter. We cut back to Mary's close-up (shot 19) as she smiles and steps to the counter to pick up her cat. We hold this shot and allow Mary to exit close to the camera rather than panning with her. Letting Mary exit emphasizes the fact that the question of what caused the noise that woke her up has been answered. It also allows time to be compressed and motivates a cut to whatever shot we choose for Mary's walk back to her bedroom.

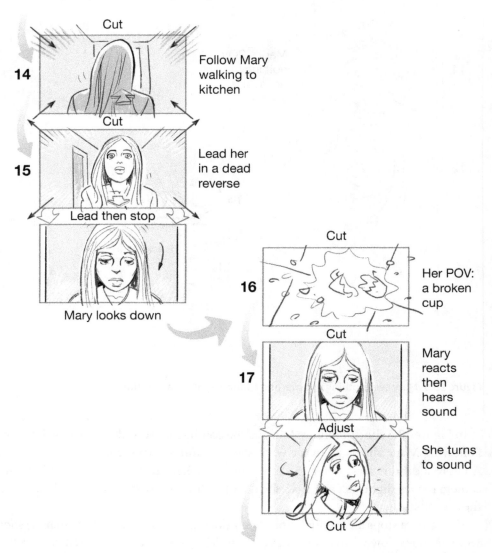

Figure 13.6 Mary stops at the kitchen door and looks down at a broken cup on the floor. She hears a scratch and turns to look at the counter.

In shot 20 we see Mary framed in the doorway to the hall walking away from us toward her bedroom carrying her cat. This shot seems like the end of the story in several ways: it's symmetrical, it has a frame within a frame, and Mary is walking deep towards her bedroom. But as Mary becomes smaller as she approaches her bedroom door and the story seems to have ended happily, a dark figure steps in close to the camera from the left side of frame! There's an intruder, and Mary is now in jeopardy even though she thinks all is well. The figure steps in from the left because it would seem strange to have an entrance from the cat's side of the kitchen, since Mary would have seen something.

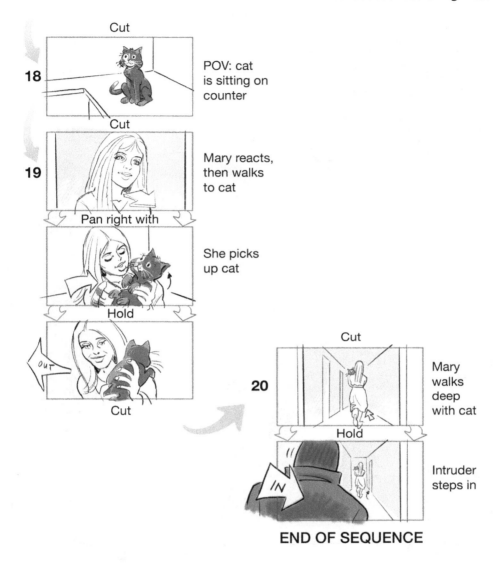

Figure 13.7 Mary sees her cat sitting on the counter. She smiles, picks it up and starts to walk toward the hallway and her bedroom.

The script could continue a little with a cut back to the exterior establishing shot of the house. Over this shot we could hear an off-camera scream. We could perhaps even see a stranger who happens to be walking past the house react to Mary's scream.

Making a Shot List and a Map

Maps are always useful to clarify the action of a scene and the shots that cover it. Three maps that show the movement of the characters and the camera positions

Figure 13.8 These maps show the action of the characters as well as camera placement and movement. The camera positions would often be farther back than shown, but were placed closer to Mary for clarity.

during the beginning, middle and end of the story are contained in Figure 13.8. A shot list is shown below. The numbers in this shot list correspond to the labeling of the storyboard panels and map. Shot list entries that begin with several numbers indicate shots that will be divided into pieces during editing. The pieces will be intercut with other shots in numerical order as shown in the storyboard.

1.	Exterior establishing shot of the house.
2.	Push in on Mary asleep in her bed. A crash awakens her and she exits left.
3.	Medium shot of Mary as she finishes putting her robe on and steps into the hall.
4 and 14.	CU of Mary standing and looking left and then right. As she starts to walk the camera pans and follows her to the kitchen.
5, 7, 10, and 12.	Lead Mary as she walks toward the kitchen. She stops at the study door to look in. She reacts to a noise from the kitchen, looks toward the kitchen, and exits right.
6.	Full shot of Mary as she walks past an open door as seen from inside a second bedroom.
8.	In the study, pan left from a stuffed owl to a closed door. Mary opens the door and looks into the room.
9.	A low-angle wide shot from the kitchen shows Mary in full shot closing the door to the study. Something crosses the lens, making a noise that causes Mary turn to look toward the kitchen.
11.	Mary's stationary POV of the kitchen from her position at the study door.
13.	Tracking shot of Mary's feet moving right as she walks along hallway and exits right.
15, 17, and 19.	Mary walks into the kitchen from a medium close-up into a close-up. She reacts to the broken cup on the floor, then looks from the cup to the cat. The camera pans as Mary walks to pick up the cat, turn, and exit left.
16.	Mary's POV of a broken cup on the kitchen floor.
20.	Mary walks deep toward her bedroom carrying her cat. The intruder steps into the shot from camera left to watch her walk deep.

14

Stories about Following or Chasing

This chapter illustrates several useful techniques for telling the story of one character following another. Such stories can be told either from the point of view of the character being followed, or from that of the follower. Detectives, reporters, jealous lovers, hitmen, and others could all have reasons to pursue someone.

While there are many ways to design a pursuit, certain types of shots and cuts are very effective and are commonly used. The cinematic storytelling ideas that are employed in the following examples have wide applicability. Additional ideas can be discovered by studying pursuit scenes in movies and by brainstorming while studying potential locations. How the story of a pursuit is best told will depend on whether the story should be told from the POV of the follower or the one being followed. It will also be influenced by which character (if any) is a "good guy" or a "bad guy." Here I will use the terms "the follower" and "the target," but neither is necessarily a bad guy, as the pursuer's motive could be good or evil.

General Considerations

- The scene must be designed while keeping in mind whose scene it, the follower's or the target's.
- Continuity of screen motion must be observed to keep it clear that this is a pursuit.
- Tie-up shots help maintain the spatial and story connection between the characters.
- The coverage of the characters should be varied, and the shots should provide cutting points such as wipes and exits to help make the cuts back and forth between the characters smooth.
- The ambiance, whether busy or deserted, day or night, and so on, is important to a suspenseful sequence, and should be worked into the shots.

Showing That a Follower Is Menacing

- Use low-angle shots of the follower.
- The follower can enter or be revealed unexpectedly coming from around a corner, stepping out of shadows, or appearing in silhouette.
- The follower's POV can lean out from behind a tree or a wall, and be followed by the pursuer's close-up.

The Art of Cinematic Storytelling. Kelly Gordon Brine, Oxford University Press (2020). © Oxford University Press.
DOI: 10.1093/oso/9780190054328.001.0001.

- Follow close behind the follower and lead the follower in close shots.
- Tie-up shots make a threat to the target seem more real.
- A rack focus can unexpectedly reveal the follower watching in the foreground, background, or seated behind a window that was reflecting the person pursued.
- The follower's pace can quicken as the scene progresses, and the follower can be shown to be gaining ground on the target.
- If the follower is seen to be overcoming obstacles, such as crowds, traffic, or fences, then the target will seem to be in greater jeopardy.
- If the target suspects that he is being followed, he can also be shown working to overcome obstacles to his escape.

Adding More Variety to the Coverage

- Pedestrians and traffic can cross through the foreground of the shots.
- Tracking shots with interesting foreground and background are immersive and can often be used in a pursuit. A tracking shot of the target's legs is often effective.
- Shots that use a frame within a frame of the pursued character reinforce the feeling that he is a target, as, for example, when the target is framed walking past the entrance to an alley or seen through a window or door frame.
- Unusual angles, high angles, and canted shots can help build suspense.
- Strangers can be shown reacting to the pursuit if it's obviously a chase.

Starting a Pursuit from the Follower's POV

As mentioned, the story of a pursuit can be told as the follower's story or the target's story. The next few pages describe and illustrate some of the techniques that can be used to tell the story from both perspectives. In this scenario the target is not aware that he is being followed. The first set of examples is the follower's story. He's favored by being given closer shots, by the camera traveling with him, and by showing his POV of the target.

Figure 14.1 illustrates the first two of six techniques. In the first sequence, the story begins with a full shot of the target as seen from across the street. We cut to a reverse-angle close-up of the follower, and we realize that what we just saw was the follower's POV. (There is always the choice of who is seen first, the target or the follower.) These two shots are intercut: the target starts to walk away, and a cut back to the follower's close-up shows him exiting in pursuit. There is no tie-up unless we see the follower enter the shot of the disappearing target.

The second technique begins with the follower's POV, and he steps into it. Perhaps he turns and glances to one side, and we recognize him in his profile. Now the target starts to walk away, and the follower walks deeper into the shot in pursuit. This

FOLLOWER: *Technique 1*

No tie-up shot

FOLLOWER: *Technique 2*

Follower enters POV

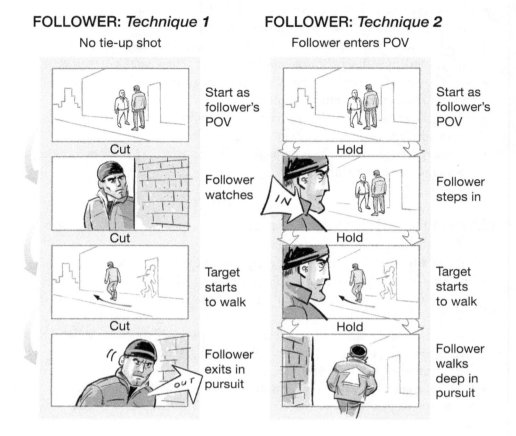

Start as follower's POV

Cut

Follower watches

Cut

Target starts to walk

Cut

Follower exits in pursuit

Start as follower's POV

Hold

Follower steps in

Hold

Target starts to walk

Hold

Follower walks deep in pursuit

Figure 14.1 These storyboards show the first two of six techniques that begin the story of a pursuit as told from the follower's point of view.

approach ties the two characters together in space, and sets up the pursuit in a single shot. As the follower walks deep, the shot could continue with the camera following him. Now a cut could be made to a shot that leads the follower.

The third approach is illustrated in Figure 14.2. Once again we begin with the follower's POV, but this time the target starts to walk away before we know that this is a POV. We use the target's movement to motivate the camera to pan with him, and while panning we discover the follower in a rear three-quarter angle shot. It's best if the pan that finds the follower is short. The follower should look to the side or put out a cigarette before starting to walk so that we can identify him.

Figure 14.2 also shows the fourth technique. Here we once again begin with a POV, but this time it's a low-angle one, and as the follower steps into the frame we see his flank and his hand. This shot ties the follower and the target together in one shot. Now we cut to the reverse angle, which is a close-up of the follower. He starts to walk. We could let the follower exit and pick him up in a shot that follows him, but it's more cinematic to pan with him and fall in behind him. As we follow him we may catch

FOLLOWER: *Technique 3* FOLLOWER: *Technique 4*

POV pans from target to follower

Follower enters POV; pan and follow

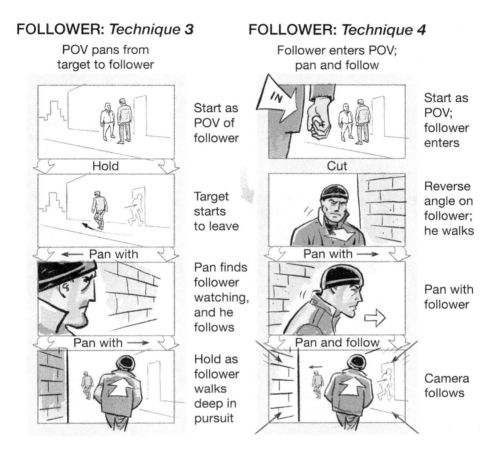

Technique 3:

Start as POV of follower

Hold

Target starts to leave

Pan with ←

Pan finds follower watching, and he follows

Pan with →

Hold as follower walks deep in pursuit

Technique 4:

Start as POV; follower enters

Cut

Reverse angle on follower; he walks

Pan with →

Pan with follower

Pan and follow

Camera follows

Figure 14.2 These storyboards illustrate the third and fourth of six techniques that begin the story of a pursuit as told from the follower's point of view.

a glimpse of the target. Technique number 4 is more intimidating and suspenseful than the first three because of the low angle and the pan-and-follow shot.

The fifth pursuit technique is shown in Figure 14.3. The fifth technique begins with a low-angle moving shot that follows the target. Although this shot is low, it serves the purpose of being the follower's moving POV. Suddenly the follower's feet walk into this shot, and we continue with him for a moment or two. Tying the follower and the target together in the same space makes the pursuit seem more real. The low angle graphically emphasizes the pursuit by showing the follower's legs as he walks, and keeping it a mystery at first who the follower is creates suspense. Now we cut to the reverse angle, which is a moving shot that leads the follower, and his identity is revealed.

Figure 14.3 also illustrated the sixth technique, which begins with the target reflected in a restaurant or shop window. The target starts to walk away down the sidewalk. A rack focus is done, and now we no longer see the target's reflection, but we

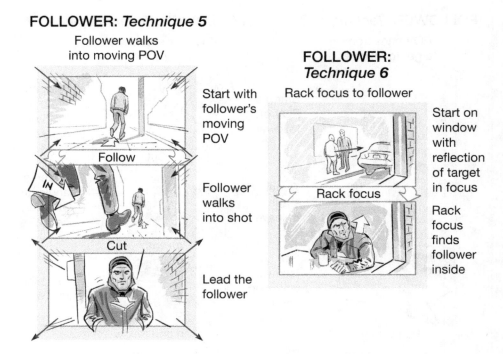

FOLLOWER: *Technique 5*

Follower walks
into moving POV

Start with
follower's
moving
POV

Follow

IN

Follower
walks
into shot

Cut

Lead the
follower

FOLLOWER:
Technique 6

Rack focus to follower

Start on
window
with
reflection
of target
in focus

Rack focus

Rack
focus
finds
follower
inside

Figure 14.3 These storyboards illustrate the fifth and sixth of six techniques that begin the story of a pursuit as told from the follower's point of view.

see in its place the follower seated or standing behind the glass. We realize that this character has also seen what we've witnessed, and when he stands and turns to leave, we understand that he will follow the target.

Starting a Pursuit from the Target's POV

Now the story will be told from the target's perspective. He's favored by being given closer shots and by the camera traveling with him. But it's also necessary to see the follower in a close shot to make it clear that he's following the target. Four techniques that begin to tell the story from the target's perspective are described here.

In Figure 14.4 the first technique shows the target positioned in the foreground of the shot, perhaps in conversation. The follower stands far back on the sidewalk, but a rack focus brings him into focus in the distance to highlight him. Viewers will find this unexpected, and highlighting the distant character makes viewers consider what the story connection is. The distant character may turn his head to look at the target to reinforce this connection. A couple of over-shoulder shots could allow the two foreground characters to finish their conversation, and the target exits in one

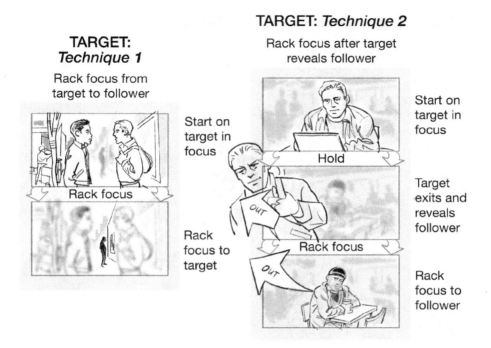

TARGET: *Technique 2*

Rack focus after target
reveals follower

TARGET:
Technique 1

Rack focus from
target to follower

Start on
target in
focus

Rack focus

Rack
focus to
target

Start on
target in
focus

Hold

OUT

Rack focus

OUT

Start on
target in
focus

Target
exits and
reveals
follower

Rack
focus to
follower

Figure 14.4 These storyboards show the first two of four techniques that begin the story of a pursuit as told from the target's point of view.

of them. Now we cut to a much closer shot of the follower, who has turned to look down the sidewalk in the direction of the target. He walks toward the camera and could exit in the same screen direction. Viewers will understand that the follower is pursuing the target.

In technique 2, which is also in Figure 14.4, the target and the follower are both seated in the same restaurant. We don't see the follower until the target gets up to leave, revealing the follower. A rack focus is done to the follower, who now also rises from his chair. He exits the frame in the same screen direction as the target. Viewers understand that he is following the target.

Technique 3 in Figure 14.5 begins with a subjective shot in which the target is being led. We pass a corner, and a moment later the follower is seen stepping out to pursue the target. The target walks toward the camera, which is moving backward slowly enough to allow the target to exit. A moment later the follower exits this shot in the same screen direction as the target did. We understand that he's in pursuit.

In technique 4, also in Figure 14.5, the camera is once again leading the target. As we come to an alley we slow down and angle slightly as we let the target exit the frame, revealing the follower in the alley. He begins to follow the target, coming into

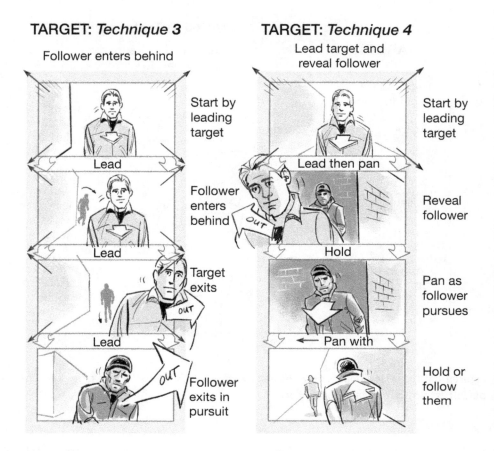

Figure 14.5 These storyboards illustrate the third and fourth of four techniques that begin the story of a pursuit as told from the target's story.

focus as he approaches the camera. We continue the shot by panning with the follower 180 degrees. Now we either follow him or leave the camera in this stationary position to see what has become a tie-up shot of the follower walking a few steps behind the target.

Tie-Up Shots during a Pursuit

Once a pursuit has started, it usually continues for several scenes. The characters are typically shown moving through a variety of settings, and this prolongs the suspense. In addition to traveling shots, wider static shots can be used to keep the coverage interesting and to tie the two characters together in the same space. Figure 14.6 shows

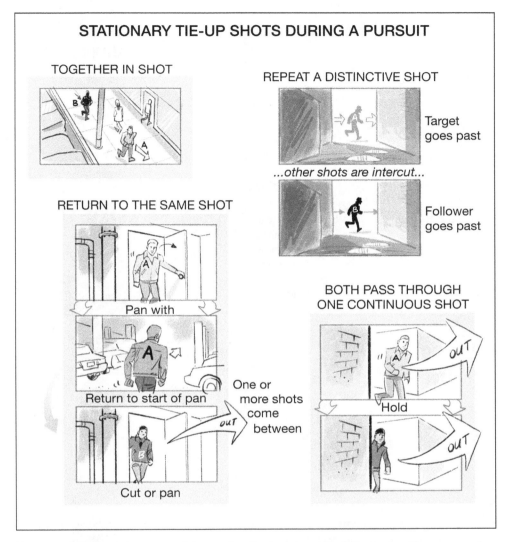

Figure 14.6 To show that a pursuit is ongoing, the target and the follower must be seen passing through the same space moments apart.

several ways that wide stationary shots can be used to tie a target and a follower together during a pursuit.

An easily recognized landmark makes it clear that the follower is on the trail of the target, and this is especially useful when several minutes have gone by since the story of the pursuit began (Figure 14.7). To show that the follower has lost the target, the follower can take a wrong turn at the landmark. Another way to connect the characters spatially is to pan with the target as he walks along, and then suddenly swish pan backward to find the follower retracing the target's steps not far behind him.

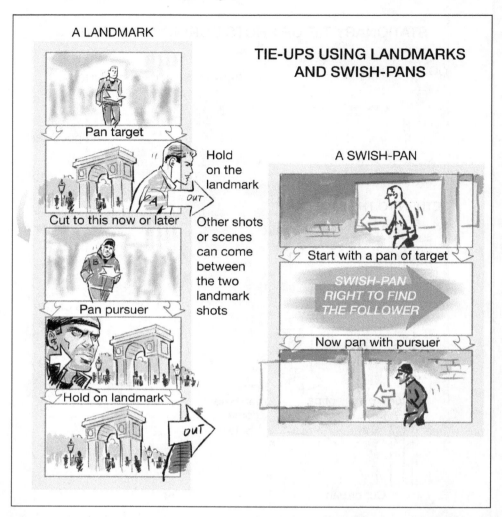

Figure 14.7 Landmarks and swish pans can be used to tie the target and the follower together and show that the follower has not lost the trail.

15

Two-Character Dialogue

In film two-character conversations are by far the most common. The characters who are talking are usually standing, seated, walking, lying in bed, or on the telephone. Dialogue looks better on the screen if the shots are designed to have similarities in their compositions and to conform to the same screen geometry. The best results are achieved when the shots of the characters are mirrored for most shots. Several common configurations of two characters are explored in this chapter, including face to face, side by side, and walking.

There are a few standard templates of shots that can be applied to dialogue, although not all of these shots are necessarily needed for every scene that involves a two-person conversation. If a template is used as a guide, a varied set of attractive shots that cut well with each other can be created. Later in this chapter several blocking techniques are explained that can be used to get two characters into position for dialogue as well as several techniques for ending dialogue with one character's exit.

The Geometry of Two-Character Conversations

Dialogue When Characters Face Each Other

Many scenes have dialogue between two face-to-face characters, whether standing or seated. The coverage is very similar. These scenes often start with a wide shot, although there are other options, such as panning an arriving character who joins another in a two-shot. A conversation is typically covered in two or three pairs of matching shots in various sizes, and they are usually edited so that the sequence begins with the wider shots and moves to tighter coverage as the conversation progresses.

The camera height is often a little below that of the shorter actor's eye level, as this angle is flattering and makes the characters seem more important. Wide shots may be shot from a higher or lower angle if this improves the composition or somehow graphically supports the story. The following list describes the shots that are typically used, although not every one of them will be shot for every scene. They are illustrated in Figure 15.1, while the map in Figure 15.2 shows the approximate camera positions for these shots.

The Art of Cinematic Storytelling. Kelly Gordon Brine, Oxford University Press (2020). © Oxford University Press.
DOI: 10.1093/oso/9780190054328.001.0001.

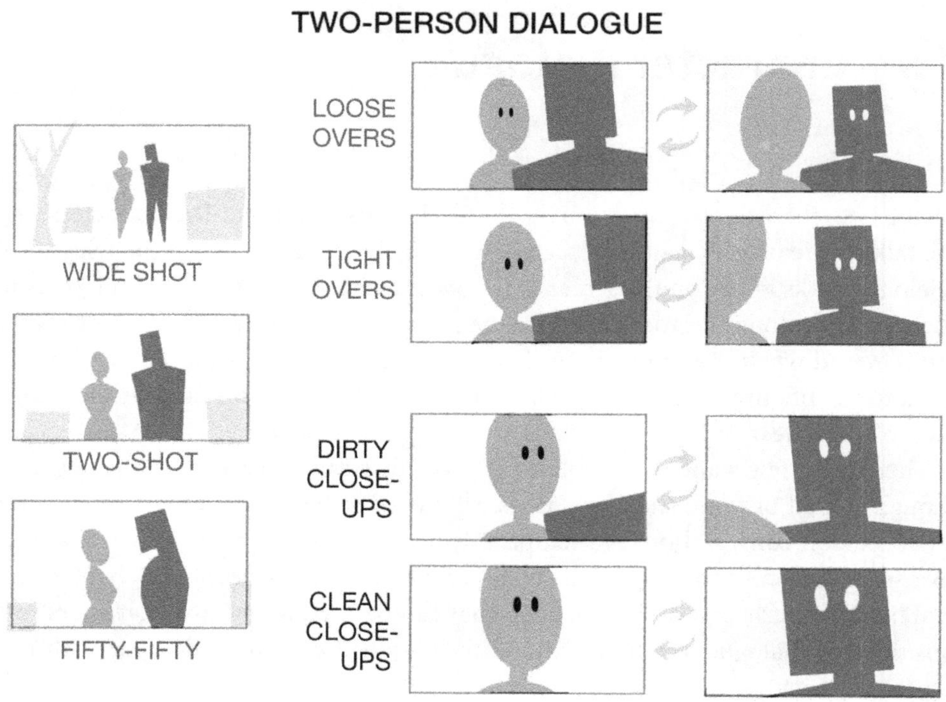

TWO-PERSON DIALOGUE

Figure 15.1 A face-to-face conversation can be covered in these classic shots. Coverage consists mainly of pairs of matching shots that mirror each other and therefore cut smoothly. The camera positions are shown in Figure 15.2.

- A wide *master shot* establishes where the characters are and covers the scene. It will sometimes slowly dolly sideways for visual variety and increased tension, and the scene may return to this shot several times.
- An attractive *two-shot* emphasizes the characters and downplays the setting.
- A *fifty-fifty two-shot* can show equality, permanence, or confrontation. When placed in front of an attractive background, it can have a timeless quality.
- *Loose over-shoulder shots* that show both sides of the foreground character's head tie two characters together both in space and emotionally. They are shot in matching pairs.
- *Tight over-shoulder shots* crop the foreground character's head and keep the characters tied together spatially and emotionally with more intensity.
- Matching *dirty close-ups* put the story's focus on one character while retaining the spatial connection to the other character. Only a small piece of the foreground character's shoulder is included in the shot.
- Matching *clean close-ups* are effective for strong reactions, for separating a character psychologically from the other character, and for shots that tilt up or down between the hands and the head.

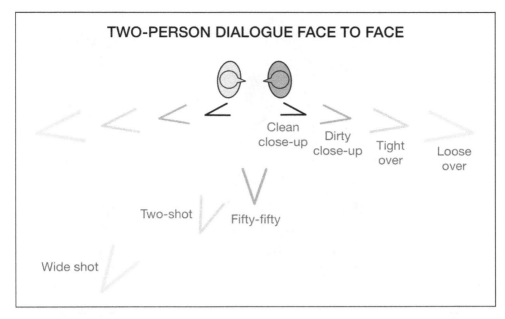

Figure 15.2 The camera positions in this map correspond to the shots of a face-to-face two-person conversation that are illustrated in Figure 15.1.

The Camera Crosses behind a Character

In film much of a conversation takes place in matching over-shoulder shots. An interesting way to vary the coverage is to slide the camera across the axis. A dramatic moment such as a confession can be emphasized by using one of the over-shoulder shots as a starting point and dollying the camera behind the character who is listening. The shot ends as a new over-shoulder on the other side of the line as the startling news from the character facing the camera ends (Figure 15.3). The final position is a shot that mirrors what was seen from the dolly's starting position. Now a new over-shoulder to match this one is recorded to show the surprised reaction of the character who was listening.

Over-Shoulder Shots and Camera Height

A conversation can be made to seem more important by keeping the camera height lower than the eye levels of the actors. The matching shots should be from equivalent heights. Low-angle over-shoulder shots make the characters seem stronger, and can reinforce conflict, mystery, and suspense, or simply show an interesting background (Figure 15.4).

Two characters can have different eye levels for three reasons. One actor may be much taller than the other, one may be standing on a step or other object, or one

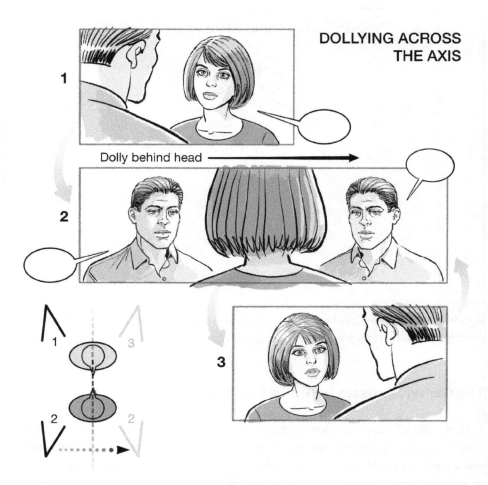

Figure 15.3 At a dramatic moment during dialogue, the camera can cross the axis behind one character's head to become an over-shoulder shot on the other side. A new matching over-shoulder shot is added.

character may be seated while the other stands. If the actors are not too dissimilar in height the camera is often set just below the shorter character's eye level. When there is more height disparity the camera height can favor the character who drives the scene. Figure 15.5 illustrates the three approaches to matching shots for characters of different heights. Note that when there is a great difference in height the shots do not mirror each other as completely. Shot 3 is an "over-shoulder" shot that is actually over the taller character's arm and flank, while shot 4 is an "over-shoulder" in which no shoulder is visible because the foreground character is too short to be seen.

LOW-ANGLE
OVER-SHOULDERS

Figure 15.4 Low-angle over-shoulder shots make the characters seem stronger and make the conversation seem more important.

Conversation in a Doorway

A character ringing a bell, knocking on a door, or opening a door is often shot in pro-file or in a rear three-quarter shot. When the door opens, coverage usually consists of over-shoulders as could cover any face-to-face conversation. At the end of the dialogue one or both characters may exit in the same overs. The final image in such a sequence is often a character's reaction shot. Figure 15.6 illustrates typical over-shoulder shots for a conversation in a doorway, while Figure 15.7 shows the camera positions for these shots.

Telephone Conversations

The classic approach to phone conversations in film is to match the two characters' shots. Even though the two characters are in two different settings, matching the shots reinforces the fact that they are talking to each other (Figure 15.8). Today many directors still give characters on phone calls opposed looks and keep the characters

OVER-SHOULDERS WHEN HEIGHTS ARE DIFFERENT

Figure 15.5 When two characters are of very different heights, there are three options for the heights of over-shoulder shots. The camera can be positioned as shown in pairs of positions that can be described as *low-high, low-low*, and *high-high*.

on separate sides of the screen, but in general they are less concerned about matching. This is probably because mobile phone calls can take place in any setting, and callers are often walking.

Conversation When Seated Side by Side

Side-by-side conversations can occur while people are driving, dining, sitting on benches, looking through fences, and watching performances. Figure 15.9 provides a map that is a template for the classic shots that cover side-by-side conversation. The essential shots are a wide master, a two-shot, matching raking over-shoulder shots, and matching close-ups. If they are appropriate for the setting, extras can cross the foreground to bring the environment to life.

Angles from behind the characters can be used instead of or in addition to shots from in front. The shots from behind are a reverse master, a rear two-shot, and French overs. French overs can make a conversation seem more intimate, more

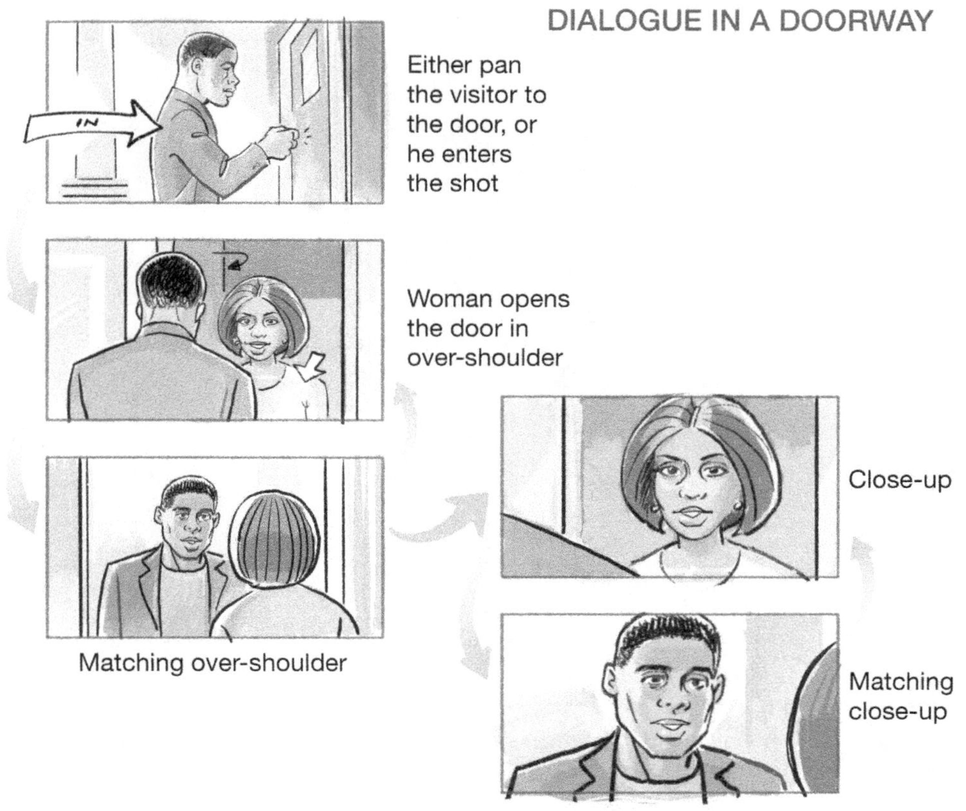

DIALOGUE IN A DOORWAY

Either pan
the visitor to
the door, or
he enters
the shot

Woman opens
the door in
over-shoulder

Close-up

Matching over-shoulder

Matching
close-up

Figure 15.6 The minimum coverage of a conversation in a doorway includes over-shoulder shots and matching close-ups. The corresponding map is in Figure 15.7.

conspiratorial, or edgier. They may also be used because they show a background that is more attractive, more relevant, or more controllable. French overs shot from the back seat of a car are often used for conversation between a driver and a front-seat passenger. For conversations on a park bench or a couch, there is an opportunity to move the camera from its position shooting a French over to a position where it shoots a normal over-shoulder by dollying sideways and crossing behind the head of one of the characters. Other ways of crossing the axis smoothly are to bridge it with a POV or a cutaway, or to use one of the wide shots. Wipes can be used as cutting points from the wide to the tighter shots.

Conversation When Seated at Right Angles

In some settings it's natural for two characters to stand or sit at right angles to each other. Their conversation can be covered in a wide shot, a two-shot, over-shoulders,

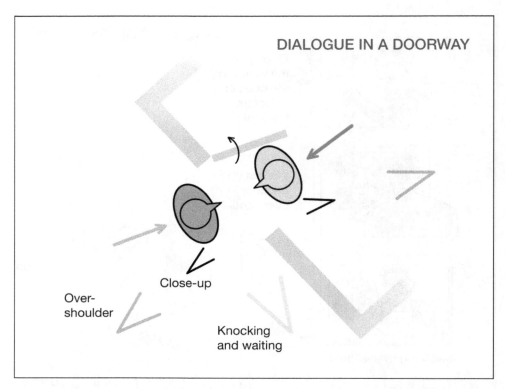

Figure 15.7 This map shows the camera positions for conversation in a doorway as illustrated in Figure 15.6.

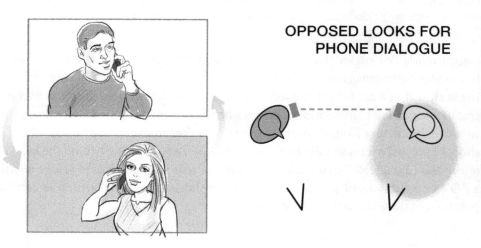

Figure 15.8 The shots of two characters having a phone conversation cut more smoothly when they are matching even though the characters cannot see each other.

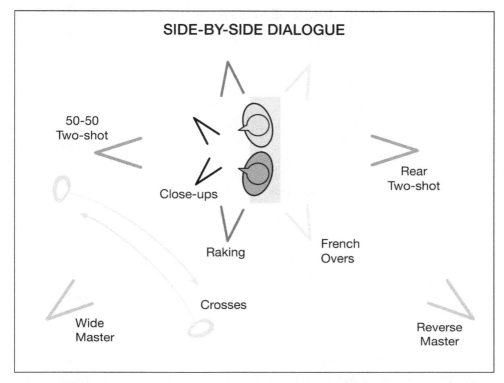

Figure 15.9 This map shows the classic camera angles for a conversation between two characters who are seated or standing side by side. Shots from in front, from behind, or a combination may be used. Coverage in a car is similar.

and close-ups. There is also the option of using French overs if this improves the backgrounds of the shots. Figure 15.10 shows the camera positions that are typically used. As usual the wide shot of seated or standing characters can slowly dolly sideways to add visual interest and tension. Depending on the setting, waiters, office workers, or pedestrians can cross the frame to bring the environment to life.

A Two-Character Walk-and-Talk

The camera can lead two characters as they walk and talk: this creates continuous and attractive changes to the background. Walk-and-talks are cinematic, immersive, and more interesting than static ones, and they make conversations seem more urgent. The fact that the camera is moving with the characters makes the storytelling subjective. Scenes that call for a seated conversation are sometimes converted to walk-and-talks to add urgency and visual variety. A Steadicam is usually used for walk-and-talks to avoid the shakiness of handheld shots.

Figure 15.11 illustrates a walk-and-talk with two characters. Such a scene can begin with a wipe, or the camera can pan quickly with a passing extra, land on the

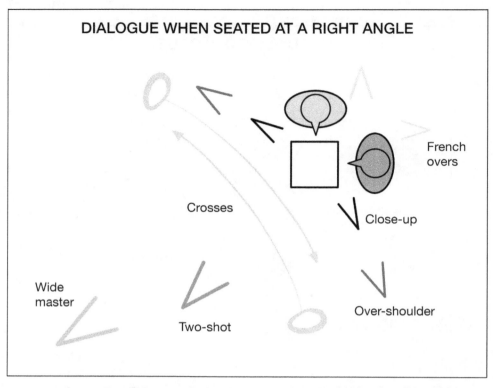

Figure 15.10 This map shows typical camera angles for a conversation between two characters seated at a right angles. Not every shot is always necessary.

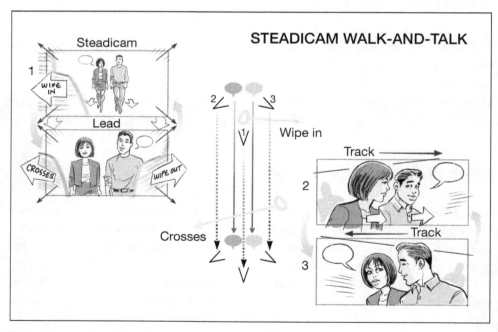

Figure 15.11 A Steadicam walk-and-talk is an active and immersive way to cover a conversation. Two Steadicam raking shots can be added for a longer conversation.

approaching characters already in dialogue, and immediately lead them. Crosses by pedestrians or coworkers make these scenes more visually interesting and realistic, and they also provide cutting points.

For longer dialogue in a walk-and-talk, close tracking shots from each side will add emphasis and variety. These matching raking shots will have the characters facing in opposite screen directions, but these shots cut well because the axis is between the two characters as they talk. This axis is not based on the direction in which they are looking or walking, but on the story's psychological connection between the two characters, as is the case in interior car scenes. An optional additional angle is a wider tracking shot that sees the characters through a fence, foliage, or equipment as the camera moves along with the characters. Such a shot can begin by coming off foreground to reveal the characters as they walk and talk.

At an appropriate point in the dialogue one character can stop for dramatic emphasis, while the other character continues one step past and turns back to face the stopped character. The characters are now stationary and can be covered in overs and close-ups.

A walk-and-talk can also be shot using a stationary camera and a long lens (Figure 15.12). A long-lens walk-and-talk looks very different and has a different feeling because of the flattened perspective, the limited depth of field, and the fact that the shot is not as subjective. The two characters talking may seem lost in the crowd, to be in their own world, or not to be making progress. The reduced perspective change of a long lens means that the dialogue can continue for a considerable length of time before the characters have grown too large in the shot. The compressed perspective and restricted depth of field minimize movement and detail and help to create an attractive composition. A long-lens walk-and-talk can begin or end with a wipe and is more exciting and visually interesting if occasional crosses by pedestrians or coworkers are added.

Beginning Dialogue

When a scene starts with a conversation that is already underway, a transition helps to start the scene smoothly and naturally. For example, a shot can start by panning a waiter who is walking past. At the moment the waiter crosses the characters, the camera holds on the them as the waiter exits. Other options are a tilt down to find the characters, or a dolly sideways off a wall or someone's back to find the characters whose dialogue we already hear. Another alternative is to prelap the first few words of dialogue of the new scene over the last shot of the previous scene. In this case a hard cut is suitable.

Dialogue often begins in combination with movement by a character. Characters may also come closer to each other or move farther apart at some point in a conversation. Several useful blocking techniques for bringing two characters together for dialogue are described in the following pages.

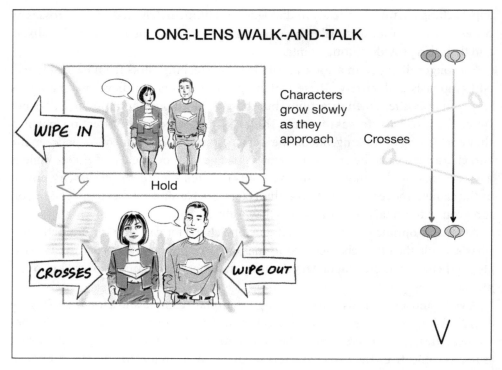

Figure 15.12 A long lens walk-and-talk is an attractive shot that conveys a dreamlike feeling of detachment and sometimes a lack of progress. The compressed perspective can make the environment seem more crowded than it is.

Pan One Character to Another

Panning one character to another is often done as a conversation begins (Figure 15.13). The shot starts on a single character and ends as a two-shot. This approach is cinematic and is both more visually interesting and more dramatic than using a wide shot. It can be useful for taking the first character away from a busy and complicated background so that the additional shots that cover the conversation can be recorded against a simpler and more manageable background. The first character may deliver the first line during her approach, before the second character is visible in the shot.

Start on What Is Being Handed to a Character

The camera can start close on a drink, letter, or other item as the first character hands it to the second character. The shot widens during the action, ending in a two-shot (Figure 15.14). Starting close on what's being delivered can create a transition to a new scene, while at the same time showing an item that is important to the story, or that signals the type of setting that the new scene takes place in. This technique can

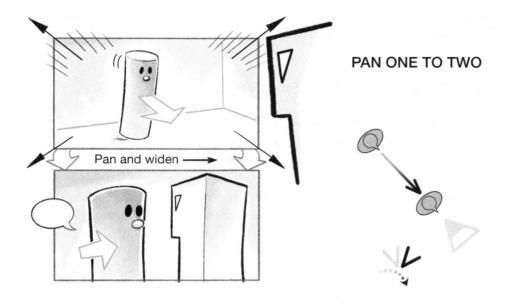

PAN ONE TO TWO

Figure 15.13 Panning one character to another is often done as a conversation begins. This approach is cinematic and can be used to pan away from a busy background to simplify the shots that cover the conversation.

PANNING WITH A PROP

Figure 15.14 Panning with a prop to begin a conversation can be an effective transition to a new scene. The item being handed can be significant to the story or reflect the type of setting. The dialogue can begin before the characters' faces are seen.

also be used mid-scene to compress time. The first character may start to deliver her first line before either character's face is visible.

Pan a Character to an Over-Shoulder

As shown in Figure 15.15, another way to begin a conversation is to start with the camera on the first character, who is entering through a door or coming around a corner, and then pan 90 degrees with that character until the character stops in an over-shoulder shot onto the second character. The first character may deliver her first line before the second character is visible. The camera may push in slightly during the first character's arrival to land in a suitable framing of the over-shoulder shot.

The Characters Do-si-do

A *do-si-do* is a dance figure in which two partners pass each other back to back before returning to their original positions. It is a convenient term to describe a theatrical turn in which a walking character crosses a standing character, stops, rotates 180 degrees past the audience, and comes face to face with the standing character. By rotating in the unnatural direction *toward the camera* a character's face remains visible to viewers throughout the turn (Figure 15.16).

Figure 15.15 An arriving character can deliver a line as he or she is panned 90 degrees into an over-shoulder shot in which we now see the second character.

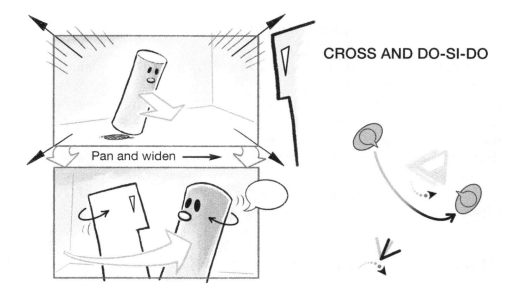

CROSS AND DO-SI-DO

Figure 15.16 *Do-si-do* is a dance figure in which two partners pass each other back to back before facing each other again. It is a convenient term to describe a theatrical turn in which a character crosses a standing character, stops, and rotates 180 degrees face to the audience before facing the standing character.

Having the first character walk past the second character and then rotate in a direction that favors the camera creates a cinematic shot that is preferable to one in which the character simply walks up, stops, and talks. The camera begins this shot on the walking character, and it pans and widens with that character until the two characters are framed in a two-shot for their dialogue. The walking character may deliver the first line while walking and rotating to face the stationary character, or may arrive and turn before speaking.

Ending Dialogue

Dialogue at the end of a scene often culminates with the reaction shot of one of the characters, with one character exiting, or with both a reaction and an exit. If a character leaves, this can be done in several ways. One way is for the character who leaves to walk deep, away from the camera. The character can remain in focus while walking away, enter soft focus, or exit. The shot that follows is the reverse angle reaction shot of the character who remains while watching the other character leave.

Leaving by Walking Forward in an Over-Shoulder

A popular technique to show characters walking away is to have them come toward the camera from their starting position in an over-shoulder shot. As the actor approaches, the camera moves backward to widen the shot slightly to make room for the departing character to walk between the remaining character and the camera during the exit (Figure 15.17). The remaining character's eyes have followed the departing character, sweeping past the lens and ending with an off-screen look that is a reaction shot. This exit seems more urgent, and it is cinematic because it is done in a single shot. There is the option of showing the remaining character's POV of the departing character.

A Theatrical Exit from a Conversation

There is a common variation on the way a character exits from an over-shoulder shot in the direction of the camera. In this variation the departing character does not come forward to walk between the remaining character and the camera, but instead leaves by traveling on the *far* side of the remaining character (Figure 15.18). What makes this exit theatrical is that the closer character does not watch the

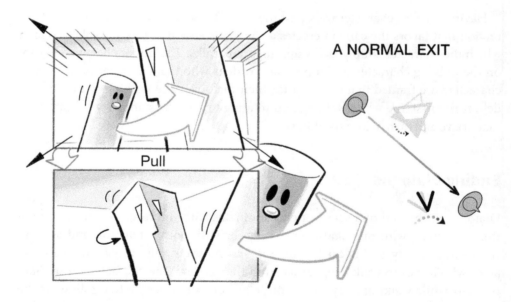

Figure 15.17 At the end of a conversation a character in an over-shoulder shot can "push" the camera as the character exits between the camera and the second character. The remaining character watches the departing character in what is now a reaction shot.

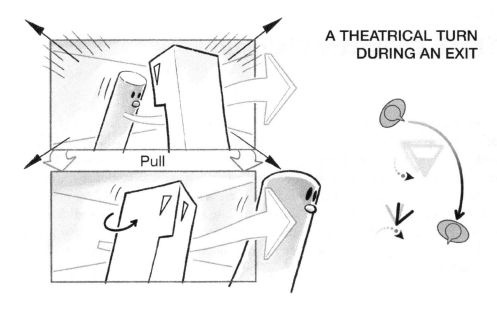

**A THEATRICAL TURN
DURING AN EXIT**

Pull

Figure 15.18 When the more distant character in an over-shoulder shot leaves the shot by traveling behind the remaining character, that character can spin in the opposite direction to remain visible to the audience as might be done on the stage.

departing character leave, but instead does a head rotation in the *opposite* direction, favoring the camera. Only after the remaining character's gaze has swept past the camera and completed 180 degrees of rotation does the remaining character see the departing character once again. This blocking is not unlike the do-si-do that was described earlier. Viewers do not find this blocking unusual or artificial. They focus on watching the expression on the face of the character who is turning.

16

Three-Character Dialogue

There is always a geometry to the configuration of characters who are talking to each other. When two characters talk their configuration is usually quite symmetrical, and their shots can be mirrored so that they match so that cuts are smooth. There is less symmetry to the coverage of three people engaged in conversation, because two of the characters usually face the third. But there is usually also a need for matching shots between pairs of characters who are talking to each while the third character listens. For these pairs the mirrored shots are similar to those used for two-person dialogue. This chapter looks at examples of sets of shots to cover three characters who talk while standing, while seated, and while walking.

Three Standing Characters Talk

As shown in Figure 16.1, conversation among three characters can often be covered in five shots, although more may be used. The two characters who have the most dialogue are usually positioned on the left and right sides of the group. The character who has the least dialogue is placed between the other two, positioned beside the character that this character is teamed with in the scene as they face the third character who stands on the opposite side.

Dialogue scenes often begin with a wipe or a reveal that finds the characters in the middle of a conversation. In other cases two characters approach a third, or one character joins two. A third possibility is that three characters are walking together and they all stop to continue their conversation while standing. However the characters assemble, the ideal final configuration is one in which two characters stand facing one. The coverage is an extension of that for two-character conversations. The standard shots that are used are shown on the map in Figure 16.2.

The storyboard panels in Figure 16.3 illustrate conversation among three characters. Pairs of gray arrows indicated the smoothest cuts that can be made. When a character has a split eyeline, care must be taken in editing to make sure that pairs of characters who are talking to each have opposed looks at the moment a cut between them takes place. The cuts are described below:

- A *wide master shot* (not illustrated) that can be used to establish the setting. This shot can slowly move sideways to add visual variety and tension to a stationary scene. Extras may cross the foreground to make the setting seem busy and real.

The Art of Cinematic Storytelling. Kelly Gordon Brine, Oxford University Press (2020). © Oxford University Press.
DOI: 10.1093/oso/9780190054328.001.0001.

Figure 16.1 Dialogue among three standing characters can be covered in five shots. A wide shot and additional close-ups can be added.

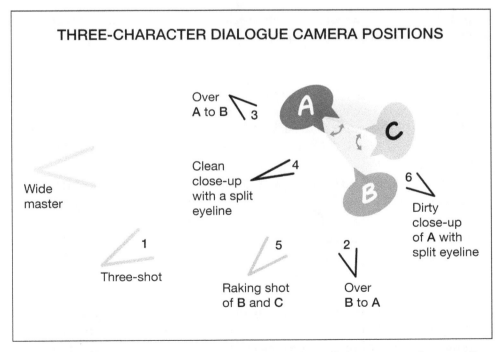

Figure 16.2 This map shows camera positions that cover basic dialogue among three standing characters. In this configuration **A** and **B** have the most dialogue, and **B** and **C** are in some way a team. These shots are illustrated in Figure 16.3.

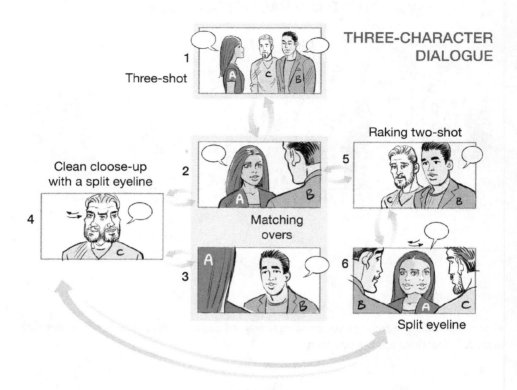

Figure 16.3 The gray arrows beside these storyboard frames indicate cuts that work well. The shot numbers correspond to those in Figures 16.1 and Figure 16.2.

- A *three-shot* (shot 1) that isolates the group from their surroundings and focuses on the conversation.
- *Matching over-shoulder shots* (shots 2 and 3) cover dialogue between **A** and **B**.
- A *clean single shot* of **C** (4) looking left and right at **A** and **B** for dialogue and reactions.
- A *raking shot* of **C** and **B** looking at **A** (5). Often in this shot **C** glances at **B**, which sets up an axis between **A** and **C** for their dialogue and overs if they have more than a couple of lines of dialogue with each other.
- A *clean single shot* of character **A** framed between **B** and **C**, with a split eyeline (shot 6).
- *Close-ups* of all characters (not illustrated).

In this example of conversation among three people, there could be several lines of dialogue between the character on the left and the middle character. Two extra shots could be created to cover this dialogue. These shots are illustrated in Figure 16.4 and are described below:

ADDING AN EYELINE BETWEEN THE FIRST AND THIRD CHARACTERS

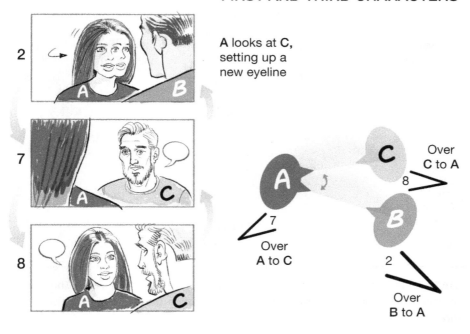

A looks at C, setting up a new eyeline

Figure 16.4 If there are several lines of dialogue between two characters who do not have over-shoulder shots, those shots can be added so that their dialogue is well covered.

- From **A**'s look to **C** in shot 2, a cut can be made to **A**'s *over-shoulder shot* onto **C** (shot 7).
- The *over-shoulder shot* of **C** onto **A** (shot 8) matches shot 7, and these two can be intercut while the dialogue is between **A** and **C**.

Three Seated Characters Talk

When three characters are seated at a table talking, the two most important characters are not usually seated beside each other but are opposite each other. This allows the two main characters to be connected visually and dramatically in over-shoulder shots. From the camera's angle, the least important character is placed between the other two, and should be covered in a clean single with a split eyeline. The three characters may be seated on three sides of a table, as shown in Figures 16.5, or on two sides, as shown in Figure 16.6.

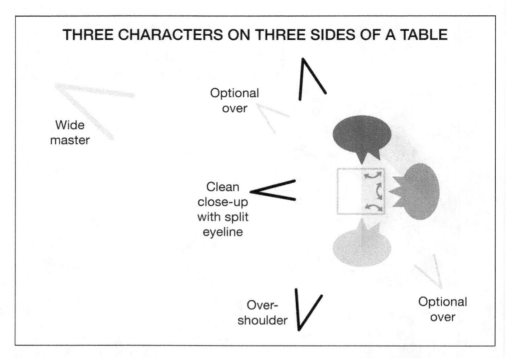

Figure 16.5 Characters can be seated around three sides of a table for dialogue. This map shows standard camera positions to cover their conversation. Clean close-ups can be added for all three characters.

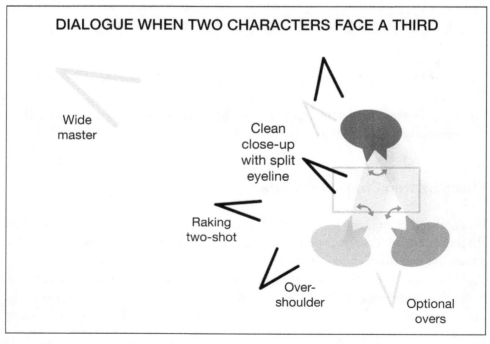

Figure 16.6 Three characters at a table can be seated with one opposite two. The camera positions are similar to those used in Figure 16.5, but a raking two-shot has been added to this configuration. Clean close-ups can be added for all characters.

Three Characters Walk and Talk

A Steadicam walk-and-talk is a popular option for a conversation among three characters. A walk-and-talk creates a more immersive, fluid, and fast-paced dialogue scene than can be achieved if the characters are standing or seated. Often some additional action can be added, such as dropping off some papers, pouring coffee, or using a vending machine. The feeling of a walk-and-talk is subjective because the camera travels with the group. Steadicam punch-ins can be used to isolate individual characters in a close-up. If extras cross the frame the environment seems busier and more real. Figure 16.7 illustrates a walk-and-talk with three characters.

A walk-and-talk can also be shot using a long lens, as shown in Figure 16.8. The feeling is quite different from a Steadicam walk-and-talk, partly because the camera is stationary and partly because of the effects of the long lens. Space is flattened, less of the setting is shown, action is minimized, and the characters progress slowly

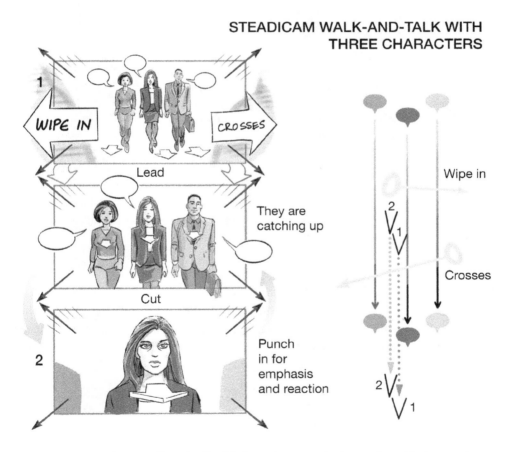

STEADICAM WALK-AND-TALK WITH THREE CHARACTERS

Figure 16.7 A Steadicam walk-and-talk with three characters is cinematic and feels urgent. A punch in to a Steadicam close-up isolates and emphasizes one character or a pair of characters.

The Art of Cinematic Storytelling. Kelly Gordon Brine, Oxford University Press (2020). © Oxford University Press.
DOI: 10.1093/oso/9780190054328.001.0001.

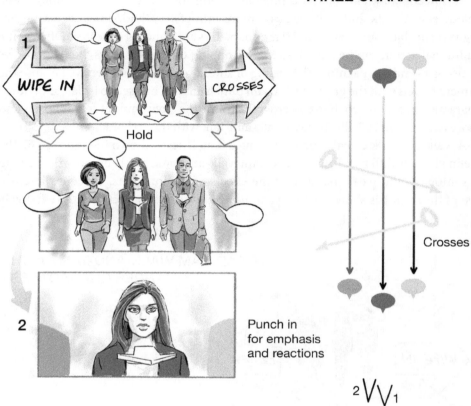

Figure 16.8 A dialogue scene among three characters who are walking toward the camera can be shot using a long lens. The mood seems dreamier and less urgent than a Steadicam walk-and-talk. One or more punch ins can be added.

toward the camera. The limited depth of field throws much of the image out of focus. The characters are somewhat isolated from their surroundings, and the shot can be more dreamlike. As a storytelling tool, a long-lens shot can imply that the characters are making slow progress toward their objectives, or that they are not in a hurry.

17

Group and Crowd Scenes

Films often show scenes of families at the dinner table, business meetings, speeches, performances, crowds and other gatherings. These scenes need clear geography so that viewers can get their bearings and keep them. In spite of there being many people in such scenes, there is often little action. This makes it more important to add visual interest in various ways, such as through camera movement, wipes, and shots through whatever foreground is available or can be added.

General Considerations

Groups of various kinds can often be covered in similar ways, and techniques that work for one type of gathering can often be applied to another type with minor adjustments. This chapter's suggested ways of blocking and shooting groups will be seen to have similarities whether people are at a table, at a performance, or at some other type of gathering. Keep in mind that within most large group scenes there are what might be considered sub-scenes in which two or three characters talk to each other, and these can often be blocked using the techniques that work for two- and three-character dialogue.

Keeping the Geography Clear

- Keep the camera on one side of the space as much as possible to create a principal axis of action that will keep the geography consistent. This will reduce the complexity of lighting and shooting as well as make it easier for viewers to understand where everything is throughout the scene.
- More often than not the focus of an event, whether it's the stage, the podium, the altar, or something else, is placed on the left of the screen and the audience on the right.
- The speaking characters should be seated strategically to keep their eyelines as simple as possible.
- Tie-up shots should connect the speech-giver or leader of the group to the audience.

Movement and Visual Interest

- Even if it's not in the script, where possible it is advisable to have a character or extra arrive or leave to add some movement to the scene. Another option is for

The Art of Cinematic Storytelling. Kelly Gordon Brine, Oxford University Press (2020). © Oxford University Press.
DOI: 10.1093/oso/9780190054328.001.0001.

a speaker to walk to a window or elsewhere while speaking. In the case of group at a table, an extra can serve food and drinks or deliver documents for interest or to motivate a pan.

- It's important to use dolly shots to create visual variety in otherwise stationary scenes.
- Whenever possible, shoot a wide shot through blinds, at a high angle, or framed through a window or doorway to add visual variety.

Cuts and Transitions

- Build transitions such as reveals into shots. This is helpful for shot contrast, time transitions, movement, and variety.
- Tilt ups from hand, plates, documents, and so on, to characters' close-ups are effective transitions.
- The start of a scene involving a large group is often an entrance, an establishing shot, or an in-camera transition such as a reveal off a wall or someone's back. A subjective way to start such a scene is to follow the character whose scene it is into the gathering.
- A short scene-within-a-scene between a couple of characters can start with a wipe or a reveal to isolate it from the larger action of the scene.

Four People Seated at a Table

Table scenes can require many camera positions to cover the dialogue of all the characters. The seating arrangement should be designed strategically to keep the number of shots as low as possible. In a scene where four people are at a table, someone in a position of authority is usually seated at the head of the table. But the scene may not belong to that character. The main axis is between the two most important characters in the scene.

Additional axes between other sets of characters may be needed. An important goal is to have as few axes as possible. When a new axis has to be introduced, it should be done in such a way that it is not more different from the main axis than it needs to be. The more similar two axes are, the less complicated the lighting and the more likely that existing shots will still have eyelines that can be matched with those of characters in the new shots.

Characters who look at each other should always have opposed looks. An on-screen head turn is often helpful to take us from one axis to another. Sometimes the head turn of a character who is only listening can provide a useful bridge to a character who has a line of dialogue. Another option is to use a cutaway to something such as food on the table, something being served, a wide shot, or a view out the window. The shot immediately after the cutaway will create a new axis between any pair of characters for their dialogue.

Here are some of the shots that are likely to be needed at table scenes:

- A *wide master shot.* Options include very slowly dollying sideways to add movement to the scene. The wide shot may introduce the scene, so it should have an in-camera transition such as a reveal built into it.
- *Over-shoulder shots* of pairs of characters with dialogue.
- *Clean close-ups* of characters who have lines or who react to what is said and done.
- Shots to cover the action of characters who are arriving or leaving the table.
- *Insert shots* of important items on the table, such as food, phones, keys, cards, or documents.
- An interesting *re-establishing shot* from a new angle, such as framed in a doorway or a window.

A simple way to provide characters with opposed eyelines is to leave one of the longer sides of a table empty. Two characters can sit side by side on one long side of the table while leaving the opposite side empty, even though this is somewhat theatrical. It will not work for some activities such as card games. Figure 17.1 shows camera positions for a configuration in which the two characters with the most dialogue are seated at opposite ends of the table.

A seating arrangement in which one character occupies each side of the four sides of a table is the most naturalistic. To reduce camera positions the least important character can be seated on the long side closest to the camera in the master shot, facing away from the camera. This simplifies the screen geography of the main three characters, who are covered as though the fourth character is not present. If the character whose back is to the camera in the master shot enters into conversation with a character at one end of the table, French overs are helpful because they maintain the usual look of the characters at the ends of the table. Figure 17.2 shows pairs of matching shots that cover dialogue between pairs of people who are talking to each other. The more verbal exchanges there are between different pairs of characters, the more shots will be needed to fully cover the scene.

A short pan can add variety to the standard template of dialogue at a table. At an appropriate moment in the script the camera can pan from one character to another who is seated beside the first character to see a reaction to something that was said. If the first character looks to the second, this can motivate such a pan. This can provide welcome movement and visual variety in a largely static scene, and it highlights a story connection between two characters.

A Boardroom Meeting

Boardroom scenes are common, and in these scenes most participants remain seated. If participants can be made to enter or exit, the shots become more visually interesting. The camera can also be used to compensate for the lack of movement by

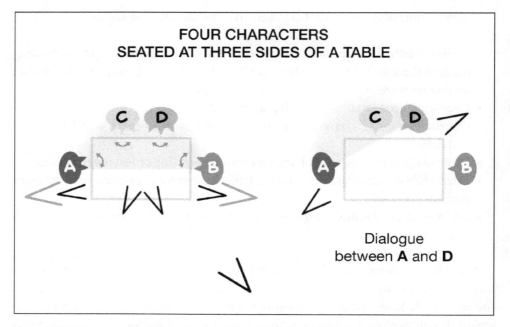

Figure 17.1 Four people can be seated at three sides of a table to simplify the eyelines and reduce the number of shots that are required. The main camera positions are shown, and the directions of characters' looks are indicated using noses and arrows.

dollying behind the heads of people at the table, tracking someone who is arriving, dollying as someone speaks, or panning from one close-up to another.

The point of view of the scene will be either that of the person leading the meeting or one of the participants. Coverage should favor this person's end or side of the table. If there are exchanges between a few pairs of participants, they should be covered in over-shoulders or close-ups unless the dialogue during their exchange is very brief. The main participants in the scene should have close-ups. Raking shots are almost always useful when shooting groups of people, especially to show several people who may have no lines and no close-ups, such as miscellaneous business people at the boardroom table. These shots add visual variety and may be used to graphically reinforce a feeling of the board acting in unison, much like a raking shot of soldiers at attention.

An example of a sequence that covers simple action in a boardroom is shown in Figure 17.3. In this scenario the leader labeled **A** arrives, and the camera tracks left behind participants' heads and then pans left as **A** walks to the chair at the head of the table. The reverse angle shows the group as **A** sits down on the left of the frame in the foreground. **A**'s close-up plays against group shots to the left and the right. **A** and the participant labeled **B** exchange several lines of dialogue in over-shoulder shots. A wide shot from outside the glass room tracks past vertical blinds. This shot provides visual variety and re-establishes the scene. Figure 17.4 provides a map of the shots in this sequence. Other shots that could be added include close-ups, pans

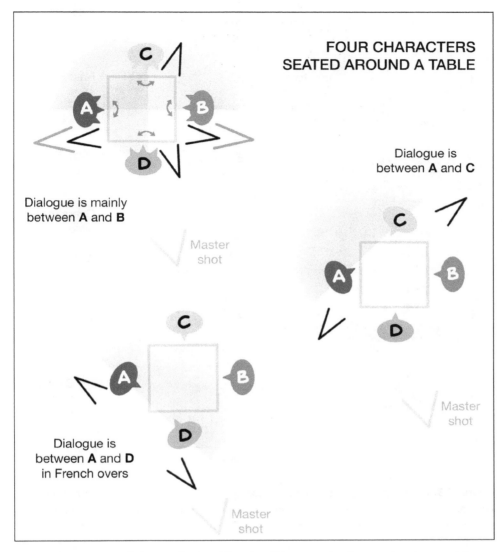

Figure 17.2 Covering dialogue of pairs of people talking to each other may involve several sets of matching over-shoulder shots. A close-up would normally be shot in addition to each over-shoulder shot.

between neighbors, and a sideways dolly alongside the table that focuses on the attendees on the far side.

Formal Gatherings

There are similarities in the seating arrangement of many large organized gatherings, whether lectures, speeches, religious services, or performances. Typically the

CLASSIC BOARDROOM BLOCKING

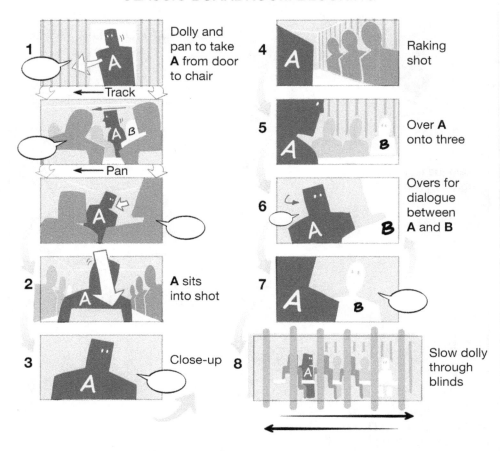

Figure 17.3 This simple sequence in a boardroom shows the types of shots that are often used. The tracking shot of the leader's entrance and the slowly moving wide shot through vertical blinds add movement to a fairly static scene. Figure 17.4 contains a map of this scene.

audience is in rows, and they all face and pay attention to one speaker or a small group of speakers at the front of a room. The symmetrical layout and the lack of action in many such scenes limit the type and number of shots. By convention camera positions are mainly on the side that keeps the stage on the left of the frame and the audience on the right, but this can be flipped.

The main axis of a formal event runs from the speaker to the important characters in the audience. In such scenes shots are often cut to alternate between angles on the speaker and angles on the audience to see reactions. In this geography the speaker will almost always have a right look, and the members of the audience will almost always have a left look. Anyone in the room can sweep the lens if required to look at someone on the other side, but this will be an exception and may never be required. For example, a member of the audience might turn away from the speaker to make a comment to a companion.

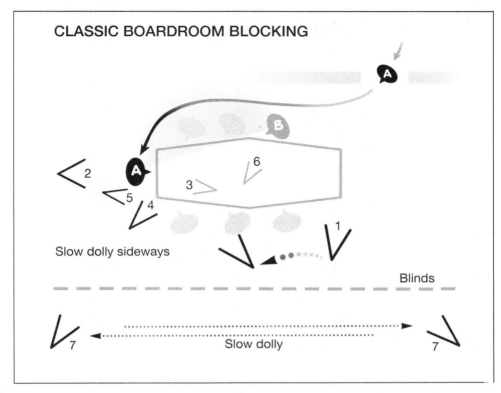

Figure 17.4 This map shows the camera positions and movement as illustrated in the boardroom scene storyboarded in Figure 17.3.

A key element of cinematic storytelling is movement. Two possibilities in these scenes are the arrival or departure of the speaker or of members of the audience. Camera movement can be used substitute for the lack of human action: dolly moves, tilts, and pans can all be used to introduce visual variety. Figure 17.5 is a map that provides a template of useful angles for a scene involving a speaker and a crowd. These shots are described in the sections that follow. Not every shot would necessarily be needed. They are not listed in story order, but are grouped based on who is in the shots. Other shot possibilities could arise depending on the script, the type of gathering, and the location.

Establishing Shots

1. High wide establishing shot from the front left corner, with the crowd facing screen left. If there is a chandelier, the camera can crane down off this to reveal the scene. Another option for a transition is a tilt down from the ceiling.
2. Low wide establishing shot from the back left corner, toward the stage.
3. Camera moves off foreground, such as a pillar or a flower arrangement, to reveal the scene in a wide shot.

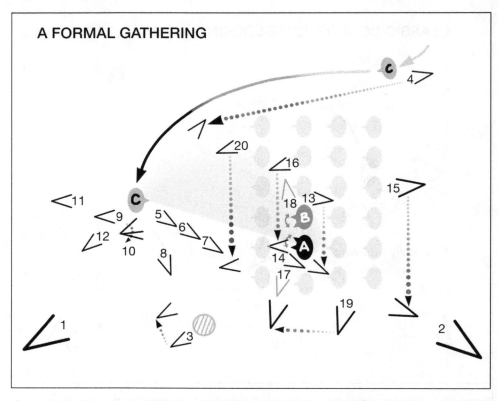

Figure 17.5 This map provides a template of shots that can be used to cover a formal gathering such as a lecture, a speech, a religious service, or a performance. Camera movement is used to create cutting points, transitions and visual interest.

Close Shots of the Speaker

4. Follow the speaker to the podium in a medium shot (if this action is in the script).
5. Low-angle, clean close-up of the speaker (with a right look).
6. Low-angle, medium close-up of the speaker (right look). It includes a piece of the podium.
7. Cowboy shot of the speaker (right look) that includes others on the stage or important props or set decoration that evokes the type of setting.
8. Low-angle raking shot of the speaker (right look), with a piece of the podium, or if there are several speakers, a raking shot of all of them.

The Speaker's POV of the Audience

9. Over the right shoulder of the speaker onto the audience. The speaker can look left and right so that the speaker's profile is sometimes seen.

10. Speaker's clean angle POV as it pans to the right across the audience.
11. Medium wide shot over the speaker onto the audience.
12. Low-angle shot from behind the speaker's silhouette against flaring spotlights.

The Audience's POV of the Speaker

13. Over A's left shoulder to the speaker. This could begin as a dolly left.
14. A's clean POV of the stage, possibly in two sizes.
15. Dolly left behind the heads of a row of people in the audience, with the speaker in focus.

Close Shots of the Main Characters in the Audience

16. Dolly to the right across A's and B's row and land on A in a single with a left look. This shot can also pan between the two characters to connect their singles cinematically.
17. Raking two-shot of A and B looking left.
18. Matching raking two-shot of A and B looking right for conversation between A and B. Because of their right look, we must return to shot 17 before cutting to any shot of the stage to return to the main axis of the scene, which was crossed. These shots are similar to the coverage of a driver and passenger in a car.

Moving Shots of the Audience Watching and Listening

19. Dolly left along the side aisle to see down the rows. The audience members have left looks in these raking angles. Land on the row with our characters.
20. The camera is one row in front of A's and B's row. It dollies to the right across the faces of members of the audience. The camera is angled very slightly left so that all the audience members have a left look throughout. This shot lands on A and B as they react to something that is being said by the speaker.

Informal Gatherings with a Speaker and a Crowd

Shooting a crowd outside often presents the problem of containing what's visible. Seeing down streets must often be avoided for many reasons, including control of traffic and pedestrians, distracting signage, and the style of vehicles and buildings. The problem is worst for stories set in the past. Some of these issues can be eliminated by keeping the background out of focus. Often what should not be seen by the camera can be blocked by using large vehicles, temporary structures, greenery, and objects such as crates or barrels. Items that selectively block the camera's view can also be used within a shot to give the illusion that a crowd is larger than it is.

Another helpful technique for containing what's visible when shooting exterior scenes is to use buildings as backgrounds. For example, more contained views are achieved by having the main line of action run across a street from storefront to storefront rather than down a street, which would allow the camera to see great depth in both directions. Choosing the right line of action can reduce the number of extras that are required as well as making a scene simpler and cheaper to shoot.

An informal gathering with a standing crowd could be a protest, a political rally, or a musical performance. The same types of shots that cover large formal gatherings effectively can be used to cover an informal event. These scenes are often quite static, and they can be made more cinematic by using camera movement and by adding the arrival of the speaker or of characters in the crowd. If a scene begins with the event already underway, a transition such as a dolly reveal or a dolly tilt can start the scene. Figure 17.6 shows a typical gathering of a standing crowd and a speaker, and

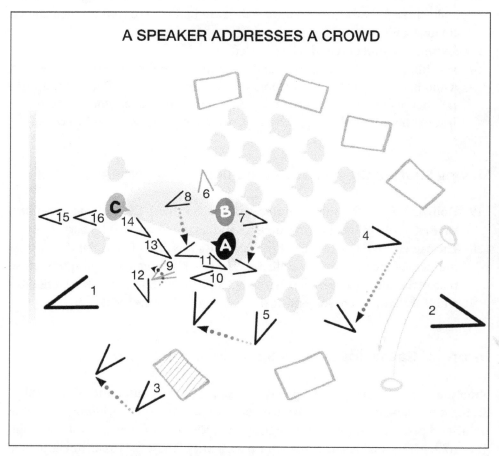

Figure 17.6 This map provides a template of shots that can be used to cover a crowd listening to a speaker. Note the camera moves that are used to create cutting points, transitions and visual interest.

common camera positions are indicated. The shots are described in the following sections, grouped by subject and not in story order. These shots are similar in many ways to those that are used to cover a more formal gathering where the audience is seated, as described earlier.

Establishing Shots

1. Wide establishing shot favoring the crowd.
2. Wide high-angle establishing shot favoring the speaker.
3. Medium wide shot that starts as a reveal for use when returning to this setting after cutting away to parallel action in another scene.

Shots of and over the Crowd

4. Dolly left behind the crowd the backs and heads of members of the crowd with the distant speaker in focus.
5. Dolly left to see raking views of the crowd, and land on **A** and **B** in profile (with left looks).
6. Raking shot of **A** and **B** that matches shot 5.
7. Dolly left off **B** to land over **A**'s shoulder onto the speaker.
8. Dolly right across the crowd and land on **A** in a medium close-up with a left look.
9. This angle provides close-ups of both **A** and **B**, as well as connecting them using short pans. **A** and **B** maintain a left looks to the speaker, but **B** has a right look to **A**.
10. Several crowd reaction shots.

Shots of and over the Speaker

11. **A**'s clean cowboy shot of **C** (with a right look).
12. Three-quarter angle shot of the speaker and others behind speaker.
13. Low-angle cowboy shot of speaker against a building or other background.
14. Close-up of the speaker with a right look.
15. Medium wide over the speaker to the crowd.
16. Over-shoulder of the speaker onto the crowd.

A Crowd Watches a Fight

In this chapter's final example a fight is taking place and the crowd forms a circle around it. **A** and **B** are in the crowd watching **C** and **D** fight. This scene would seem

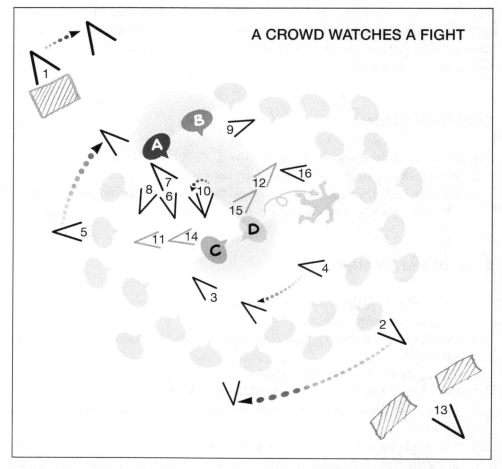

Figure 17.7 This map shows a generic fight scene in which a crowd forms a circle around the action. The numbered shots are typical camera positions and camera moves that could be used to cover this type of scene cinematically.

more real if shot using a handheld camera, and some of the shots of the fight could be in slow motion. This scene would look best if the room is hazy and illuminated by shafts of light from high windows. Figure 17.7 is a map of potential shots to cover the action of such a scene, and they are described in the remainder of the chapter.

Shots of the Fight Scene

1. Come off foreground rafters, a wall, or another object to reveal a high-angle, wide shot of the scene.
2. Dolly left behind the crowd with the fight in focus.
3. The crowd watches the fight (with a left look).
4. Dolly right across the reactions of the crowd (with a neutral or left look).

5. Dolly left behind the crowd seeing the fight and landing in an over-shoulder onto **A**.

Shots of the Two Characters Who Are among the Observers

6. Close-up of **A** (right look).
7. **A**'s clean POV of the fight.
8. Raking shot of **A** and **B** as they watch the fight and talk. They will normally have a right look, although **B** will have a left look while talking to **A**.
9. Optional reverse-angle raking shot of **A** and **B** if needed for a longer conversation (left look).
10. Pan between **B**'s close-up and **A**'s close-up (both have right looks except whenever **B** turns to **A**).

Shots That Are with the Fighters

11. Loose shot over **C** onto **D** as they fight.
12. Loose shot over **D** onto **C** as they fight. Shots 11 and 12 are intercut.
13. Full shot framed by a doorway or a window of the fight in progress with **A** and **B** in the background watching.
14. Tighter shot over **C** onto **D** as they fight and **C** punches **D** and **D** falls backward.
15. Tighter shot over **D** onto **C** as they fight and as **C** punches **D** and **D** flies backward out of frame.
16. Medium close-up as **D** enters the frame moving left and his head and shoulders hit the floor.

18

Shooting Driving Scenes

Driving scenes are found in almost every movie and television show. This chapter presents many options for shot design for both interior and exterior car shots. In this chapter the term "car" should be considered to mean any kind of vehicle. Driving sequences usually require cuts between exterior shots of the car in motion and interior shots of the occupants as they drive, talk, and look out the windows. There are many exterior shot possibilities for cars, while the interior shot choices are limited by the fixed positions of the seats.

Exterior shots may serve to say something about a car's character, its condition, the environment through which it's being driven, the style of driving, or the length of the trip. Interior shots are mainly concerned with the occupants' conversation and sometimes with what they see through the windows. Early in a story more detail may be given about a character's car and the action of getting into and out of it. Later on the storytelling pace is quicker and hard cuts are often made to a driver who is already on the road. This reflects how settings are generally handled: when first introduced they are shown in more detail, whereas later on the audience is expected to recognize the settings quickly without much time spent reintroducing them, which would slow down the pace of the storytelling and may bore viewers.

A Car Drives Away

The Driver Is Already in the Car

There are many ways that a car can be shot as it drives away. These possibilities have to be evaluated to determine which ones are appropriate for a particular story, as well as for which ones are possible in the location under consideration. Some of the most useful options are described in what follows and are shown on the map in Figure 18.1.

1. Often it's important to show someone drive away as the POV of a character left behind.
2. The car's exit can be shown in a full shot from an objective angle in front of the car. The car may go straight out or turn to cross the frame before exiting on the other side of the camera. This shot has the advantage of holding on the

The Art of Cinematic Storytelling. Kelly Gordon Brine, Oxford University Press (2020). © Oxford University Press.
DOI: 10.1093/oso/9780190054328.001.0001.

setting and whoever was left behind. If the camera is low this angle is more dramatic.

3. An objective three-quarter angle can show a car headed deeper into the shot from an angle near one of the rear fenders.

4. A more unusual and sometimes comic angle begins with the camera framing a tight shot of the rear of a car's trunk, license, and bumper, and as the car drives deep it is revealed.

5. The driver can be seen framed in one of the front side windows, and the camera pans as the car drives deeper. This highlights the fact that the character is going away.

6. The driver can be seen framed in one of the front side windows, and the car can simply exit this shot. This is a quick departure that might be used because a pan would not look attractive or even be possible in a busy environment, because the departure is urgent, or because it creates a better cutting point.

7. The camera can be on the front passenger seat and stay on the driver in profile. This can be used if the story continues with the driver.

8. The camera can be in the back seat looking out the windshield over the driver's shoulder. This is useful as a longer shot if it's important to see some of the driver's trip.

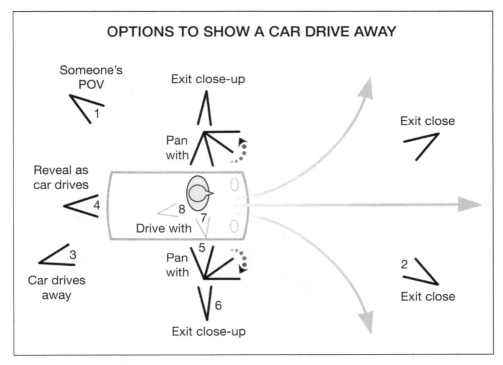

Figure 18.1 The camera positions shown on this map illustrate some of the many choices of angles that can be used to show a car driving away.

The Driver Gets into a Car and Drives Away

A character who walks to a car, gets in, and drives away can be shot in several ways. The options must be evaluated to see which ones work for the story and the location. Figure 18.2 illustrates six common ways of covering this action in one shot, and these shots are shown on the map in Figure 18.3.

1. The car is seen in a full shot. A man enters from beside the camera, possibly in a low-angle shot. The car exits close to the camera. This seems urgent if it starts a scene.
2. The man is led briefly as he comes out a door, and then he is panned to the car, ending in a wider shot. This starts as a subjective shot and makes the man's trip seem urgent.

OPTIONS TO TAKE A CHARACTER TO A CAR

Figure 18.2 These storyboards illustrate six common ways to shoot a character getting into a car and driving away. A map of these shots can be found in Figure 18.3.

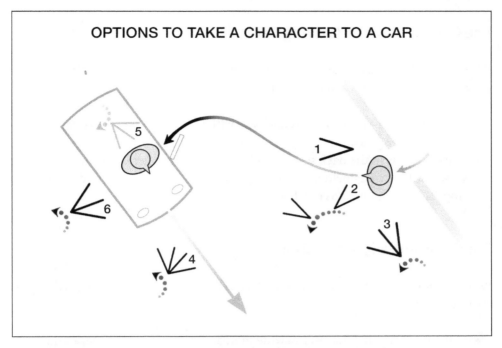

Figure 18.3 This map shows the car, the driver, and the camera positions for the six shots illustrated in Figure 18.2.

3. A man suddenly enters the shot (or comes out a doorway) in profile. The camera immediately pans with him as he heads to the car, ending in a wider shot. He drives away. This seems urgent and may be chosen for its attractive background.

4. We pan the man to his car. The car leaves deep or exits close to the camera. This highlights the setting he is leaving.

5. The camera is in the back seat looking out the side window, and it pans as the driver approaches and gets in. This could be the POV of someone hiding in the car. This becomes a subjective shot, and it makes the driver seem vulnerable. The shot may continue as the trip begins.

6. The camera is on the opposite side of the car and booms down with the driver as he gets in and drives out of the shot. This is subjective and could serve as a reaction shot to something that has just happened.

A Car Arrives

There are many ways to shoot a car's arrival. It is time well spent to consider several options and then choose the one that works best for the story.

The Camera Is in the Arriving Car

If the camera is inside the car, the driver's arrival is told from that character's point of view. The two most common ways of doing this are:

- The camera is in the front passenger seat with the driver in frame as the car stops and the driver gets out.
- The camera is in the back seat, shooting an over-shoulder of the driver and the view out the windshield as the car approaches its destination and comes to a stop. The camera pans as the driver gets out.

The Car Is Already in the Shot

When a stationary camera records a car's arrival the shot is objective unless the angle is someone's POV.

- The car pulls in off the street in a wide shot, drives closer to the camera, and stops.
- The camera is on the street, and it pans the arriving car 90 degrees into a driveway or parking lot, thereby establishing the setting.
- The car arrives from the distance. This might suggest the end of a long trip, an unwanted visitor, or some uncertainty about what the driver will find here.
- The car's arrival is seen as someone's POV from outside, in a doorway, through the foreground, or through a window on the ground floor or on a higher floor.
- The camera pans with an arriving car and continues until it lands on the profile of someone watching, or in an over-shoulder of the character who is watching.

The Car Makes an Entrance

If a car makes an entrance before it comes to a stop, this can help begin a scene by providing shot contrast and a time transition.

- The car comes through an opening such as through a large door into a warehouse or industrial building.
- A car emerges around the corner of a building, or from behind foreground objects.
- The car pulls into the shot suddenly from close beside the camera, possibly turning before it stops.
- The camera is angled toward the ground, and the car's fender and wheel come into the frame. Sometimes this shot continues as we see the lower part of the driver's door open and feet step out.

An In-Camera Transition Begins the Shot

A transition can be built into the beginning of a shot that shows a car's arrival. The shot contrast and feeling of the passage of time can help both the cut and the storytelling.

- The camera tilts down to find a car arriving.
- The camera dollies sideways off something in the foreground to reveal a car arriving.
- The camera cranes down off a branch or a sign to reveal a car arriving.

A Car Travels

A car that is traveling can be shown in many creative ways. Both the driver's POV and the moving background that is visible in the background of shots of the driver and the passengers make it clear that the car is in motion. In general, shots outside the car emphasize the journey itself, and in these shots the car itself is the character. In addition to showing that someone is traveling, an exterior shot can be used to say something about the type of car, the locale, and the length or urgency of the trip.

Objective Stationary Shots of a Car Going By

There are many ways to shot a car as it drives past. The diagram in Figure 18.4 shows the camera positions for 11 common types of stationary exterior shot of a moving car. Each shot gives a different feeling to the same action. Eight of these shots are described below and illustrated in Figures 18.5, 18.6 and 18.7.

Four wide stationary exterior car shots that are shown in the diagram in Figure 18.4 are illustrated in Figure 18.5 using the same shot numbers. These shots can be part of a montage or can begin a scene.

1. A long shot shows a car going across the screen. It emphasizes a long journey and the nature of the locale. Often the camera is stationary and the car is allowed to drive across the shot. This shot can be used to end a scene.
2. A car rises up over a hill into view as seen through a long lens. This shot is usually attractive, gives the car an entrance, and may suggest power or progress.
3. A high angle can be recorded from an overpass, crane, drone, bridge, balcony, or any other elevated vantage point. A high angle from an overpass can start on an approaching car and tilt down as the car disappears under the overpass, or begin by looking straight down on the pavement, and tilt up with the car as it suddenly enters the shot and drives away.

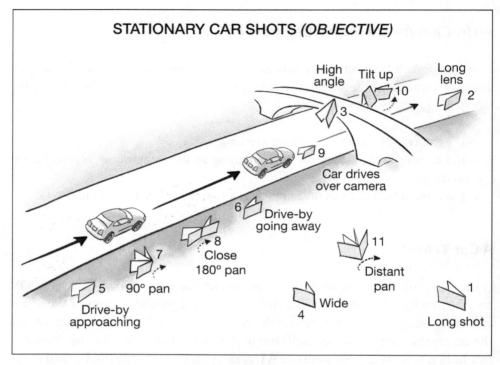

Figure 18.4 This diagram shows often-used stationary camera positions for exterior shots that create objective coverage of car travel. Eight of these eleven numbered shots are illustrated in Figures 18.5, 18.6 and 18.7.

4. A wide shot may begin with the car driving into the shot, or the car may emerge from behind a building, fence, foliage, or any other large object.

Two common drive-by shots that do not pan with the passing car were shown in the diagram in Figure 18.4 and are illustrated in Figure 18.6 using the same shot numbers. The camera is often set at a low angle to make such a shot more exciting.

5. A drive-by toward a low-angle camera sees the car grow as it approaches and then exits close to the camera. The dramatic exit can motivate a cut to the interior of the car or it can end a scene.
6. A drive-by of a car approaching from behind the camera sees it enter the shot dramatically and quickly recede into the distance. A low angle and a wide lens increase the drama. This shot can end a scene.

Two common drive-by shots that pan with the passing car were shown in the diagram in Figure 18.4 and are illustrated in Figure 18.7 using the same shot numbers. These shots are exciting and convey a feeling of urgency.

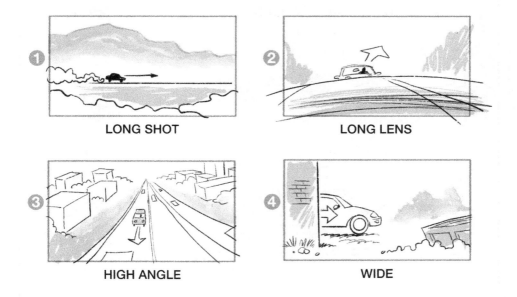

Figure 18.5 These wide shots are effective at placing a car in its environment. The shot numbers correspond to the camera positions shown in Figure 18.4.

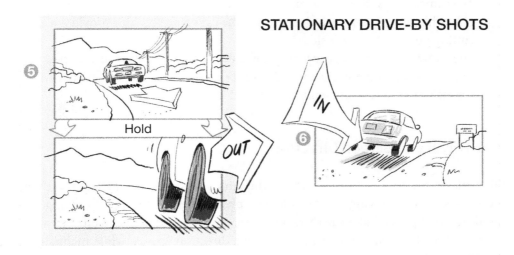

Figure 18.6 These two exciting drive-by shots do not involve a pan. Shot 5's exit makes a good cutting point. The shot numbers correspond to the camera positions shown in Figure 18.4.

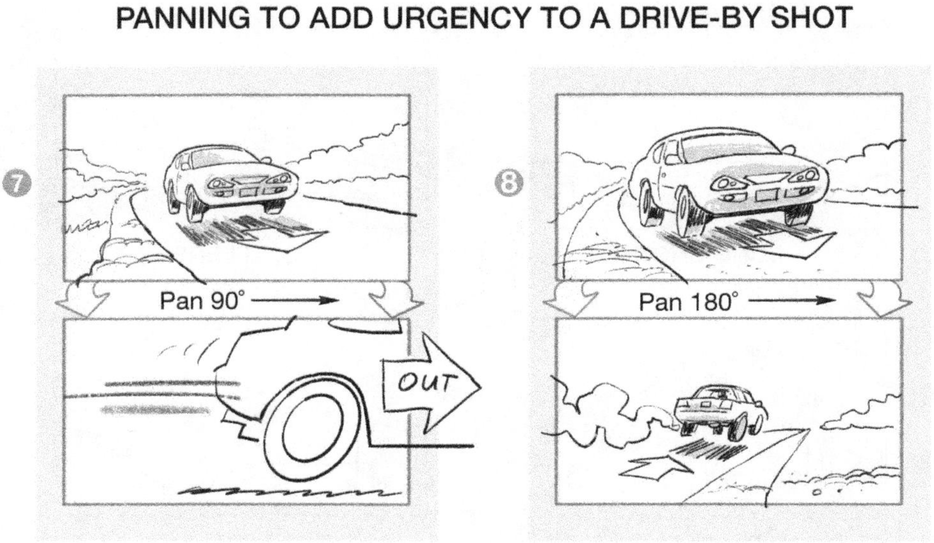

PANNING TO ADD URGENCY TO A DRIVE-BY SHOT

Figure 18.7 These two *panning* drive-by shots signal even greater urgency than drive-by shots without pans The shot numbers correspond to the camera positions shown in Figure 18.4.

7. The camera pans the approaching car through an angle of 90 degrees, but at this point the camera stops panning and lets the car exit right. This provides a good cutting point to a scene inside the car.
8. The camera pans the approaching car a full 180 degrees as it drives past and starts to recede into the distance. This shot's story beat is that the car's occupants are making progress on their journey.

Car Travel and Screen Direction

To achieve continuity of screen motion the same ideas must be applied to the cuts between shots of a moving car as would be applied to a character who is walking. The guiding principle is that a car should not change screen direction arbitrarily from shot to shot. There are many ways to make a direction change while maintaining continuity. The most obvious one is to see the car turn on camera. Another is to use a neutral shot to bridge the two shots with opposite screen directions.

If a Steadicam is looking down the road at a distant car that is approaching, the camera operator can walk cross the road in order to change the car's screen direction. And as always a cut to a new scene erases the geography of the car's journey in the minds of viewers, and allows it to be re-established in the opposite direction when the story returns to exterior shots of the car. A cut inside the car will serve this purpose.

Subjective Shots that Travel with a Car

Subjective car shots are those in which the camera moves with the car. The diagram in Figure 18.8 shows 10 commonly used angles, and these are described below and illustrated in Figures 18.9 and 18.10.

Subjective shots that lead and follow a car can be intercut in the same ways as a walking character's shots. These shots can also be embellished in the same ways that those of walking characters are. These camera angles that are shown in the diagram in Figure 18.8 and are illustrated in Figure 18.9 using the same shot numbers.

1. Leading the car centered in a full shot. The car can be allowed to slowly catch up and grow larger in the frame to make the shot grow in intensity.
2. Starting on the grill and widening or moving up to reveal the driver and passengers. This shot is a transition.
3. Starting with the camera looking down at the road surface or up at the sky, and tilting up or down to find the car. This shot is a transition.
4. Following the car in a centered full shot or a tighter shot. This can begin with the camera pointing down at the pavement or up at the sky, and tilting up or down to create a transition.

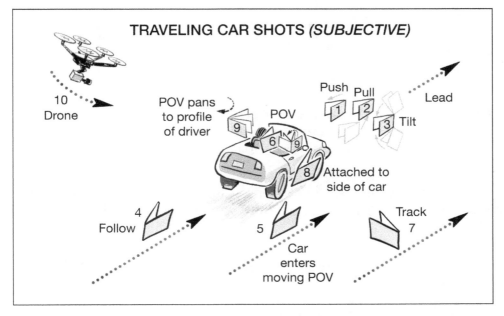

Figure 18.8 This diagram illustrates camera positions for drone and camera car shots that can be used to create subjective exterior shots of a moving car. If desired a car can enter or exit leading, following and tracking shots. Shots one through eight are illustrated in Figure 18.9 and Figure 18.10.

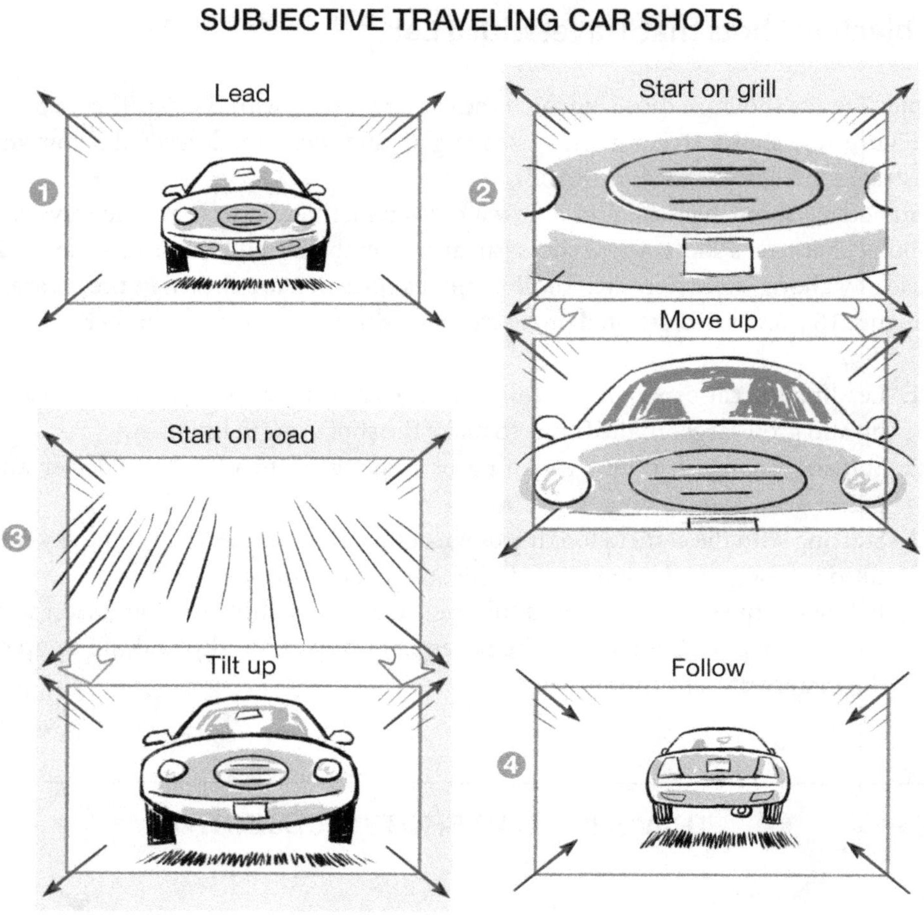

SUBJECTIVE TRAVELING CAR SHOTS

Figure 18.9 These exterior shots travel with the car to cover the action subjectively. When a tilt or move up or down is included it creates a transition that can begin a scene. The shot numbers correspond to the camera positions shown in Figure 18.8.

The remaining camera positions for moving coverage of a moving car that were shown in the diagram in Figure 18.8 are described below and illustrated in Figure 18.10.

5. The car enters its moving POV just as a character would walk into a moving POV.
6. The driver's moving POV is shown through the windshield.
7. The camera is attached to the car at an angle that shows the front wheel and fender and the road ahead.
8. A wide tracking shot shows the car in a full shot. The car can enter this shot. This can also be a tighter shot that crops the car.

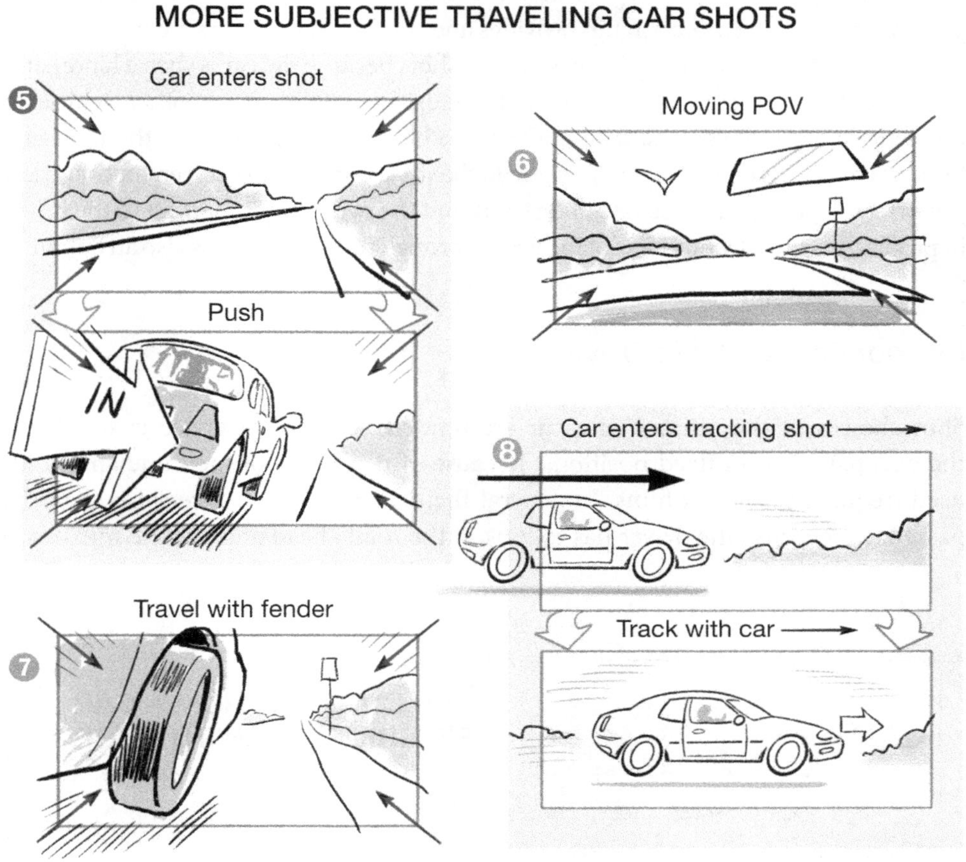

MORE SUBJECTIVE TRAVELING CAR SHOTS

Figure 18.10 Some additional options for subjective traveling car shots are illustrated. The shot numbers correspond to the camera positions shown in Figure 18.8.

9. What starts as a clean POV from beside the driver's door pans to become a profile of the driver (not illustrated). This pan can also be done from the front passenger seat.
10. A drone shot has many possibilities (not illustrated). It is most often flown high above the car and shows it following a road in a rural setting.

A Driver with No Passengers

Cutting from an Exterior to an Interior Shot

An interior car scene is often preceded by an exterior shot of the traveling car. A drive-by with an exit is one good choice. For continuity the driver should be seen headed in the same direction in both shots. Some directors flip the screen direction of the driver when cutting from a drive-by to a shot of the driver. The arguments in favor are the good shot contrast a direction flip provides and the fact that viewers are not confused by this because the geography is clear in both shots because the car is such a landmark.

But continuity would be important if the driver is following another vehicle or hurrying to a particular destination. On the other hand, if the driver's thoughts and feelings are what is important at this point in the story, continuity of screen motion is less important. Figure 18.11 illustrates a drive-by and the two options for a cut to the driver in profile. A cut to a frontal view of the driver through the windshield is also an option.

Interior Car Shots of a Driver

Shot choices in the interior of a car are limited because the space is small and the occupants are in fixed positions. Because of this many of the same angles are used frequently in most films. In general the driver requires more shots than the passengers because the driver has to look at the road ahead and use the mirrors to

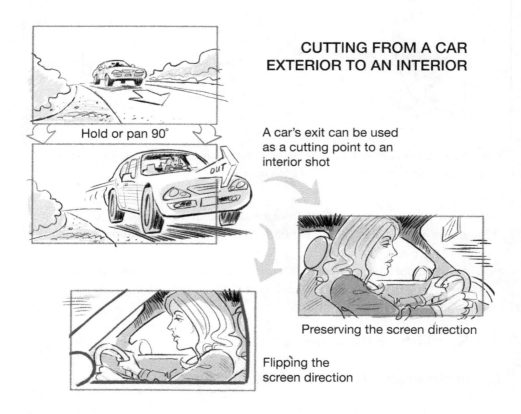

CUTTING FROM A CAR EXTERIOR TO AN INTERIOR

Hold or pan 90°

OUT

A car's exit can be used as a cutting point to an interior shot

Preserving the screen direction

Flipping the screen direction

Figure 18.11 A drive-by can be used as an establishing shot for a moving car. If the car exits close to the camera, a cutting point is provided that makes the cut smoother. Some directors flip the driver's shot to create shot contrast.

look at what's behind, including traffic and passengers. Figure 18.12 shows the usual angles used for the driver and the driver's POV through the windshield and in the rear-view mirror, and these are described here.

1. The driver can be covered in a wide or tight shot through the windshield. This shot can show glances into the rearview mirror, as well as a piece of any vehicle that is following.
2. The driver's POV seen through the windshield may be clean or it may include the driver's hand, the dashboard, and the rearview mirror.
3. The driver is often shot in profile in two or more sizes from the passenger seat angle. The driver's POV and his profile can be combined in a pan.
4. The driver is often shown in a close shot of the rearview mirror. This may be either a POV of a back-seat passenger or an objective shot.
5. The driver and the driver's POV can be combined in one over-shoulder shot.
6. The driver is often shot facing left as seen through the driver's window
7. The driver's POV of the vehicle behind or a back-seat passenger can be shot in the rearview mirror.

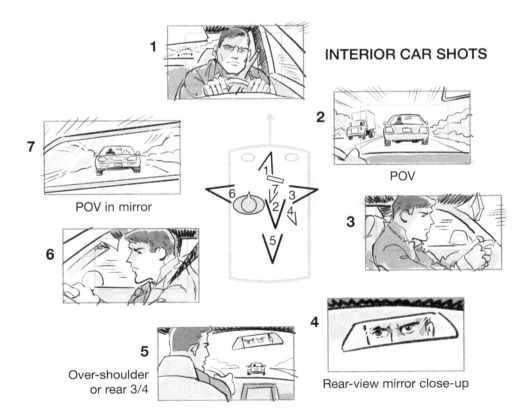

Figure 18.12 The standard layout of cars and the fixed position of the driver limit the shot options, and therefore the types of shots illustrated are used very often.

Motivated by a desire to create something that differs from the usual interior car coverage, some filmmakers experiment with unconventional angles and compositions. Sometimes an unusual shot at the right moment can suggest a character's state of mind quite effectively, while at other times odd shots draw attention to themselves. Figure 18.13 shows some options for unusual shots, and these are described here:

1. Reflections racing over the windshield and the driver not visible
2. Crowding the driver and car to one side of the frame
3. An over-shoulder from outside the car
4. A very wide over-shoulder from the back seat with the driver on the far left and no passenger
5. A high angle from outside that crowds a passenger or driver and shows the pavement racing past

UNUSUAL ANGLES OF DRIVERS AND PASSENGERS

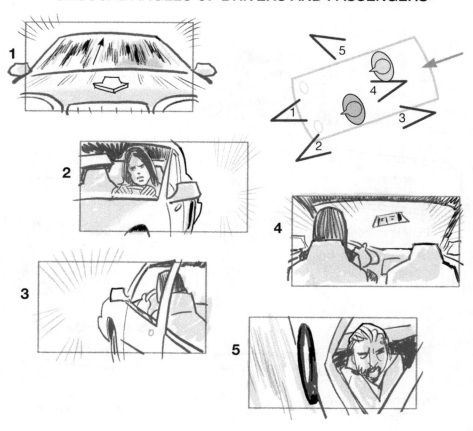

Figure 18.13 Unusual car shot angles and compositions can be used to suggest a character's state of mind, create tension, or foreshadow a problem ahead.

A Driver and a Front-Seat Passenger

Front-Seat Conversation Shot through the Windows

Coverage of a driver and a front-seat passenger can be shot in a limited number of ways because of their fixed positions. The fact that the characters sometimes look screen left and sometimes right does not matter, because the important axis is not the direction in which they are traveling, but the psychological connection between them. The camera angles that are used are illustrated in Figure 18.14, and are described below. These shots are also suitable for conversation in a parked car.

1. A symmetrical two-shot through the front windshield. This may start as a tilt up or down, or even as a pan that begins with the camera pointed at the buildings and foliage alongside the road that appear to race past.

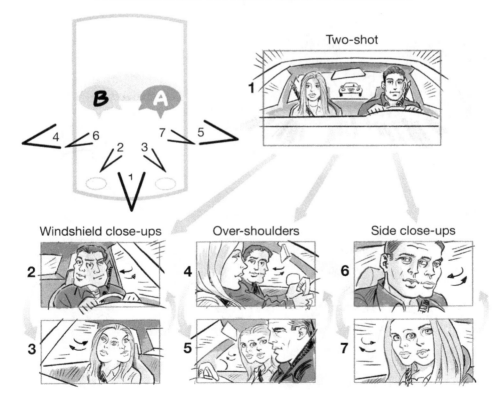

Figure 18.14 These storyboards illustrate the classic angles for dialogue between a driver and a front-seat passenger.

2 and 3.   Matching close-ups through the windshield

4 and 5.   Matching raking over-shoulder shots through the side windows. This shoot can boom up or down to move with the more distant character as that character gets into or out of a car.

6 and 7.   Matching close-ups through the side windows

French Overs for the Driver and the Front-Seat Passenger

Dialogue in a car's front-seat is often covered using French over shots from the back seat. This can make the conversation seem more private, personal, or intense. Figure 18.15 illustrates these angles, and they are described here:

1. A symmetrical two-shot from the back seat that also shows the occupants' POV through the windshield

FRENCH OVERS FOR FRONT-SEAT DIALOGUE

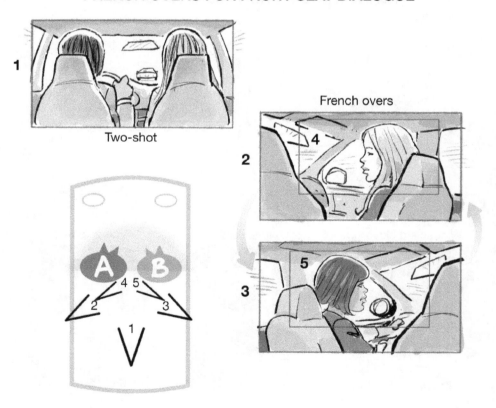

Figure 18.15   French overs are often used for front-seat dialogue. They make a conversation seem more private, personal, or intense.

2 and 3. Matching French overs shot from the back seat
4 and 5. Tighter matching French overs shot from the back seat

A Driver with One Back-Seat Passenger

If the driver and a back-seat passenger are talking or looking at each other there is an axis between them that should be respected for continuity. The rearview mirror is useful for close-ups. The coverage can favor the passenger or the driver, as shown in Figure 18.16.

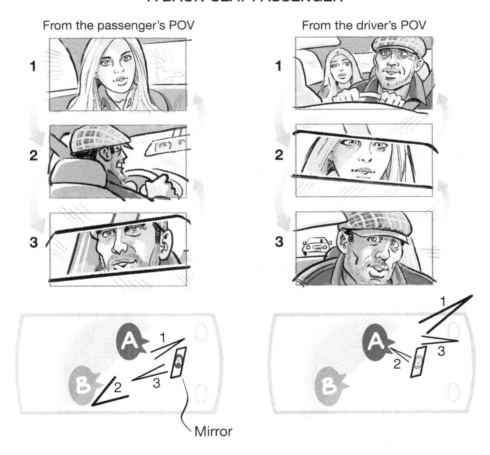

Figure 18.16 Conversation between a driver and a passenger in the back seat makes use of the rearview mirror. There is a choice of who is reflected in the mirror.

A Driver with Passengers in the Front and Back

There are several approaches to shooting three characters in a car. The coverage can be built on standard shots of the front-seat passengers either from the front and sides or in French overs. Three options for covering this arrangement are described below and illustrated in Figure 18.17.

1. A three-shot covers the group, and a clean single with a split eyeline is the close-up of the back-seat passenger. Matching raking shots cover conversation between the front-seat passengers. Close-ups through the front windshield or the side windows can be added.
2. If it is important to begin the scene on the back-seat passenger, the scene can start with a shot from outside the car on the back-seat passenger in profile, and this shot can dolly along the side of the car to find the front-seat passengers in

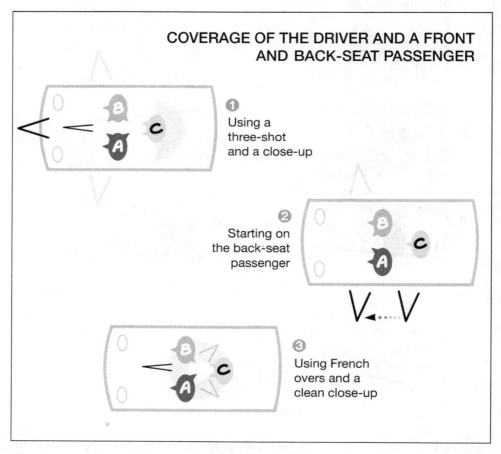

Figure 18.17 This map illustrates three approaches to interior coverage for a driver, a front-seat passenger, and one back-seat passenger.

a raking two-shot. This connects the occupants spatially and psychologically. Now the scene can continue with front-seat overs.

3. French overs can be used for the front-seat occupants. These shots can have split eyelines. A clean single with a split eyeline can be used for the back-seat passenger.

A Driver with Two Back-Seat Passengers

There are sometimes two passengers in the back seat. There could be two children in the back seat who are being driven somewhere by a parent, or the car could be a taxi. As shown in Figure 18.18, two back-seat passengers can be covered in overs and close-ups that are identical to the ones used for the occupants of the front seats. If one of the passengers interacts with or looks at the driver, that passenger should be seated so that any of the camera positions shown in Figure 18.16 can be used. A close-up of the driver shot through the windshield or from the side is often used even if the driver has no dialogue.

Four Characters in a Car

The coverage of four occupants of a car is easiest if one of the passengers has no dialogue or important reactions. If all occupants must be covered, the coverage can be the same as for three occupants, with the addition of a clean single shot of the fourth passenger, who should have a split eyeline.

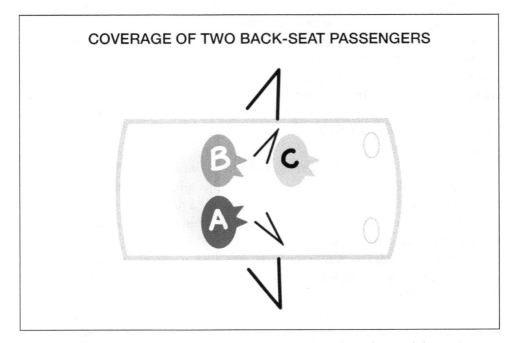

Figure 18.18 Two back-seat passengers can be covered using raking shots and close-ups.

19

Blocking for Cinematic Storytelling

The process of blocking, in which the movements of actors in relation to camera positions, lens choices and movement is worked out to best support the drama of a scene, is perhaps the most important part of directing. Blocking can be thought of as the choreography of the actors and the camera. The action of actors on the set does not always have to be perfectly natural to be effective and to seem natural to viewers. Actors are blocked to favor the camera, just as stage actors are directed to favor the view of their audience. But because the camera can be moved to any position, blocking in film is more flexible than in theater. Although every scene and every location is unique, there are certain techniques that can be applied to enhance the drama visually in most kinds of scenes. This chapter describes some useful ideas for approaching the blocking of scenes and for cinematic storytelling.

An Overall Plan for the Scene

There are usually many ways to block and shoot a scene. As much of the blocking as possible should be developed during preproduction. This not only helps the filmmaker, but it helps virtually every other department and thus saves time during the production phase. Actors often have ideas about where their characters should move during a scene. While some of the cast's ideas will be helpful, their suggestions focus mainly on character and not shot design, cuts, and transitions.

Some scenes provide fairly limited opportunities for blocking because the characters are constrained by the set. Examples are scenes in elevators, at tables, and in cars. On the other hand, blocking can become very complicated on a large set when there is action that involves several characters or vehicles and many possibilities for the staging.

A storytelling plan to stage a scene's action has to be developed by brainstorming and experimenting. It's natural that during this process many ideas will be considered. Some are kept, while others are modified or rejected. Every filmmaker learns how to block through practice and by watching the films of other directors. Speed comes with experience.

It's always important to think about how each shot expresses its story beat graphically. Using the graphic design of an image to emphasize the drama of a story beat is akin to the dramatic emphasis that a good layout gives to a comic book panel. But shots can be much more powerful than comic book panels because the movement of the characters and the camera can create major changes in a shot's design

The Art of Cinematic Storytelling. Kelly Gordon Brine, Oxford University Press (2020). © Oxford University Press.
DOI: 10.1093/oso/9780190054328.001.0001.

from beginning to end. This can be used to change the dramatic emphasis during a single shot.

Choosing Locations

When scouting for locations there are practical considerations such as availability, cost, travel time, parking, and noise levels. From the perspective of storytelling the location has to have the elements the script requires, although sometimes the script can be modified to suit what's available. Often a location can be used in a story in a way that does not reflect its actual use by being redressed to appear on film as something different.

Film has the strange power of being able to take locations that are far apart in the real world and bring them together to look like they are connected. For instance, a character can enter a building on film and then be seen continuing to walk inside the building. In fact the exterior and interior may be situated in different locations that are far apart. Another example is that two characters in the same scene can have their reverse angles recorded in two separate locations. On film it can seem like the castle wall behind one character faces the forest behind the other, when in reality these environments are not in the same location.

Scenes can be shot in rooms, staircases, and hallways that will seem spatially connected on film in ways that are quite different from a building's actual layout. For instance, two rooms could seem to be on different floors but in reality they are on the same floor. Sometimes it is helpful for a single set to be redecorated to appear to be a different set. For example, a character may seem to walk from one hallway to another, but it is actually the first hallway again. This fact is hidden by redressing and relighting the set to appear dissimilar enough to convince viewers.

Improving the Background

The background of a shot is always an important consideration. A background has to support the story, be visually interesting, and appear consistent with the backgrounds visible in other shots in the same scene. It's often better to play a scene against a background with depth than against something close by, such as a wall. When one side of the line of action has a better background, this normally means that the camera is placed on the opposite side of the axis so it will see this background. If the angle in one direction is good but the reverse angle doesn't have a good background, it is sometimes possible to cheat the positions of the characters and the camera to improve the background of the reverse angle. Viewers don't notice these cheats, but they do notice backgrounds that are unattractive, distracting, or so different from each other that they seem to be in a different setting. Figure 19.1 illustrates changing the camera angles to cheat the background.

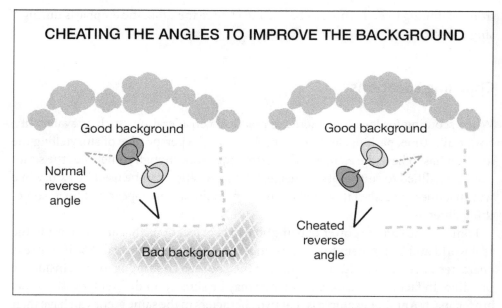

Figure 19.1 Sometimes the background of a reverse angle is unattractive or seems to be in a different setting from the first angle. The positions of the actors and the camera can be cheated to improve the background.

Shot Sizes throughout a Scene

The blocking should always be designed with a view to which character's scene it is. The camera will often move with that character, show that character more often in closer shots than other characters are shown, and show the action in the scene more often from that character's POV.

There is often a pattern of characters moving physically closer to each other as the drama of a scene increases. The characters may have a friendly or an antagonistic relationship and still move closer to each other as the drama of a scene develops. The actors can be directed to move apart again at an appropriate point, only to move closer once again as the scene progresses.

It's generally true that the visual pattern of a scene is to start with wide shots and gradually change to closer ones until the scene reaches its climax (Figure 19.2). Wider objective shots establish the setting and the geography, while closer ones convey a character's subjective experience.

The wide-to-close approach to scene design is a good starting point, although it would be too repetitive if every scene followed the same pattern. In practice some scenes are made more effective by starting with a close shot, by cutting wide again in the middle, or by ending with a wide shot that shows that we are leaving a character in a new environment or facing a problem. It's helpful to approach a new scene with the general idea of starting wide, but to consider if starting it with a close-up could be more effective.

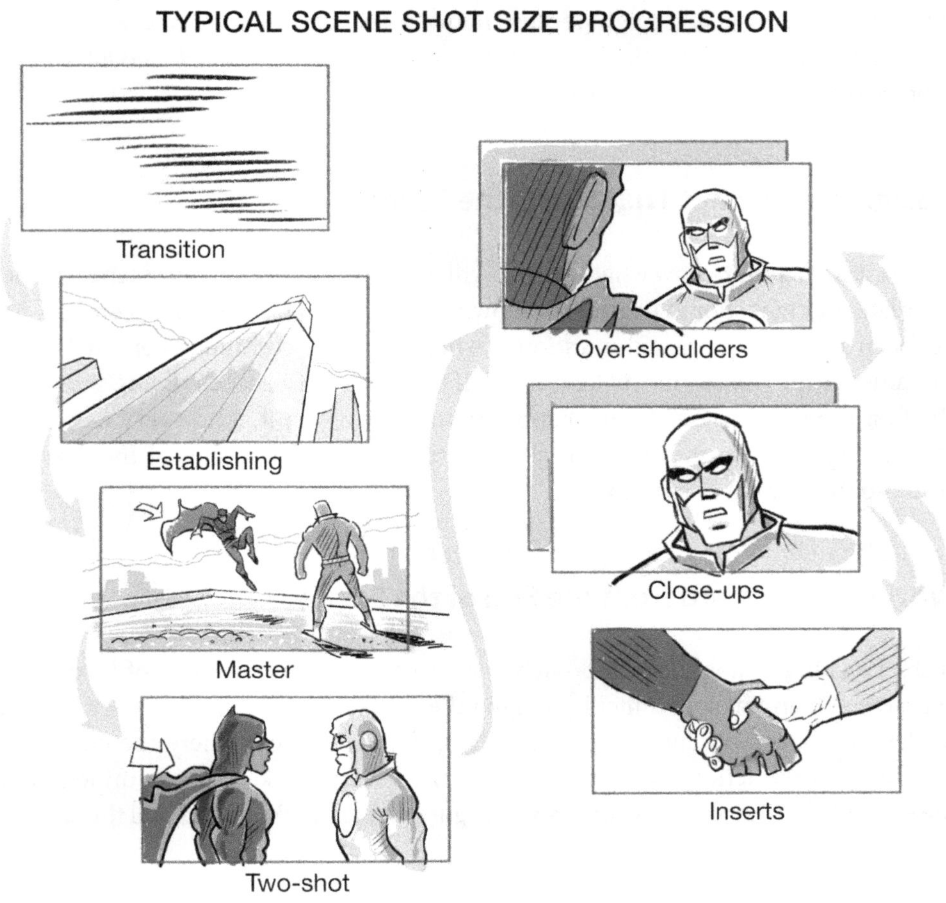

TYPICAL SCENE SHOT SIZE PROGRESSION

Transition

Establishing

Master

Two-shot

Over-shoulders

Close-ups

Inserts

Figure 19.2 Scenes often begin with wider shots that establish the setting and the spatial relationships of the geography. As a scene progresses the shots become closer and more subjective.

Simplifying the Shooting and Editing

Long and involved scenes are a challenge to block, but often a complicated scene can be looked at as several smaller parts that can be blocked separately. The geography of these pieces may have to be consistent with the others if they are connected through the movement of characters or through their looks and POVs. For instance, if a shootout is taking place, and in the scene three groups of police are positioned in three places, the dialogue within each of these groups could be thought of as individual scenes. But for consistent screen geography, these officers should all be facing the same direction toward their enemies.

It's generally safer and faster if a scene is covered in several shots and not just one complex long take. These shots will be shorter and simpler, and they can be cut together in various ways. If a long take is used to shoot a scene or a complicated sequence within a scene, it might require many takes before a good one is shot. If it's discovered in editing that the long take is not working, there may be no alternative footage that can be used in its place.

Designing the Shot That Starts the Scene

A filmmaker should know what the shot will be that ends the previous scene in order to create the right shot to begin the following scene, even if the earlier scene has not yet been shot. An important question is whether time is continuous or whether an in-camera time transition will be needed. If the setting of a scene is being shown for the first time, it may need one or more shots to establish it. And every new scene should begin with a shot that has shot contrast with the last shot of the previous scene so that the cut is smooth.

Working Backward from the End of the Scene

If the blocking of a scene is approached in story order, there's a risk of boxing the characters in and having difficulty staging the final action and finding good camera angles for it. A good approach for avoiding this is to know where the characters should be for the action that comes later in the scene, and to keep this in mind so that the earlier blocking works toward this configuration of the characters and the camera.

Some Classic Blocking

Many blocking and shooting techniques are used frequently because they are effective for storytelling, and several useful ones are described here.

Blocking for the Camera

Blocking for the camera is the staging of the action and the positioning of the camera so that the camera is favored. This includes such actions as a character turning to look closer to the camera in reaction to something that has happened off-screen, a character who turns doing so with face to the camera rather than away from it, and a character who walks somewhere to get something moving toward the camera rather than away from it. For example, if a character hears a phone ringing and walks to answer it, it's usually better to have the camera positioned behind the phone so that the character walks closer to the camera to answer it. Now the character's reaction to the call will be seen in a close-up.

Shooting Down the Tube

Many directors like to shoot "down the tube" when they can make a scene work this way. The tube is what the camera sees from a given position. Shooting down the tube is staging the actors' action and positioning the camera so that movement is reduced between the left and the right and takes place in depth instead, along the camera's line of sight. Characters can move both toward the camera and away from it. This reduces the number of shots needed and produces a more immersive cinematic effect because of the perspective changes that occur as characters move in depth. Shooting down the tube also reduces the camera's need to pan with moving characters. Figure 19.3 illustrates shooting down the tube.

Rack-Focusing to Another Character or Object

When shooting down the tube, the focus can be changed from one character or object to another to redirect viewers' attention (Figure 19.4). This changes the center of interest and allows multiple beats to be shown in a single shot. A second rack

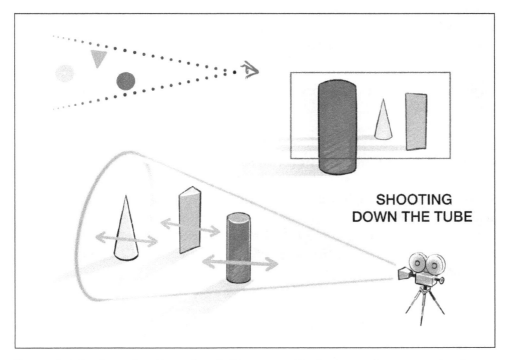

Figure 19.3 Staging action "down the tube" means positioning two or three actors at various depths in one shot and having them walk closer or farther from the camera for their dialogue and action.

Figure 19.4 A rack focus to a character or an object at a different depth draws the audience's attention to what is important for the next beat. It avoids a cut and is very cinematic.

focus that returns focus to the first character or even goes to a third character is also sometimes done.

A Handoff from One Character to Another

A handoff occurs when the camera pans with a moving character to a second character who is stationary, and the camera now holds on that character as the first character exits the shot (Figure 19.5). Handoffs are cinematic and tie the characters together in the same space. They a line of dialogue, an exit and a reaction to be artfully combined in a single shot.

Cross and Walk into Close-Up

Suppose two characters are talking to each other as they stand facing each other at different distances from the camera. The closer character's back is to the camera, while the more distant character is facing the camera. At an appropriate dramatic

A HANDOFF

Pan right and pull →

Figure 19.5 A handoff occurs when the camera pans with a walking character and discovers a second character. The camera now holds on the second character and lets the first character exit. The second character often watches the first character leave.

moment the more distant character walks toward the camera, crosses the closer character, and now stops near the camera in a close-up (Figure 19.6). The stationary character who was passed has turned to watch the walking character move close to the camera. The character who walked up into close-up now delivers an important line that is made more dramatic by being in a close-up. Note that the camera is adjusted by pulling back a little and panning slightly to keep the shot attractively composed.

This blocking puts the emphasis on the character who comes forward, while the stationary character reacts in the background. If it suits the script, the line of dialogue from the character who walked up can be followed by a rack focus to the more distant character. If the closer character has another line to deliver, then the rack focus can return to that character, or this character could start to turn. A new reverse-angle shot would be used to complete the turn, and this new shot could be either the stationary character's clean POV or an over-shoulder onto the character who just turned.

Countering

A countering move is one in which the camera travels in the direction opposite to that of a moving character, but keeps that character in frame by panning. It is similar

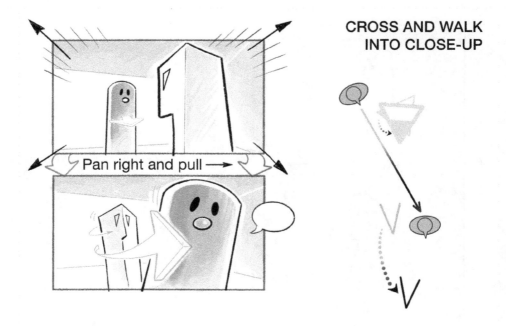

Figure 19.6 In an over-shoulder shot the more distant character can come forward and cross the stationary character to deliver a dramatic line in close-up. The stationary character has turned to watch the moving character.

to two adversaries circling each other. If the movement of a character and the camera seems to rotate about an unmoving character, the countering move is said to *hinge* on that character.

One example of countering is shown in Figure 19.7. Here two characters are talking to each other in over-shoulder shots, and at an appropriate dramatic moment in the dialogue one character walks to stand beside but at a right angle to the one who remains stationary. During this short walk, the camera keeps the walking character in the frame by simultaneously moving forward and panning with the walking character. This camera move hinges on the stationary character. The character who has remained stationary continues facing forward and the new camera position sees this character in profile, while the other character stands face-to-camera behind. This type of countering move is often used when a character is being interrogated, but it can be done for other reasons, such as changing the background during a conversation. The camera movement is similar to that of a wrap, and the camera's path can be either a straight line or an arc.

Counter, Then Lead

A fast-paced transition to a walk-and-talk scene begins with the camera quickly countering an extra who is walking toward two approaching characters, whose off-screen dialogue we already hear. Starting on the extra makes the office or other

Figure 19.7 When the camera counters a character it moves in the opposite direction to that character but pans with the character to keep the character within the frame

environment seem busy and makes the conversation we are hearing seem more urgent. The characters come into view and the extra disappears behind them. The instant the camera lands on these approaching characters, it begins to pull backward and the shot becomes a Steadicam walk-and-talk (Figure 19.8).

Stepping into a Shot

If a character is in a profile close-up looking at something off-camera, a second character can step into the shot in profile closer to the camera (Figure 19.9). This is surprising, and it emphasizes the importance of what the characters are looking at. Often the second character delivers a line after stepping in. They could be watching anything, but this blocking is often used when two characters are doing surveillance through a window. As a general rule, if one character is already in a shot, an entrance that is between the camera and that character is more dramatic than one in which the entrance is more distant. The second character may also cross the first.

Adding a Cinematic Tie-Up to an Exit

Two characters who are shown in conversation only in clean shots can be united at the end of their conversation. The departing character exits his clean shot, and the

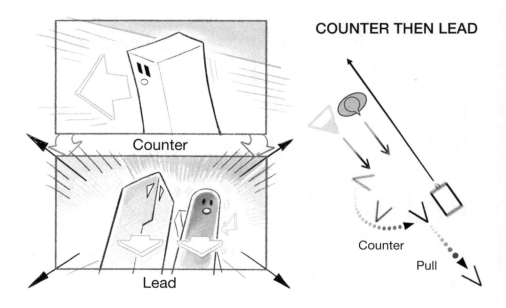

Figure 19.8 An exciting transition to a walk-and-talk scene begins as the camera counters an extra who is headed toward two approaching characters, whose dialogue we already hear. As the pan brings these characters into view, the extra disappears behind them, and the camera immediately leads the newly-discovered characters in a walk-and-talk.

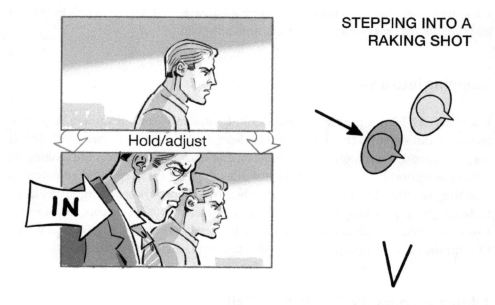

Figure 19.9 The short-sided raking shot of a character can be designed to leave room for another character to step into the shot in profile closer to the camera. The second character's sudden entrance is dramatic and more cinematic than a deeper entrance.

Figure 19.10 Two characters who are not seen in the same shot can be tied together at the moment one of them exits. The character who leaves crosses through the foreground of what was a clean shot of the remaining character, turning it into a tie-up shot.

clean shot of the remaining character is wiped by the departing character (Figure 19.10). Although it comes late in the scene, this technique serves to tie up the two characters in the same space. It unites the characters dramatically, as well as adding motion to the otherwise static shot of the remaining character.

Combined Choreography: Reveal—Pull—Wrap—Follow

Often several blocking techniques can be combined into one shot. Imagine the simple action of a woman entering a room, approaching a second woman, and talking with her. This scene could be shot in many ways, and Figure 19.11 illustrates one cinematic approach. It starts with a dolly-reveal transition that

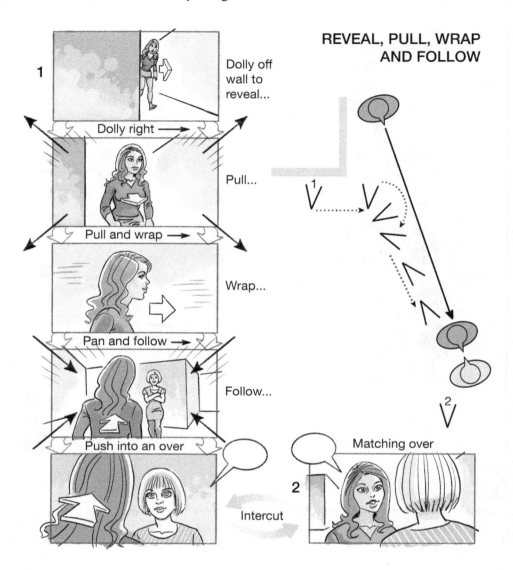

Figure 19.11 The entrance of a character can be dramatized cinematically through creative blocking and the combination of several techniques in one shot. Here the camera does a reveal, and then it leads, wraps, and follows a character until she stops in an over-shoulder as her dialogue begins.

finds the first woman. This reveal signals the start of a new scene, provides a time transition, and ensures shot contrast with the last shot of the previous scene. As soon as the camera finds the woman, it begins to lead her, but then it does a quick wrap that brings the second woman into view as the camera now follows the first woman.

The combination of a pull, a wrap, and a shot that follows the woman creates more excitement and a faster pace than would be achieved by the woman entering through a door. The pan also establishes the room. The shot ends as an over-shoulder, and a matching over-shoulder allows us to see the face of the first woman once again. This cinematic blocking of one character's entrance shows what a difference interesting blocking can make.

Examples of Storytelling Approaches

In this set of simple examples what is essentially the same story is told using a variety of approaches to visual storytelling. The differences are a result of the directorial choices made in the blocking, shooting, and editing of the same action.

In television shows that involve police investigations, it's not uncommon for a detective to receive an urgent phone call late at night informing her of the discovery of a new murder victim whose death must be investigated. The detective heads to the crime scene at the end of one scene and arrives at the beginning of the following scene.

Ten potential approaches to telling this story are described here, and each approach might suit a particular script, although the director has considerable latitude much of the time. These ideas show the great variety in possible ways to tell a story visually. Any director who is brainstorming how to shoot a detective's arrival at a crime scene would likely consider some of these possibilities.

Show the Detective's Journey to the Crime Scene

Here are the shots and cuts for this sequence:

1. A close-up of the detective asleep in bed. Her phone rings and she answers it. She reacts to the news, gets out of bed, and exits close to the camera. She could optionally be seen putting her coat on and heading out the door.
2. A low-angle shot in the detective's driveway as she leaves in her car. The car exits close to the camera.
3. A moving POV shot through the windshield. This shot pans left to find the detective in profile as she drives.
4. A drive-by shot in which the detective's car exits.
5. A shot from the back seat of the car, including a piece of the detective's head and shoulder. Through the windshield we can see emergency vehicles, police, and onlookers as the detective drives closer and stops.
6. The detective gets out of her car.
7. A cowboy shot of the victim lying on the ground; tilt up to reveal the detective approaching and stopping to look. Other police officers are beside her.

This approach emphasizes the detective's drive to the scene. This gives more of a feeling of the time and distance involved, and may highlight the type of neighborhood because we see her POV out the windshield in two of the shots.

The Detective Quickly Drives Up to the Crime Scene

Here are the shots and cuts for this sequence:

1. A close-up of the detective asleep in bed. Her phone rings and she answers it. She gets out of bed and exits close to the camera.
2. The detective's car drives toward the camera in an alley and stops. She gets out and exits.
3. Tilt up from victim to the detective approaching and stopping to look. Other police officers are accompanying her.

The detective arrives at the crime scene so quickly that this almost seems like a jump cut. A greater sense of time and distance could be created by using a transition. Two examples are panning with some police officers or forensics specialists to an angle where the detective's car can be seen arriving, or using a wipe to reveal her arrival.

Jump Cut to the Detective Driving, Then Arriving at Crime Scene

Here are the shots and cuts for this sequence:

1. A close-up of the detective asleep in bed. Her phone rings and she answers it. She does not exit this shot.
2. Jump cut to her driving as seen through the windshield in a close-up.
3. Tilt up from victim to the detective stopping to look at the victim and then have dialogue with the officers beside her.

The jump cut to the detective driving conveys urgency. The tilt up from the victim establishes where we are, provides a time transition, and shows the detective's arrival.

Jump Cut to the Detective Already at the Crime Scene

Here are the shots and cuts for this sequence:

1. A close-up of the detective asleep in bed. Her phone rings and she answers it. She gets out of bed and exits close to the camera.

2. Start with a wipe that reveals the detective. We lead her as she walks toward the victim.
3. The detective's POV of the victim as she steps into the shot.
4. Reverse-angle three-shot of the detective with an officer at each shoulder.

This storytelling is very fast paced and urgent, with only a wipe as a time transition Perhaps this is the latest of several murders and things are spinning out of control. There is no establishing shot, but we discover the setting with the detective.

We see the detective exit, indicating she's headed somewhere. Starting the next shot on the victim and tilting up to find the detective provides a transition that signals both the start of a new scene and that some time has passed. The pace may be too fast.

Pull Straight Up from the Victim

Here are the shots and cuts for this sequence:

1. A close-up of the detective asleep in bed. Her phone rings and she answers it. She gets out of bed and exits close to the camera.
2. Start with the camera looking straight down at the victim, who is framed in half shot and possibly angled diagonally with the head low in the frame. Pull straight up, rotating slowly. The shot grows wide enough to include the small circle of detectives surrounding the victim.
3. A close-up of the detective looking down at the victim.

The pull-up shot emphasizes the tragedy of this murder, and perhaps some specific information about the type of victim and the method used by the killer. There may be a mystical feeling of the victim's spirit rising. It may seem that the detectives will have difficulty solving this case.

Tilt Down from a Known Building

Here are the shots for this sequence:

1. A close-up of the detective asleep in bed. Her phone rings and she answers it. She gets out of bed and exits close to the camera.
2. Tilt down from a building that identifies this setting to a wide establishing shot of the crime scene with activity.
3. A raking shot of the detective and her colleagues.

The tilt provides a time transition, and if the building is recognized by viewers from a previous scene, it can suggest who the victim or murderer is, or indicate a pattern to the murders.

Discover the Crime Scene with This Detective

Here are the shots and cuts for this sequence:

1. A close-up of the detective asleep in bed. Her phone rings and she answers it. She gets out of bed and exits close to the camera.
2. The camera follows the detective's back as she walks from her car toward the site of the crime and stops. Push past her to the victim, or she turns into profile as she turns to talk to a colleague for an update.

Following the detective to the scene of the crime makes viewers experience events subjectively. An intermediate shot of the detective driving could improve the pacing of the storytelling.

Come Off a Wall or Other Object to Find the Detective

Here are the shots and cuts for this sequence:

1. A close-up of the detective asleep in bed. Her phone rings and she answers it. She gets out of bed and exits close to the camera.
2. We track the detective's walk as we see her through police car windows. She emerges and several officers join her as she continues toward the crime scene. Emergency personnel cross the shot.
3. The detective stops in a cowboy shot and looks down. On her look we tilt down to the victim that the detective now sees.

Starting on emergency vehicles helps to describe the crime scene, and the flashing lights dramatize the detective's arrival. The dolly reveal provides a transition.

Show Community Interest in This Crime

Here are the shots and cuts for this sequence:

1. A close-up of the detective asleep in bed. Her phone rings and she answers it. She gets out of bed and exits close to the camera.
2. We pan across the crowd of onlookers and stop at the point where the detective pushes through the crowd and ducks under the police tape. She stops and looks.
3. An over-shoulder shot or the detective's clean POV of the victim on the ground.

Panning the crowd of onlookers provides a transition at the same time as it emphasizes the community's reaction to this crime.

Tie the Detective and the Victim Together

Here are the shots and cuts for this sequence:

1. A close-up of the detective asleep in bed. Her phone rings and she answers it. She gets out of bed and exits close to the camera.
2. A close-up on the profile of the victim. Rack-focus to the detective arriving in the middle ground.
3. The detective's POV of the victim on the ground.
4. Close-up reaction shot of detective, or a raking shot with colleague beside her.

This sequence might be chosen if the detective knows the victim, or if there is something relevant about the type of victim. By starting shot 2 with the profile of the victim and rack-focusing to the detective, a time transition is created.

These ten examples illustrate that even for relatively simple and straightforward action, many creative possibilities can be imagined for the design of shots, cuts and transitions. And even once a sequence has been blocked and shot and no more action or angles can be added, the visual storytelling can still be refined and enhanced very creatively during editing. The best takes must be assessed, the exact ordering of the beats is determined, shots are trimmed and intercut, transitions are chosen, and the pacing is fine-tuned to maximize the storytelling power of the available footage.

Glossary of Filmmaking Terms

action line See *axis*.

animatic A prototype version of a video sequence in a movie or a game, originally produced by shooting successive frames of a storyboard and adding a soundtrack, but now often created using 2D and 3D computer animation and visual effects.

animation The illusion of motion that is created when successive still images with slight differences are shown in sequence. An object can be animated unintentionally in a live action film if a cut is made between shots with significant similarities in size, position, color, or pattern.

anticipatory framing The technique of beginning to move or stopping the camera to accommodate changes in the subject's position an instant before the movement starts or ends. One example is to begin a pan the instant before a character starts to walk.

arc See *wrap*.

arm An articulated structure that the camera can be mounted on so it can be positioned out some distance from the tripod or dolly, as well as higher or lower than its usual position. The arm can swing or extend smoothly while recording.

aspect ratio The relative size of the height and width of the part of the camera's image that will be seen on the screen. The camera will either capture more than this or crop the image immediately to save storage. If the image is not cropped immediately, then the option of recomposing a shot during editing is available.

axis Any imaginary line used for spatial reference. It can be the line of sight of the camera, the imaginary line between two characters who are looking at each other, the line between a character and what that character sees, or the direction in which something is moving. *Line* and *axis* can be used interchangeably.

background What is farthest away in an image.

background actor An actor with a nonspeaking role; also called an *extra*.

backlighting Creating an attractive band of light along the contour of persons or objects by illuminating from behind. This separates the subject from the background and highlights it.

backstory A history of fictional events that took place prior to the start of the current narrative. Backstory is created for characters to explain their actions and to add depth and believability to a story. It can be revealed through dialogue, flashbacks, photos, or props.

beat See *story beat*.

beta effect An unintended secondary illusion of motion on the screen due to a cut between images with visual similarities.

blocking Working out the details of the movements of actors and vehicles in relation to camera positions in order to design shots, not unlike choreographing a dance. Key considerations are storytelling, composition, continuity editing, and efficient shooting. Also called *staging*.

block shooting Often two episodes of a television series have scenes in some of the same settings. If the same director is shooting both episodes, then for efficiency all scenes that take place on one set can be grouped and shot at one time.

boom The horizontal pole or lattice structure that the camera can be mounted on the end of to record high and arcing shots, as well as to be able to move over furniture, water, or a crowd. It is attached to a tripod, a dolly, or a crane. Also called a *jib* or a *jib arm*.

bridging shot (1) A shot of movement in a neutral direction that facilitates a screen direction change. (2) A cutaway shot that suggests time passage between scenes. (3) A cutaway that is used to change to a new angle on a scene that creates new screen geometry.

camera move Sometimes used to mean any adjustment to the camera beyond a slight reframing to maintain an attractive composition. True movement of the camera is translation or travel in space, which means movement up, down, left, right, forward, or backward. Pans and tilts are not translations but are rotations of a stationary camera.

canted angle A shot taken with the camera tipped sideways so that the horizon is not level and the image seems off balance. Also called a *Dutch angle*.

center of interest The element of an image that is most important to the story that is being told. Viewers' eyes should be drawn to this area. Also called the *focal point* in the nontechnical sense of being what an observer is looking at.

character A person in a story. Any animal, vehicle, robot or object that is portrayed as having a mind can also be considered a character.

cheat (1) Any adjustment to the placement of actors, objects, or the camera to improve the composition without spoiling continuity or drawing the attention of viewers. (2) Two separate sets can be made to seem connected even though they are far apart through the use of doorways, POVs, and cuts.

choreography The art of designing combinations of movements of the human figure to form dances. In film the blocking of the action of actors and the positioning and movement of the camera resembles choreography.

cinematic The characteristic visual storytelling of film, especially when at its best by being three-dimensional, immersive, realistic, attractive, exciting, and fluid. Careful choreography of the actors and the camera make shots more cinematic, as do good cuts and transitions.

cinematographer The head of the camera and lighting crews. The cinematographer creates the lighting and oversees the creative and technical aspects of the camerawork to shoot scenes in accordance with the director's intentions.

circular dolly See *wrap*.

clean entrance A clean entrance begins with no part of what will be the subject yet visible, and then a person, a hand, or other object enters.

clean exit The subject leaves the shot completely before the shot ends.

clean shot A clean shot does not include any foreground piece of another character or what the character is looking at. A clean POV does not include the observer's head or shoulder. The opposite of a dirty shot.

clean single A close shot of a character that does not include a foreground piece of the person the character is talking to or the object near the camera that the character is looking at.

close-up (CU) A shot that tightly frames a character's upper body or an object for emphasis. A close-up of a person includes the head and some part of the shoulders and chest. The frame's lower edge crops the subject at either the level of the collar-tips or at the base of the chest. If the shot includes the chest, this framing is often called *medium close-up*. Extreme close-ups of objects are sometimes called *macro shots*.

composite shot A shot that is a combination of several elements, often including live action shot against a green screen; a visual effects layer of computer-generated creatures, vehicles, explosions, or magical effects; and a background. Also called a *composited* shot.

composition Creating a pleasing arrangement of elements in the camera's field of view to tell a story with the right meaning, emphasis, and mood.

compressing time Using cuts and transitions to shorten the screen time needed to tell the story of a character's actions that would in reality take place over a longer period of time.

constant object size The size of an image as viewed through a lens will remain constant as the focal length increases if the distance from the lens to the object increases by the same factor. A 50mm lens focused on an object at a distance of 10 feet produces an image that appears the same size as one produced by a 100mm lens focused on the object at 20 feet. But the other objects in the image that are situated at different distances will change in size.

continuity editing The technique of combining shots into sequences that tell a story with consistency and logic. Shots are designed and cuts are made in ways that maintain the narrative flow without abrupt jumps. This creates a logical coherence that smooths the discontinuities in time and space between shots and scenes. The techniques of continuity editing are known as *film grammar.*

continuity of screen motion The technique of maintaining logical consistency to the direction of movement of people, vehicles, and objects as seen on the screen.

countering A camera move in which the camera travels a straight line or arc in the direction opposite that of a moving character, but keeps that character in frame by panning.

coverage All of the shots of various sizes, from different camera angles, with and without camera movement, that are used to record the action of a scene.

cowboy shot A standing character framed from head to mid-thigh. If the person were a cowboy the shot would show the holsters.

crane shot The camera is raised or lowered, usually in an arcing movement, while fastened to the end of the crane's boom or jib. The camera can also be controlled remotely to pan and tilt.

cropping To compose a shot in such a way that part of a person or object is not visible because the frame cuts off the person or object.

cross (1) Something traverses the frame. (2) A character travels between the camera and a more distant character. (3) The camera moves in such a way that the character's eyeline changes from looking camera left to looking right, or vice versa.

cross cutting An editing technique that establishes simultaneous or parallel action. Cuts are made back and forth between action taking place in two or more settings that seems simultaneous.

crossing the axis Shooting a camera angle that reverses the screen geography of people and objects as established in a master shot.

cut Any point in a film where the shot currently playing is replaced by a different shot.

cutaway A brief cut from the main action to something else. Common uses of cutaways are to show reactions, to re-establish a setting, to create a sense of urgency, or to reinforce a mood. A cutaway can also provide information that's relevant to the story, serve as a bridge to a new camera angle, or suggest the passage of time.

cut in See *insert.*

cutting on action (1) Using an action such as lifting a glass that begins in one shot and is completed in the next to bridge two shots and hide the cut. (2) Using an action such as an exit or a gun being fired to create a diversion that makes the cut that follows less noticeable.

cutting point A suitable point within a shot to cut to another shot. Cutting points are created by action or sound. Wipes, exits, head turns, almost any type of action, and loud noises all provide good cutting points.

dead reverse A camera angle that is at 180 degrees to the previous shot.

deep Farther from the camera. A character who walks deep is moving away from the camera.

deep focus Great depth of field that makes objects appear sharp at a wide range of depths.

depth of field The distance between the nearest and the furthest objects that are in reasonably sharp focus when viewed through a lens. Smaller aperture sizes create greater depth of field. Wide lenses make more of an image appear sharp.

dirty shot A shot of a person or object that includes in the foreground a piece of someone or something. The opposite of a clean shot.

dissolve An editing-room transition between two shots that briefly blends them by smoothly fading the first one out while fading the second one in.

dolly shot Moving the camera forward, backward, or sideways on wheels.

do-si-do A dance figure in which two partners pass each other back to back. In film this term can be used to describe a walking character crossing a standing character, stopping, and then turning to look back at the standing character by rotating her head 180 degrees in such a way that her face is always visible to the camera.

down the tube Blocking action so that it is directed more toward and away from the camera rather than left and right across it. This reduces the need for additional shots and cuts, and can be used to create visually interesting and dramatic shots through perspective changes, crosses, and rack-focusing.

dramatic beat See *story beat*.

drive-by shot A shot from the shoulder of a road as a vehicle approaches and passes the camera. Also called a *pass-by shot*. Optionally the camera pans with the vehicle.

Dutch angle See *canted angle*.

editing Selecting, cutting, trimming, and assembling the footage of a film into a sequence that artfully and coherently tells a story, as well as adding the additional layers of visual effects, dialogue, sound effects, and music, etc.

entrance A character, vehicle, or object comes into a shot. The entrance may be the subject coming through a door or around a corner, stepping into frame, falling in, standing up, emerging from water, stepping out of fog, or any other type of movement by the character but not by the camera.

establishing shot A shot at the beginning of or early in a scene that shows viewers the setting that the current scene takes place in.

exit A character or vehicle leaves a shot. An exit occurs when the subject walks out a door, goes around a corner, steps out of frame, or by any other means, but the exit must be due to the subject's movement and not the camera's movement. The term *clearing frame* is also used.

extra An actor with a nonspeaking role; also called a *background actor*.

extreme close-up A very close shot. An extreme close-up of a face crops it from the middle of the forehead to below the lower lip.

eyeline The imaginary line from one character to another, or from a character to the object the character is looking at.

eyeline match When two characters are looking at each other, they are framed to be looking in opposite directions in their respective shots. Viewers understand this to mean that they are looking at each other. Also called *opposed looks*.

fade A fade in starts as a black or a white screen, and the image of the first shot gradually appears until it has fully replaced the black or white. A fade out is the opposite of this, as the image of a shot gradually disappears as it is replaced by black or white.

falloff The reduction in the intensity of a light source's illumination as the distance from the light source increases. The intensity dims at the rate of one over the square of the distance. For example, doubling the distance reduces the intensity to one quarter. Sunlight has no visible falloff because the sun is so far away that the falloff is too small to be measured.

false POV A shot that seems to be a character's POV but is not truly from the character's angle. For storytelling it serves the purpose of a POV.

favor the camera Actors sometimes perform an action such as walking or turning in a way that shows more to the camera, much as theater actors favor the view of the audience when performing on the stage.

field of view What is visible through a camera's lens. A wide lens has a greater field of view than a long lens both horizontally and vertically.

fifty-fifty shot A shot that is composed so that two people facing each other nose to nose are posed symmetrically by being centered and at the same distance from the camera.

film grammar The techniques for designing shots and cuts to tell a story in a way that maintains clarity of time, space, and motion in order to achieve continuity editing's goal of a logical and coherent narrative.

flashback A cut to an earlier time in a story.

flipping screen geography Moving the camera to the far side of the line of action and creating shots that reverse what appears on the left and right of the screen.

focal plane The plane that contains the focal point is at a right angle to the camera's line of sight.

focal point The point along a camera's line of sight that is in sharpest focus. This term is also used loosely to mean the center of interest or anything in an image that captures a viewer's attention.

forced perspective Exaggerating or reducing the effect of perspective by using wide-angle or long lenses to make objects and distances appear larger or smaller than they would to the human eye.

foreground What is closest to the viewer in an image.

foreshadowing Giving signs that hint at character traits and attitudes, as well as future conflict and events, both good and bad. Foreshadowing plants seeds that will later be harvested. It creates suspense and makes later events seem more plausible.

fourth wall The convention on stage and in film is that actors act as though they are unaware of the audience and the camera, being separated from them by an invisible fourth wall. When an actor looks into the camera lens and addresses the audience, this violates the verisimilitude of the storytelling and makes it more difficult for viewers to suspend their disbelief. Doing so is called breaking the fourth wall.

frame A rectangular shape visible within a camera's viewfinder that delineates what the edges of the images in the finished film will be. Professional video cameras display this frame within a larger image that extends beyond its edges. This additional area may be recorded if desired to provide the option of reframing shots during editing.

framing The view that the camera has of its subject when it is cropped by the frame of the chosen aspect ratio. How a shot is composed is mainly determined by the way the camera is positioned, including its height and degree of tilt, and the length of its lens.

frame within a frame The compositional technique of using a window, doorway, arch, or other shape to create a frame that partly or completely surrounds the subject within a composition.

French over An over-shoulder shot taken from a camera position behind two actors who are either standing or seated shoulder to shoulder, such as when they are in a car or sitting on a bench. Also called a *negative over*.

full shot (FS) A shot that includes a character from head to toe without cropping, but which uses most of the height of the frame so that there is not a large gap above the head or below the feet.

geography The three-dimensional reality of objects and their spatial relationships in any setting. See also *screen geography*.

green screen The use of a single shade of green as a backdrop when filming. During editing the green areas are eliminated to allow the shot to be combined with a live-action or computer-generated shot.

half shot A shot that crops a single character just below the belt. The terms *medium shot* and *belt shot* are also used.

handheld shot A shaky shot produced by a camera that is held by the operator and does not have an image stabilization system.

handoff reveal The camera pans with one character to a second character, and the camera holds on the second character as the first character exits.

hard cut A standard cut from one image to another. The term is usually used in reference to how a new scene begins. A hard cut is not jarring within a scene, but when used to begin a scene, its lack of a transition can make it abrupt. Within one scene most cuts are hard cuts.

head to toe See *full shot*.

headroom The space between the top of a character's head and the top edge of the frame.

high-angle shot A shot in which the camera is angled downward. Also called a *down shot*.

insert A cut to a closer shot of something that is also visible in the master shot. Its purpose is to highlight it or to provide more detail. Examples are text on a mobile phone, a sign on a door, or a hand reaching into a pocket.

intercutting Cutting to a different shot or scene and then back to the current shot or scene. Intercutting is done frequently during dialogue and between scenes with parallel action. Also called *cross cutting*.

invisible cut Dissolving from a plain image at the end of one moving shot to a similar plain image at the beginning of a second moving shot to make it seem as though they form one continuous shot. The camera is thereby made to seem to move continuously past a dark foreground object or through a cloud of smoke or fog.

J-cut The audio from the scene that follows can begin before the current scene has ended, creating an audio transition to the next scene. It is also called an *audio lead* or an *audio advance*.

jib See *boom*.

jump cut A cut from a character or other subject to the same subject at a point ahead in time and often in a different setting. Jump cuts break continuity editing but quicken the pace of the storytelling.

juxtaposition One image following another in a sequence. Viewers draw inferences from juxtapositions about space, time, and the story being told.

Kuleshov effect A mental phenomenon first demonstrated by Soviet filmmaker Lev Kuleshov, in which viewers derive more meaning from two juxtaposed shots seen in sequence than from single images viewed in isolation.

L-cut The audio at the end of one scene continues playing over the beginning of the next scene, connecting the two scenes.

leading look See *look-space*.

left look A character's eyes are looking (even slightly) toward the left side of the screen. The exact angle formed with the camera's line of sight is unimportant for screen geography.

lighting The careful selection and placement of lights to illuminate the action, establish a mood, create a dramatic effect, and maintain continuity with the quality and look of related shots.

line See *axis*.

line of sight The imaginary line that extends straight out from the center of a lens in the direction in which a camera is pointed.

location A film production term that refers to real places situated away from the studio that are used as settings for scenes. One location may contain several sets, each of which is used for one or more scenes. Locations are modified to suit a story's requirements.

lock-off A camera operator normally makes continuous slight adjustments to maintain a good composition as characters move. A lock-off keeps the camera completely motionless. Locked-off shots can be combined with each other or with visual effects. The other option is to combine shots that have both been recorded using motion control.

long lens A lens that has a focal length greater than 50mm, which is that of the human eye. Long lenses magnify what's seen, they compress space, and they make objects that are approaching the camera seem to make slower progress.

long shot The subject of a long shot is far away and has a height that is less than two-thirds of the height of the frame. A long shot emphasizes the environment over the subject.

long take A shot that lasts much longer than usual, and typically involves elaborate action, blocking, and camera movement. It is made with the intention of being used without being intercut other shots.

look The direction in which a character is looking relative to the left and right of the camera and the screen. Characters are said to have a left or a right look regardless of how great or slight the angle of their look is relative to the camera's line of sight.

look-space A small amount of extra space added to the composition on the side of the image in the direction in which a character is looking. This helps to balance the composition of shots in film, photography, and portrait painting. Also called a *leading look*.

loose shot A wide shot.

low-angle shot A shot in which the camera is angled upward. Also called an *up shot*.

macro shot An extreme close-up of an object.

master shot Most scenes are given wide master shots that cover long sequences of action. Sometimes there are several *mini-masters* that cover parts of the action. The closer shots that the master intercuts with are filmed with the same action, and closer shots usually conform to the screen geography established by the master shot.

match cut A cut from a wide to a closer shot (or from a close shot to a wider shot) of a particular subject. The matching requires having the subject in the same screen position with a similar eyeline. The second shot is at a camera angle that differs by about 30 degrees.

matching shots Shots of two characters talking to each other cut more smoothly if their designs are similar. Pairs of close-ups and over-shoulder shots mirror each other in their framing.

medium shot A shot of a character that is approximately from the waist up. For storytelling a medium shot balances the environment and the character. Also called a *half shot* or a *belt shot*.

medium close-up (MCU) A close shot from the chest to the top of a person's head. Sometimes the top of the head is cropped. This is a subjective shot that is about the character.

middle ground The plane in the middle of a composition, between the foreground and the background.

misdirection Intentionally presenting images that will cause viewers to draw the wrong conclusions about characters, objects, places, or events, thereby setting up a surprise for viewers when the story reveals what actually happened.

mise-en-scène This is an older and more theoretical term for what today's directors call blocking or staging. See *blocking.*

montage A series of shots that tell a story, show that an activity has taken place or is underway, describe a setting, create a mood, or show that time has passed.

motivation (1) The knowledge or emotion that causes a character to do something. (2) The movement of characters or vehicles that prompts the camera to pan or follow them. (3) The emotional reaction of a character that causes the camera to push closer. (4) Anything that causes the camera to pan or tilt to see something, such as a character's look, an off-screen noise, birds flying, or shoes entering the frame.

negative over See *French over.*

neutral screen direction Movement directly toward the camera or directly away from it, usually of a person or a vehicle.

objective shot A fairly wide shot that is not the subjective POV of any of the characters in a scene and in which the camera does not move with a character. It is the view of an uninvolved observer.

off-screen Something that happens or is positioned outside the camera's view. An on-screen character may hear dialogue or sound effects from off-screen, or may be looking at something off-screen that viewers cannot see.

opening shot The shot that begins a movie or a scene.

opposed looks When two characters are looking at each other, they are framed to be looking in opposite directions in their respective shots. Viewers understand this to mean that they are looking at each other. Also called an *eyeline match.*

overlapping action An action is filmed in its entirety in two or more shot sizes so that a cut can be made at any point and the action will appear to be continuous.

over-shoulder shot A shot can be taken from behind a character that includes some part of the head and shoulders, in addition to what the character is looking at. Also called *over* and *over-the-shoulder shot.*

pacing The speed at which a story is being told. This is continuously refined during editing. Choices include the ordering of beats, how much the shots are trimmed, whether time is compressed, and the amount of intercutting. Pacing is a key element of storytelling that can make a story seem real, interesting, and exciting.

pan The camera rotates or swivels sideways as it records, sometimes in order to keep a moving character or vehicle in the frame and sometimes to show an environment.

panel A storyboard frame.

parallel action Simultaneous action in two settings that the film cuts between. Also known as parallel editing or crosscutting.

plate The background layer of a composite shot.

point of view (POV) (1) A shot of what a character sees, or an angle close to it. (2) The shooting and editing of the action of a scene with the goal of portraying events as they are experienced by one specific character.

post-production The final phase of filmmaking, during which a film is edited.

POV See *point of view.*

prelap See *J-cut*.

preproduction The phase in which a film is designed and planned in all its many aspects. Everything that can be done to prepare for production is undertaken, including budgeting, hiring a crew, casting, finding locations, designing and building sets, planning the shots, scheduling, designing costumes, and renting equipment.

previsualization A visual approach to designing the sequence of shots that tell a story on film using storyboard drawings or animatics as a way to plan the storytelling, shots, action, stunts, and visual effects.

production The phase of filmmaking that follows preproduction. During production the script is enacted and recorded to produce raw footage of live action. Visual effects and voice-overs are also created during the production phase.

prop Any handheld or movable object that is seen or used by actors on a film set but that is not a structural part of the set.

pull The camera is moved backward while a shot is being recorded.

pull focus To adjust a camera's lens in order to keep the subject in focus. This is required if the distance from the camera to the subject changes because the subject or the camera moves.

punch in A cut to a closer shot of the same subject at exactly the same angle, created by using two cameras with different lenses that are positioned side by side. Punching out to a wider shot is also done.

push The camera is moved forward while a shot is being recorded.

rack focus The lens of the camera is adjusted so that the focus will change from a plane at one distance to a plane at a different distance from the lens. This is done to draw the attention of viewers from one person or object to another for a storytelling reason.

raking shot A shot that holds two or more characters in profile as they sit, stand or walk side by side.

reaction shot A close shot that shows a character reacting to events.

redress To redecorate a set so that it can double as a different set.

re-establishing shot A wide shot used mid-scene to remind viewers about the setting, who and what is present, the mood, and the geography of the space.

reframing What the camera sees is normally continually adjusted by the operator to maintain a pleasing composition as actors move. This is especially important when there is a major change to the composition, such as when a character enters or exits a shot.

return See *reverse angle*.

reveal (1) Someone or something not initially visible in a shot is discovered due to camera movement of any kind. (2) On-screen action shows someone or something that was not visible at first, such as when a mask is pulled off, a box or door is opened, or a figure turns toward the camera. (3) Showing a plot twist or an important clue visually.

reverse angle A shot recorded from an angle close to 180 degrees opposite the shot that precedes it. In practice this angle matches the camera angle that the first shot's line of sight forms with the axis, and therefore it will usually be less than 180 degrees unless the shot is a dead reverse. Also called a *return*.

right look A character's eyes are looking (even slightly) toward the right of the screen. The exact angle formed with the camera's line of sight is unimportant for screen geography.

scene In principle a part of a film's story in which action occurs in one setting and in continuous time. In practice characters are often traveling during a scene, time can be compressed to eliminate unnecessary action during a scene, and scripts contain scenes where characters in several settings talk to each other by phone or watch video feeds of simultaneous events.

scene transition Any in-camera or editing-room technique that is used instead of a hard cut to begin a scene. Some examples are wipes, tilts, reveals, changes of focus, montages, dissolves. and fades.

screen direction The direction of a character's look or movement as it relates to the left and right of the screen, even if this is only to a small degree because the character is also looking or moving diagonally toward or away from the camera.

screen geography The horizontal two-dimensional arrangement of characters and objects as they appear on the flat screen, without regard to depth. It is primarily concerned with the left and right of the screen as it applies to characters' positions, movement and looks. Clear screen geography helps viewers keep their spatial bearings in a scene.

sequence A series of shots that work together to tell part of a story.

set The place that will be visible on camera as a scene is enacted and recorded. It may be a part of something that already exists, or it may be specially constructed in a studio. One location can become several sets. A set can be redressed to double as a different set.

setting (1) The specific time and place of one scene. (2) The general time and place of a story.

setup A camera position with a particular lens and appropriate lighting for the recording of one specific shot.

shallow focus The use of limited depth of field in order to make objects at other distances appear out of focus or soft. This is done both to eliminate distractions and to direct the attention of viewers to the subject of a shot.

shooting storyboard A storyboard that depicts the specific shots that are proposed for a sequence accurately enough to be used as a guide during preproduction and production.

short-siding Intentionally framing characters so that they have much less look-space than they would have in a balanced composition.

shot A continuous piece of film recorded over seconds or minutes from the instant the camera starts rolling until it stops. The footage is trimmed as needed and often cut into sections that are then intercut with other shots. Each shot is generally repeated in several takes.

shot contrast The visual differences between two shots. Increasing shot contrast helps viewers understand the new shot that appears at a cut more quickly without wasting time trying to understand whether it is a continuation of the previous shot.

shot list A list of all of the shots needed for a scene or a sequence.

shot size How big the subject appears in the frame, ranging from long shots to extreme close-ups.

single A clean shot of one character that is a close-up or a medium close-up.

smooth cut A cut that does not draw attention to itself by creating a visually jarring jump, pop, turn, or transformation.

snap zoom A quick zoom that is used to tighten a close-up in order to motivate a flashback, or to draw the audience's attention to something.

soft focus Out of focus, blurry.

sound prelap and overlap Dialogue, music, or sound effects from one scene overlap the preceding or following scene for a few seconds. In a *J-cut* the sound from the following scene is heard before the current scene ends. In an *L-cut* the sound continues into the following scene.

spatial continuity Presenting a series of shots of a scene such that characters and objects do not change their actual positions, eyelines, or actions in real three-dimensional space from one shot to the next without it either being seen or an indication being given that time has passed.

split eyeline A characteristic of any shot in which a character's action requires looks to both the left and right of the lens.

stable composition A composition that is not undergoing substantial changes.

staging See *blocking*.

stationary camera The camera does not move away from its current fixed position, but in its current location it may pan or tilt by changing its aim.

Steadicam A camera stabilizer that is attached to an operator using a body harness. As the operator runs, climbs steps, or crosses rough terrain, the Steadicam's counterweight absorbs bumps and shakes to produce smooth and fluid shots.

steal focus To distract viewers from what they should be looking at.

storyboard A series of drawings that show the shot size, composition, camera movement, action, dialogue, and cuts that form a planned film sequence.

story beat The smallest division of action in a film or a play. It is anything that happens that moves a story forward. Also called a *dramatic beat* or a *beat*.

stunt A difficult or dangerous physical feat performed by a specialist instead of an actor.

subject The person or thing that a shot's composition is designed to highlight in order to convey information about the story.

subjective shot Any shot that makes viewers feel that they are experiencing events through a character. This increases the emotional involvement of viewers.

suspense Excitement or anxious uncertainty about what will happen next.

sweep the lens When characters change the direction in which they are looking from one side of the camera to the other. This sets up a new eyeline to the left or the right.

swingle A single camera position designed to shoot close-ups of two or more characters who are standing or seated in a row. It swings to shoot singles of each character. The camera can also film short pans from one character to another as needed.

swish pan A swish pan is a rapid pan *off* one character dissolved with a rapid pan *onto* a different character. It simulates the visual experience of glancing quickly from one person to another. Also called a *whip pan*.

tableau shot A wide shot whose action is carefully staged, composed, and lit to present action as it would appear on a stage or in a painting.

take A single continuously recorded version of a shot. Usually there are several takes made of each shot, and during editing the best elements of various ones are used in the edited film.

telephoto lens See *long lens*.

three-shot An attractively framed group shot of three characters, who may be standing or seated.

tie-up shot A shot that contains both a character and the person or thing that the character is looking at, talking to, or is otherwise connected to in the story.

tight eyeline The character is looking at a point near the lens but not into it. This makes the shot more subjective.

tight shot A close shot.

tilt   Recording a shot as the camera's angle changes to point up or down.

three-quarter angle shot   A shot recorded while the camera is situated at about a 45-degree angle to the subject.

time transition   The use of an image or images to indicate a change in the time of day or season, or to indicate that time has moved ahead or back. Many time transitions can be created while shooting. Fades and dissolves are created during editing.

tracking shot   A shot in which the camera moves sideways, usually in parallel to a moving person or vehicle. Sometimes the terms *dolly shot* and *tracking shot* are used interchangeably.

transition   The use of images and sound to indicate a change of time or place, and often of both. Visual transitions can be created while shooting or during editing. In-camera transitions usually involve camera movement or a change of focus.

traveling shot   The camera does not stay in a fixed position, but moves up, down, left, right, forward, or backward. Pans and tilts are not traveling shots because the camera remains in one place but rotates.

trucking shot   An alternate term for a tracking shot, that is, dollying the camera left or right.

two-shot   A shot of two characters that is usually framed closer than a full shot.

unmotivated pan   A pan that is not following a moving subject and does not have a story reason to find something that is currently off-screen.

unstable composition   A composition that is changing significantly.

verisimilitude   The quality of having the appearance of being real.

voice-over   The voice of an unseen narrator.

VFX   See *visual effects*.

visual effects   Primarily computer-generated digital imagery of environments, fire, smoke, objects, and creatures that look realistic, but that would be dangerous, expensive, or impossible to capture on film. The VFX footage is combined with live action.

walk-and-talk   A dialogue scene in which the characters are walking during their conversation.

walk-space   Extra space on the side of frame that the character or object is moving toward, put there to achieve compositional balance.

whip pan   See *swish pan*.

wide-angle lens   A lens that has a focal length of less than that of the human eye (50mm). These lenses bring more into a shot, have greater depth of field, exaggerate depth, and make handheld shots appear steadier. Movement toward and away from the camera seems accelerated.

wide eyeline   A character is not looking at a point close to the lens but farther to one side.

wide shot   The camera is positioned far enough away and with a suitable lens to show many characters and a large part of the set.

wipe   A person or object of no special importance quickly crosses the frame close to the camera, briefly hiding what's behind it. A wipe is often used to begin or end a shot, and as a transition to begin or end a scene.

wrap   The camera circles part way or all the way around the subject at a constant distance while keeping the subject framed as the center of interest. Also called an *arc* or a *rotation*.

zoom   Adjusting a lens by altering its length while recording so that the magnification level of a shot changes smoothly to produce either a wider or a more magnified view. Zooming does not involve any camera movement other than within the lens.

Index

Printed in the USA
CPSIA information can be obtained
at www.ICGtesting.com
CBHW081113151024
15678CB00004B/3

9 780190 054335